From Far and Wide

From Far and Wide

A Complete History of Canada's Arctic Sovereignty

PETER PIGOTT

DUNDURN
TORONTO

Editor: Shannon Whibbs
Design: Jennifer Scott
Printer: Transcontinental

Library and Archives Canada Cataloguing in Publication

Pigott, Peter
    From far and wide : a complete history of Canada's Arctic sovereignty / by Peter Pigott.

Includes bibliographical references and index.
Issued also in electronic formats.
ISBN 978-1-55488-987-7

    1. Arctic regions--Strategic aspects--History. 2. Canada--Armed Forces--Arctic regions--History. 3. Canada, Northern--Military policy--History. 4. Arctic regions--History. 5. Canada, Northern--History. I. Title.

FC3956.P45 2011   971.9   C2011-903770-X

1 2 3 4 5   15 14 13 12 11

Conseil des Arts du Canada / Canada Council for the Arts

Canada

ONTARIO ARTS COUNCIL
CONSEIL DES ARTS DE L'ONTARIO

We acknowledge the support of the **Canada Council for the Arts** and the **Ontario Arts Council** for our publishing program. We also acknowledge the financial support of the **Government of Canada** through the **Canada Book Fund** and **Livres Canada Books**, and the **Government of Ontario** through the **Ontario Book Publishing Tax Credit** and the **Ontario Media Development Corporation**.

Care has been taken to trace the ownership of copyright material used in this book. The author and the publisher welcome any information enabling them to rectify any references or credits in subsequent editions.

J. Kirk Howard, President

Printed and bound in Canada.
www.dundurn.com

Dundurn
3 Church Street, Suite 500
Toronto, Ontario, Canada
M5E 1M2

Gazelle Book Services Limited
White Cross Mills
High Town, Lancaster, England
LA1 4XS

Dundurn
2250 Military Road
Tonawanda, NY
U.S.A. 14150

For my parents

Contents

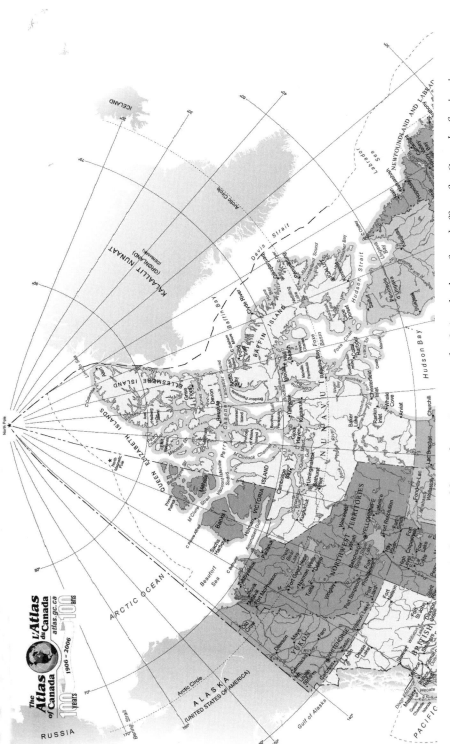

The Royal Navy's attempts to find a navigable Northwest Passage to the Orient had profound effects for Canada, forcing it to assert sovereignty over its Arctic windfall.

Introduction

*F*rom *Far and Wide* is a play in six acts. The stage setting and the back-drop remain the same throughout while the players enter in period costume, perform their lines, and exit. The arrangement of scenery and props is intended to depict the Canadian Arctic — from the 60th parallel as far north as Herschel Island in the west to the Lincoln Sea in the east. The painted backdrop could thus be icebergs, pack ice, mountains, glaciers, coastal plains, muskeg, or Baffin Island cliffs. The few props will range from simple canvas tents to empty meat tins to 1927 Fokker monoplanes to giant golf ball–like antenna.

Because this is the Arctic, the lighting will vary from high intensity to almost pitch-blackness. It will initially illuminate each scene and then a spotlight will focus on the individual central to the period — be it Sir John Franklin, Sir George Simpson, Clifford Sifton, or John Diefenbaker, keeping the remainder of the stage dark while he speaks of his particular "vision" for the Arctic. If the theatre company possesses the resources and technical wizardry to create the magnificence of the aurora borealis, so much the better.

As stage lighting tends to remove definition from a face, cosmetic makeup is essential, especially in Acts One through Three. Haggard features etched by scurvy and disease can be created by emphasizing cheek-bones, eye sockets to portray hollowed faces. Alternately, sunburn and sun blindness in such a frigid climate would cause swollen eyes and lips and the appearance of each actor in these scenes is to be made up with reddish greasepaint, creating the effect of as if boiling water had been poured on his head.

At times the action will move away from centre stage to the Norwegian or the Alaskan Arctic, or a river in the Yukon. As this is a historical drama, the dialogue and costumes of the all-male cast are appropriate to their time period. This will vary from British naval officers of the 1840s to North-West Mounted Police constables in 1898 to Prime Minister Mackenzie King in the 1940s to that of American servicemen of the 1950s, culminating with the Canadian Forces' "Frozen Chosen" in 2010. By far the most difficult task for the actors will be conveying to the audience the ever present, bone-chilling cold. Intermittently, there will be voices heard offstage, ostensibly coming from diplomats, prime ministers, and interested parties (like Lady Franklin) in London, Ottawa, Oslo, and Washington.

The audience will soon discern that the singular thread that runs through all six acts is the quest for sovereignty over 40 percent of Canada's land mass and more than 19,000 islands in the Arctic Archipelago. The actors will discuss exploration of the Arctic and protecting what they have mapped (and thus claimed for their sovereign) from the other polar neighbours such as Denmark, Norway, Russia, Sweden, and the United States. Their incentives to risk their lives in the harshest climate on the planet will range from sheer obsession about conquering the Northwest Passage to "moiling for gold"[1] to protecting the Arctic's fragile ecosystem.

Then, below the footlights, but crucial to the play, would be the Aboriginals of the Canadian Arctic — the Inuit. Referred to in early scenes as *Esquimaux* or *Eskimo*, until the last pages of Act Six, they are to be treated indifferently by those on stage. But unlike them, the Inuit are dressed appropriately for the Arctic: in double-layer trousers and waterproof parkas (double-layer pullover jackets with hoods) made of skins and furs.

Beginning as a mystery, the play is Canada's own Norse saga, an epic of adventure over two centuries, populated by men who were sometimes arrogant, greedy, and careless of their circumstances, but were always brave and determined. It wasn't that ignorance was bliss or uncertainty adventurous, but that for many who ventured into the Arctic, both would prove deadly. They were the astronauts of their day, and the Arctic was their moon.

It is hoped that the audience will come away from *From Far and Wide* with the realization that 90 percent of sovereignty is stewardship and that all sovereign rights of Arctic lands and waters by the government of Canada is owed to British exploration in the post-Napoleonic era and Inuit use and occupation of Inuit Nunangat since time immemorial.

The germ of *From Far and Wide* arose when I worked in the Treaty Section of the Department of Foreign Affairs. The original texts of all treaties that Canada is party to were stored in the Treaty Vault and, in my opinion, no other room in the Lester B. Pearson Building holds so much of the history of our country's foreign relations — even before it was a country. Within the banal facades of mobile shelving were rows of manila folders containing the original texts of agreements, conventions, protocols, declarations, memoranda of understanding, and Exchange of Notes. On all except the very recent, the signatures had faded, the vellum aged from translucent to opaque, the wax seals brittle and cracked.

I romanticized the language of the treaties and the choreography of their signing ceremonies. As history's great accomplishments, from the age of calligraphy to computers, they were proof that nations could come together to protect migratory birds, combat cyber-crime, or disarm their nuclear arsenals. Some treaties had been signed in the grandeur of Versailles or on the decks of battleships, while others were sealed in hitherto unknown places like Kyoto, Doha, or Schengen — or Osborne House on the Isle of Wight, the summer residence of Her Majesty Queen Victoria. For it was here on July 31, 1880, that all British territories and possessions in North America were given to the Dominion of Canada — the biggest land transfer in history. Within the legalese of the relevant Arctic treaties — some of which are reproduced in the book, is the subtlety and dynamism of our country's history.

Considering that most of us are more familiar with the beaches of Florida or Cuba, it is curious that a majority of Canadians consider the Arctic to be a cornerstone of national identity. In its survey for the Munk School of Global Affairs, EKOS Research Associates discovered that we see the Arctic as an integral part of our sense of national identity and favour protecting it — with the military if need be.[2] Another poll reveals that Canadians think the region should be the nation's top foreign policy priority for the military — far ahead of NATO or UN commitments.

Explored and mapped by the Royal Navy seeking a passage to the east, then transferred to the Dominion of Canada, the Arctic remained *terra incognita* until the air age. Although it could not have comprehended the size of the territorial windfall it had received, the Liberal government of Prime Minister Alexander Mackenzie accepted the transfer — if only to keep the United States and Czarist Russia out. But as the Dominion expanded along its east-west axis (dictated by the completion of the Canadian Pacific Railway), the gift was forgotten. Except for the whaling, fishing, and fur industries, the potential of the North remained unknown. It was as one astute Canadian statesman observed: "… for later."

As late as the Cold War, the Canadian military, focused as it was on battlefields in Europe, with the exception of Alert, rarely ventured north of the 60th parallel. That was understandable for as General Walter Natynczyk, chief of the defence staff has explained, even today the North is logistically more difficult for the Canadian Forces than Afghanistan. But by 2011, the concept of Arctic security had undergone a change: military threats to Canadian Arctic sovereignty had been replaced with the Whole of Government Approach for protecting the environment and maintaining a healthy, educated indigenous population.

Prime ministers from Wilfrid Laurier to Stephen Harper have regularly reminded Canadians that their governments are determined to defend this country's sovereignty in the Far North, making the term "sovereignty" as clichéd as "thinking outside the box." From my time in the Treaty Section, I know there is confusion surrounding the word. In international law, sovereignty is defined as "the totality of the various forms of exclusive jurisdiction which a state may exercise within its boundaries." This applies to land and to certain sea areas of which Canada claims sovereignty on the basis of historic title and because of straight baselines established around the Arctic Archipelago. The requirements for acquiring a historic title of the seas or sea ice are similar to those for land: the exercise of exclusive state jurisdiction, sometimes settlement by nationals, and acquiescence by foreign states, particularly those whose interests are primarily affected.

Every book is written alone, but one of this magnitude required the inspiration and help of those giants of Arctic history and poetry. Over the years, Pierre Berton, Farley Mowat, Robert Service, Jack London, and Peter C. Newman are the many authors on whose research I have drawn. All Canadians owe them a special debt of gratitude, none more than I.

Special thanks are due to many in the Department of National Defence, especially Lieutenant-Colonel John Blakeley; Director Public Affairs Canada Command, Lieutenant-Colonel Dwayne Lovegrove; Commanding Officer, 440 Transport Squadron, Lieutenant-Commander John Nethercott; Lauri Sullivan, National Defence; Captain Martine Goulet; Chief Warrant Officer Dave Mahon of the Canadian Ranger National Authority; Colonel Sean Friday (Canada COM DCOS Plans); Commander Al Harrigan, Director of Maritime Strategy, 2 Strategic Analysis; Major Bill Chambré of the Canadian Forces Arctic Training Centre; and Major Steve Burgess, CANOSCOM. Writing about 440 Squadron's Twin Otter aircraft, Lieutenant-Colonel Lovegrove put it best: "We are the physical expression of Canada maintaining sovereignty over the North."

Darryl Catton and Jerry Proc helped with the history of Alert. Catton had been posted there in 1957 and has never lost his fascination with the Arctic. A licensed amateur radio operator, Jerry Proc's interest in Alert came when a colleague asked him to identify a CRT-based direction-finding set used at Special Wireless Station, Coverdale, New Brunswick, during the war. After identifying the set, he began researching the history of the Supplementary Radio System of which Alert was one of the stations. Another of the "Frozen Chosen" was Edie Whiting, who catered to my vanity, supplying alcohol and laughter in generous measure.

My daughters Holly and Jade provided their support in the months that led to the completion of *From Far and Wide*. As with the other books, they endured their aviation-mad father, secure in the knowledge that they are his life. I must also acknowledge with sadness a special debt to my beloved aunt who passed away while I wrote the first chapters. She first encouraged me to write, typing out the stories of a six-year-old on an old Underwood.

Research for my last three books took me to Afghanistan, Sudan, and the high seas, and for this one I looked forward to exploring my own country, especially the Arctic where, Jack London wrote, it is so cold that time itself freezes. My journey to do so began in my hometown of Ottawa, not far from where on the morning of May 6, 1898, the Yukon Field Force marched from the Drill Hall to Union Station through streets lined by a cheering crowd and the band played "The Girl I Left Behind Me." May we all conquer our own Northwest Passages.

Peter Pigott, Ottawa

1

British Obsession

The first military men to venture into the Canadian Arctic were British. After 1815, having conquered both of its rivals, the navies of France and Spain, the Royal Navy looked for ways to expend its energy. With Napoleon securely in St. Helena, Nelson's navy, built up to blockade Europe, had been stood down. Ships were laid up, officers put on half pay, and ordinary seamen dismissed. In 1812, there were 131,087 men serving in 543 ships in commission, 98 of which were ships of the line. By 1817, the comparable figure had fallen to 22,944 men and 13 ships of the line. In lieu of fighting a war, exploration was an alternative — ships and crews were dispatched on what were called "Discovery Service" in the name of sovereignty, survey, and science.

That the Canadian Arctic was explored and charted was due to the Royal Navy and testimony to its efforts are the numerous islands, straits, and sounds named after the officers, their ships, their sovereigns, or their patrons. Besides the Beaufort Sea, named for Sir Francis Beaufort, the Royal Naval hydrographer, King William Island, was named for William IV and there is also Victoria Island with its Prince Albert Peninsula, Banks Island for the botanist Sir Joseph Banks, Ellesmere Island for Francis Egerton, the Earl of Ellesmere and president of the Royal Geographical Society. In ships' names — besides the *Terror* and *Erebus*, *Fury*, and *Hecla* — Resolute Bay is named after the abandoned Franklin search vessel that drifted into Baffin Bay to be picked up by the United States and returned to the Royal Navy and *Alert* after the first vessel to land at the northern part of Ellesmere Island in 1875.[1]

Britain first came to hold legitimate title over the North American Arctic region in 1763 through the terms of the Treaty of Paris, when

France ceded to her all her possessions in North America, with the exceptions of the small islands of St. Pierre and Miquelon off the Atlantic coast. For the Lords Commissioners of the Admiralty, if there were a navigable Northwest Passage to China and India, this would increase British power and commerce at the expense of the Russians, and increasingly, the young United States. Brimming with confidence to the point of arrogance, the island nation ruled supreme in the early 19th century. It was, as the popular air "Rule Britannia" went: "The dread and envy of them all." Not only had it finally defeated its traditional enemies, but its technology led the world — James Watt, Henry Bessemer, Abraham Darby, and Henry Doulton were few of a generation of Englishmen who had made major contributions to the Industrial Revolution. But the island was also happily blessed with bottomless supplies of that "crude oil" of the 19th century: coal. That an Englishman would discover the Northwest Passage was inevitable.

For the Royal Navy in the process of converting to steam and soon iron-clad ships, here was an opportunity to test out theories and equipment. Steam power, screw propellers, inflatable India rubber boats, anti-scurvy solutions, sleds hauled by men — the expeditions were ideal proving grounds for all of these. For the naval officers now on half pay, exploration among the polar snows was not only romantic, but a shortcut for awards and promotion — both meagre in a peacetime navy. They were also for the most part "deep sea" sailors who abhorred, as one wrote, "skulking around coastlines" — bringing with them where ever they went as one HBC factor wrote, their "home environment."

At a time when average life expectancy in Britain was 41 years of age, there were some in the service's senior positions who had far outlived their allotted span. Finding the Northwest Passage was to be their legacy, the last opportunity at achieving some form of immortality. Sir John Franklin, whose fate played a major role in the exploration of the Canadian Arctic, had cheated death on numerous occasions to the point of believing his own immortality. A midshipman at the battles of Copenhagen and later Trafalgar, he had accompanied his uncle Matthew Flinders on the first circumnavigation of Australia, getting wrecked on the Barrier Reef in the process. His Canadian explorations, however disastrous, had earned him a knighthood and made him eligible to marry the liberal-minded, tenacious Jane Griffin. The following decades saw a lacklustre career for Franklin, the high point of which was governing the brutal penal colony of Van Diemen's Land (Tasmania). Now at 58 years of age and, by contemporary accounts, a bumbling, genial old man, he was given one last grab at the glittering prize: to find the Northwest Passage.

A 13-year-old midshipman in the War of 1812, Sir Edward Belcher was given command of five ships to search for Franklin in 1852. Unpopular with his officers, he had been chosen because Sir Francis Beaufort had been his patron.[2] Refusing to heed the advice of experienced Arctic navigators, which resulted in his ships becoming enmeshed in ice, Belcher abandoned them all and scurried back to England. Amazingly, although court-martialed, Belcher would end his career as an admiral (the first Canadian-born to do so) and be made a Knight Commander of the Order of the Bath. Dr. Richard King, who would accompany the expeditions, observed in his "narrative" that Belcher was "… an officer advanced in years, who had spent a whole life proving himself to be the very last man fitted for so honorable a service."[3]

For Sir John Barrow, the second secretary of the Admiralty, sending Franklin to discover the Northwest Passage was the climax of a brilliant career that ranged from diplomatic service in China and South Africa to the Admiralty. During his naval tenure, he had overseen operations that included sinking the entire Ottoman fleet at Navarino to burning down Washington in the War of 1812. With the war's end, Barrow could turn his attention to the reports he had been receiving from whalers, which described an unprecedented breaking up of ice east of Greenland and vast ice packs and numerous icebergs as far south as 40° N. He concluded that the ice barrier that had prevented the successful crossing of the Northwest Passage was less formidable. Barrow had sent so many naval expeditions out to the Arctic that there are three bodies of water named after him there: Barrow Strait, Barrow Cape, and Barrow River. Now at the advanced age of eighty-one, with this the ultimate victory as his legacy, he could die contentedly.

Besides the navy, there were other interested parties in the quest to map the last blank spaces left on the North American continent — the royal family (especially the progressive-thinking Prince Albert); the Colonial Office; the Geographical Society; the Ethnological Society; the Hydrographic Office; and Number 10, Downing Street — each lobbying for their own agendas and or protégés to be paramount in any polar expedition.

For the British public, here was an adventure they could empathize with and enjoy over their breakfasts — Arctic exploration coincided with the rise in the popularity of newspapers and especially the weekly *Illustrated London News*, whose artists (before the advent of photography) drew fanciful images of what their naval explorers encountered — icebergs the size of cathedrals, ferocious giant polar bears, ships locked fast into the ice, and the elusive *Eskimaux*. As the only media of the day, newspapers and magazines shaped public opinion with their articles on Arctic exploration. In the absence of a war, Franklin's disappearance and the search for him must have been a godsend to the press, both in the amount of lines written — and in their bottom line.

Venturing into the "frozen regions" was also far more enlightened than in previous centuries of exploration. The institution of slavery had just been abolished throughout the British Empire in 1834 and the national conscience could be salved as this time there were no black or brown races to exploit or enslave. Nor were there any locals to kidnap and "Christianize." The Spanish had tainted their exploration of the New World with greed for precious metals, the destruction of native civilizations, and religious intolerance. Entering the last pristine place left in the world, the British polar explorer — devoid of imperial agenda — felt ennobled. Here he was pitted against nature itself, with a backdrop under Arctic skies where the spectral aurora borealis haunted him. Finally, Arctic exploration was in the pursuit of science. Having (it seemed) charted the remainder of the world and categorized its species — animal, vegetable, and mineral — the British scientific establishment looked to complete the puzzle. There was still coastline to be mapped, soundings to be taken, skeletons of indigenous species — man or animal — to be brought home. Portable astronomical observatories were fitted on two ships and all expeditions looked to study terrestrial magnetism and pinpoint the magnetic pole.

Englishmen had been searching for the fabled Northwest Passage since the late 16th century. Barely four years after Columbus had discovered the New World, King Henry VII gave the Venetian sailor Giovanni Caboto letters patent to exploit whatever he came across in the "new found land." The English so envied the Spanish, who had the good fortune to have colonized those parts of the world that had an abundance of gold, silver, and spices, that men like Frobisher and Drake braved the frigid temperatures for profit rather than prestige. In 1576, Martin Frobisher sailed as far as southern Baffin Island near present-day Iqaluit and into what he named Frobisher Bay. Here he mined iron pyrite ore that he brought back to London as gold. More iniquitous was his kidnapping of locals to show off at court. Queen Elizabeth I presciently named the area he had mapped "Meta Incognita" ("of limits unknown") Peninsula.[4] Seven years later, John Davis charted the eastern coast of the island, and in 1610, Henry Hudson sailed through the strait that would be named for him off the island's southern coast.

At a time when the Pacific Ocean was effectively a Spanish lake and the Portuguese and Dutch controlled the African route to India; Hudson, Frobisher, Drake, Weymouth, and Foxe all sought to reach the Orient through the Arctic. William Baffin, who incredibly ranged as far north as Ellesmere Island, charted the island he gave his name to in 1616, disappointed that the Northwest Passage did not lead through it. For a while there was the hope that the Foxe Channel might be the entrance to a southern, more ice-free route through the North American continent or that there was a shortcut to the Pacific Ocean through Hudson Bay.

But the most revered commercial adventurers of them all was the Hudson's Bay Company (HBC). Two hundred years before British North America would be governed from Ottawa, the HBC (sometimes called "Here Before Christ") was the real power in much of Canada. Canada's claim to its North rests fundamentally on the Royal Charter granted to the HBC by Charles II on May 2, 1670:

> … all the Landes and Territoryes upon the Countryes Coastes and confynes of the Seas Bayes Lakes Rivers Creekes and Soundes aforesaid [that is, "that lye within the entrance of the Streights commonly called Hudsons Streights"] that are not already actually possessed by

> or granted to any of our Subjectes or possessed by the
> Subjectes of any other Christian Prince or State …

It gave the company sovereignty to Rupert's Land (Prince Rupert was the king's cousin and the company's first governor), the watershed of rivers draining into Hudson Bay, so that they could to trade, fish, and export whatever made it a profit without having to obtain licences. Centered at Lachine, Quebec, and at York Factory on the bay itself, the HBC's governors ruled over a kingdom that encompassed all of present-day Manitoba, Saskatchewan, southern Alberta, northern Ontario, Quebec, parts of Minnesota, North Dakota, and Montana.

With an early interest in trading with China, the HBC sent out two ships in 1719 under Governor John Knight, instructing him to: "find the Straits of Anian and make what Discoveries you possibly can and to obtain all sorts of Trade and Commerce." Knight and the fleet disappeared into the polar vastness, never to be seen again.[5] It was a salutatory lesson to the HBC and its rival North West Company, and after that disaster they relied on overland exploration only, using no vessels larger than freight canoes and York boats. In their search for a river that would flow into the Pacific, employees from both companies traversed much of the North American continent. In 1771, the HBC's Samuel Hearne followed the Coppermine River to its mouth, becoming the first European to reach the Arctic coast by land. Alexander Mackenzie of the North West Company made the same error in 1789 when he went down the river that bears his name to the wrong ocean — the Arctic. His second attempt proved more successful and in an epic journey from Montreal, Mackenzie reached the Pacific Ocean on July 22, 1793.

In contrast to the commercial traders and Elizabethan privateers, the British who followed in the 18th century were disciplined, educated, Royal Naval officers. Well-travelled, many had seen action in the South China Sea, Africa, or surveyed the South Pacific. As salaried men they were motivated not by commerce, but by what this would do for their careers. There was also the celebrity circuit. In the four decades between the Napoleonic and Crimean wars, the market for books by Arctic explorers was insatiable and on return, Rae, Back, McClure, Parry, and Ross published "narratives," "reflections," and "dispatches" of their polar adventures.

In the conflicts taking place in present-day Afghanistan, Sudan, or Somalia, the humanitarian professionals in Médecins sans Frontières (Doctors Without Borders) and the United Nations World Food Programme deplored those of the media who "dropped in" for a sound bite and flew home to the New York studio. Comparatively, the men of the Hudson's Bay and the North West Companies who had chosen to make their lives in the North must have regarded the naval officers who visited to make their names and be "rotated" home within a year or two in a similar light.

The need for a route to the British possessions in India that could circumvent the Spanish and French was crucial. In 1745, British Parliament offered a reward of £20,000 to the first Englishman who could find it. Three decades later, a shortcut to the Orient's riches was becoming less important than the scientific discoveries that polar exploration would allow and the Admiralty offered £5,000 to the first Englishman who could locate the North Pole. As a result, naval expeditions were no longer only for commerce or sovereignty, but science, as well. This had its benefits as when in 1772, Captain Constantine Phipps took two vessels to find the geographic North Pole (Horatio Nelson was one of his midshipmen), the naturalist on board described and drew polar bears and Arctic birds, the first European to do so. It became customary for the British parliament to offer cash rewards to encourage expeditions to discover longitude at sea, the Northwest Passage, and the North Pole.[6]

The voyages of Captain James Cook were a precursor to the polar ones half a century later — among his officers were botanists, hydrographers, artists, and astronomers. The first to map Newfoundland and much of the St. Lawrence, in 1778, Cook (George Vancouver was one of his officers) probed for the Northwest Passage from the Pacific side of the North American continent, turning back when the ice on the Bering Strait proved impassable. His final voyage and death in 1779, would be the last such expedition before the Royal Navy needed its ships for the War of American Independence and after that the French and Napoleonic Wars.

An indication of how little was known of the North American Arctic in the postwar era is an Admiralty chart *circa* 1818. Between the Melville Peninsula at the entrance of Hudson Bay and the Bering Strait is a blank space marked *terra incognita*. On the Atlantic side is the vague outline of Greenland's west coast with the Davis Strait and Baffin Bay; to the south is Hudson Strait and its bay, well-mapped thanks to its use by the Hudson's Bay Company. Only the Mackenzie River, clearly drawn from Great Slave Lake to its mouth (through the overland efforts of Alexander Mackenzie) and the Coppermine River (because of Samuel Hearne) are drawn. No one navigator or mapmaker could guess that in the blank space lay one of the world's greatest archipelagos with ten large islands, including Baffin, Victoria, and Ellesmere. It was, wrote Hugh N. Wallace, "… like seeking a light switch in a darkened room."

The man who made it his life's work to change that was Sir John Barrow, the puppet master in the drama. When they collaborated for their operetta *HMS Pinafore*, Gilbert and Sullivan might have been thinking of Barrow for the song: "When I Was a Lad." The son of a common tanner who through his mathematical skills rose to becoming a clerk, Barrow came to the attention of Lord McCartney the first British envoy to China. An eminent negotiator, Chinese scholar, and comptroller, Barrow rose to be second secretary to the Admiralty. In this capacity he was able to indulge his obsession for Arctic exploration, sending Ross, Parry, James Clark Ross, and Franklin to search for the Northwest Passage.

Today, with satellite imagery, we can see the mistakes those Royal Naval officers made — they were unable to distinguish frozen sea from frozen land. Besides scurvy, what defeated and killed so many of the British sailors was the Boothia Peninsula, that Gibraltar of the North American mainland, the most northern tip of the Precambrian Shield that demarcates the eastern and western Arctic. Even today it is hard to imagine that the Boothia-Somerset barrier is not a series of islands, but part of the Laurentian Shield. Save the narrow 32-kilometre Bellot Strait where the Hudson's Bay Company would build Fort Ross, there was no way through it. With the polar ice and short season, Boothia was the death trap for the navy. "A wrong turning, choice of one rather than another river," wrote Hugh Wallace, "or misreading an ocean current, could stunt a career, endanger a vessel, or lose lives."[7]

At first, the Royal Navy was fortunate. In 1818, the Scottish explorer John Ross, accompanied by his young nephew James Clark Ross, entered Baffin Bay, sailing past Bylot Island down Lancaster Sound. Influenced by the mountainous terrain of Devon Island, he concluded that the sound was a dead end. His second-in-command, Edward Parry, persevered, arriving at Melville Island where he wrote he could see Banks Island to the south. Ahead of him, the McClure Strait (the entrance to the Beaufort Sea), was blocked with ice and under Ross's orders, Parry had to turn back. Astute and young enough to realize that he had more chance of finding the Northwest Passage if he hugged the shore, Parry travelled overland and down each channel and gulf — and in future expeditions he would make his name with such meticulous surveying. Had he crossed over to Banks Island from Melville and hugged its shore, he would have discovered the waterway that lies between Banks and Victoria Islands now called the Prince of Wales Strait. On sailing through it, he would have arrived at Amundsen Gulf and the open ocean, going down in history as the man who had discovered the Northwest Passage. It was not to be.

At the same time, another Discovery Service operation was making for the North Pole. The fifth rate frigate *Trent*, under Captain David Buchan and the tiny brig *Dorothea*, commanded by Lieutenant John Franklin got as far as Spitsbergen when the ice closed in around them. After four attempts to penetrate the pack, Buchan wisely turned around — to the dismay of his young lieutenants Franklin and William Beechey, both of whom no doubt silently swore that one day when they were in command of a Discovery Service ship they would push onward, regardless of the circumstances.

When the Russian explorer Baron von Wrangel explored and mapped Siberia's shore from 1820 until 1823, he must have been pleased to discover that much of it was open sea and navigable during the brief summer. Hoping that the same would apply to the North American Arctic, the Admiralty allowed Parry to mount three expeditions between 1821 and 1825. He accomplished much by wintering in the Arctic — notably in adapting to local conditions by learning from the Inuit — he was the first to make use of sleds and kayaks to travel overland, he experimented with pemmican as a food source and his men wore fur-lined jackets rather than Portsmouth issue. But none of his journeys came close to the near-success of the first. In one, on taking the Foxe Channel, he couldn't get past the ice-blocked Fury and Hecla Strait, naming it after the two ships he had. On another trip sailing through Lancaster Sound, instead of continuing west as he had done earlier, Parry turned south into Prince Regent Inlet, a cul-de-sac where one the *Fury* was caught in ice and crushed.

Making their way to rescue him were two expeditions. Franklin's colleague, William Beechey, was now a captain who commanded the *Blossom* and had penetrated the Bering Strait in 1826. He was closing in on an overland party led by Franklin — still a lieutenant.[8] Called the Northern Discovery Expedition, Franklin's party began at York Factory to follow the Coppermine River to the Arctic Ocean and then to walk east along the shore of the Kent Peninsula to Point Turnagain. Much of his supplies did not arrive in time because of rivalry between the HBC and the North West Company along the supply line. Franklin wrote that he had tried to open communication with the Natives met on the way but they were only intent on looting his few remaining supplies and he named the meeting place "Pillage Point" to mark that. As with all his expeditions, Franklin seems to have given no thought to adequate food provisioning and lost eleven of the twenty men to scurvy and starvation, his party reduced to making soup from their boots.[9] He returned home to be known as "the man who ate his boots," a label that brought him considerable fame.

But Franklin's second overland trip to the Beaufort Sea from 1825 to 1827 was a comparative triumph. On July 17, 1826, he made it as far as an island at the mouth of the Mackenzie River, which he named after the astronomer and friend John Herschel. Better still, this time he lost no one. Perhaps because of both accomplishments, he was rewarded with a knighthood. A critical observer, George Simpson, a future HBC governor and one who made several overland trips from Lachine, Quebec, to the Pacific coast, wrote that the whole Franklin trip had been: "[B]adly planned and poorly commanded by a man who could walk no more than eight miles a day and needed his three meals" and to whom, "Tea is indispensable (*sic*)."[10] As the HBC saw it, the problem with the Royal Navy explorers was that rather than adapt to the terrain they wanted to bring to the Arctic their "home environment."

The 60-year-old Captain Sir John Franklin (1786–1847), the expedition's commander, was chosen when three other officers refused the honour. For the official photo, he chose to wear outdated Nelsonian costume.

By 1825, the commercial need for a Northwest Passage by Britain had lost its appeal. The Russians seemed to have shelved their Arctic ambition and with the French, Spanish, and Portuguese empires in decline and the Royal Navy now the guarantors of peace and commerce worldwide, there was little need to traverse the unmapped Arctic to get to the Far East. An Act of Parliament in 1828 repealed the award of £20,000 that had been offered as an incentive for Arctic discovery.

But just as the Royal Navy was losing interest in mounting expeditions to discover a Northwest Passage, John Ross reappeared in 1829. He had alienated Barrow with the first expedition, so he raised the necessary funds privately — which explains why the Boothia Peninsula is named after Sir Felix Booth, a London gin distiller. And because his brother was a railway promoter, Ross brought the first steam-powered paddle-wheel ship, *Victory*, to the Arctic. He took with him his nephew James Clark Ross but like Parry, lost himself down the dead end of the Gulf of

Boothia — somehow missing the Bellot Strait. With a map drawn by an Inuit woman, he was the first to realize that the Boothia was a peninsula, not an island. However, on June 1, 1831, James Clark Ross located the North Magnetic Pole on the west coast of the Boothia Peninsula. The unreliability of the steam engine and paddlewheels proving useless in the ice floes forced Ross to abandon his machinery at Lord Mayor's Bay — so named because Sir Felix Booth was the lord mayor of London then. It took four years for Ross to be rescued, but upon his return to Britain he was knighted and given a £5,000 reward. Although he had unwittingly made the first landfall of a British officer on the northern mainland and had brought steam a new technology to the Arctic, he was overshadowed by his nephew and overlooked by Barrow for the Franklin expedition.

The Franklin Expedition was the worst disaster in the history of British polar exploration. It occurred with the complete loss of two naval vessels *Erebus* and *Terror* and all their crews. The expedition was led by Franklin, his second-in-command Captain Rawdon Moira Crozier in *Terror*, and Commander James Fitzjames in *Erebus*. How it came about and the consequences of their disappearance has had far reaching effects on present-day circumstances in the Canadian Arctic.

In 1845, the Admiralty planned the completion of the search for the Northwest Passage. Both the Atlantic and Pacific entry points had been penetrated and all that remained was to link them up. The belief that there had to be an open polar sea that would connect or at least circumvent the intricate ice-bound sounds, channels, and inlets between the Barrow Strait and the Beaufort Sea persisted until the advent of aerial photography. Given the honour to lead the ultimate expedition was the 58-year-old Sir John Franklin. He hadn't been to the Arctic for two decades and was somewhat under an official "cloud." Franklin had had just been retired from the governorship of the penal colony in Van Diemen's land (Tasmania). When he attempted to improve the lot of the convicts (many were women and children) he had come up against the local farmers who were using them for slave labour. But Barrow chose Franklin because

National Maritime Museum, Greenwich UK.

National Maritime Museum, Greenwich UK.

Left: *Commander James Fitzjames (1812–1848). A handsome young hero of the Arab and Chinese wars, Fitzjames was sure to make admiral in a few years. But he lacked Arctic experience and was thought to be too young to be given command of the expedition.*

Right: *Captain Francis Rawdon Crozier (1796–circa 1848), the expedition's able second-in-command with more Arctic experience than Franklin. He would lead the survivors in a death march to reach the HBC post at Back River. Legend has it that he alone survived to live out his life among the Chippewa.*

his knighthood gave him the right social cachet and because both were founding members of the Royal Geographical Society.[11] Also, ominously, because his first two choices, Parry and James Clark Ross, had refused.

Franklin's orders were to sail through Barrow Strait and then, avoiding the ice that Parry had seen off Melville Island on sighting Cape Walker, go south through Peel Sound and then to what was hoped to be open sea. An addition to his orders was a suggestion by James Clark Ross that while Franklin was in the Barrow Strait if he noticed that the Wellington Channel on his starboard side was ice-free, that he might consider going north instead — there might be an open sea there. Enough provisions were to be carried for three years as once through the passage, Franklin would have to circumnavigate the globe to get home.

No expense was spared with regard to the two ships that he was given. Ideally suited for the Arctic, the former bomb vessels[12] *Erebus* (built in 1826, weighing 370 tons, measuring 107 feet long with a 29-foot beam, and carrying 68 men) had been named after the son of Chaos and *Terror* (built in 1812, weighing 326 tons, measuring 102 feet long with a 27-foot beam, and carrying 65 men) had been tried in the ice already.[13] In 1836, under Captain George Back, the *Terror* had been caught in pack ice and was almost crushed before limping home, making it as far as Ireland where it had been beached and rebuilt. James Clark Ross had used both ships to explore the Antarctic ice shelf in 1839. Both three-masted, the plan was that they would sail the Atlantic, but use steam power to push through the Northwest Passage as John Ross had done. Commander James Fitzjames, captain of the *Erebus*, was a rising young star in the navy. Although he had never been to the Arctic, he was chosen because, unlike Franklin and Crozier of a previous generation, he knew steam engines. In true naval tradition, this was to be foremost a self contained, self-sufficient deep-sea expedition. There was to be no coast-hugging for scientific observations or a necessity to live off the "land" or communicate with the indigenous population. Strangely, there was no special scientific equipment or proper winter clothing. This was a naval operation and the clothing on board (like the heavy Victorian silver in the wardroom) was more suited for Portsmouth than the polar sea. Even stranger was that Barrow had made no provision for a rescue should Franklin be delayed.

With bows eight feet thick and cased with sheet iron, the ships were prepared to smash through the ice. Other improvements were double-planked hulls and keels sheathed in thick, copper plate, doubled-layered decks, and ice boards with chains projecting as far as the shrouds. Installed at great expense was the celebrated Sylvester Heating Apparatus, a central heating stove system that warmed the officers' cabins and men's berths. Learning from the failure of Ross's paddlewheels in the ice, the stern of each ship had a well into which the single-screw propeller could be lowered and raised if the presence of ice demanded. Because they were adapted for the propeller, their keels were extended to give proper vertical alignments to their sternposts and a false keel was added to both, allowing for more storage space. If they were crushed, both ships were equipped with "lifeboats" (for all the good they would do). There were 19 boats aboard — whalers and galleys — each 30 feet in length, pinnaces each 28 feet long, then cutters, gigs, and dinghies — and one India rubber Halkett boat. Finally each ship carried light sledges that the men could haul, but the ship's carpenters could build larger, stronger ones if needed. Barrow took the precaution of sending out a bulletin to the HBC that their posts in the Great Slave Lake area may receive visitors.

Steam to power ships was no longer a novelty — Samuel Cunard's steamers were already plying the Atlantic and the Royal Navy had its brand-new steam frigate, *Rattler*, standing by ready to tow *Erebus* and *Terror* out. To adapt the bomb vessels to steam, the naval engineers at Woolwich looked about for immediately available steam engines and happily seized upon two from local railways — the engine for *Erebus* from the London and Greenwich Railway and the one for the *Terror* from the London-Birmingham Railway. Rebuilt into the hulls, each engine had two cylinders, direct gearing, and could perform at 30 horsepower. In trials, off Greenwich, both ships performed at four knots under their own steam. The calculations of daily coal usage to power the engines, heat the ships for 24 hours a day through bitter below-zero weather for at least nine months each of the three years — and also melt ice for the desalinators to provide drinking water and cooking — would have been beyond the comprehension of Franklin and Crozier, but Fitzjames should have been concerned. Worse was that the two engines, central heating pipes, and the 200 tons of coal to feed both took up valuable storage space below and above decks that would be needed for three years' supply of food.

Other voyages of exploration and discovery had been lengthier — Beechey's had been three years and Darwin's had been five. But their ships could always put in anywhere in the world for water and fresh meat and vegetables. Both Franklin and Crozier had been in the Arctic before — Crozier had been with Parry's expeditions four times — and both were aware that there was nowhere in the Arctic where they could reprovision either for coal or food. It was like being launched into deep space with only what they had on board. Besides the ice and cold, what seamen feared most were the rats on board and the diseases with which their droppings infected the food stores. But more insidious was the enemy that they didn't understand: scurvy. Fresh food spoiled three days out of port and many ships took poultry and cattle with them to eke out their provision. An indication that no expense was spared with the Franklin expedition was that a supply ship with a dozen oxen accompanied it as far as Greenland. The more experienced Ross, who had always travelled light in the Arctic, had his forebodings about the amount of supplies being taken. A good friend of Crozier, he promised that if the expedition did not return in two years, he would personally launch a search for him.

Without Vitamin C over a six-week period, the human body's immune system weakens so that blood vessels tear open (first under the hair), the skin blackens as hemorrhages spread, teeth fall out, and ulcers explode in pus. After that the victim dies of any disease around him — which happened swiftly in the close quarters of a ship's hold. Over the centuries, the Royal Navy had become aware that the lack of fresh meat and fruit and vegetables inexorably resulted in scurvy. The only way food could be preserved in some edible semblance was by salting the meat (or drowning it in brine) or baking a form of biscuit that was so hard that it lasted forever. Vegetables were pickled in vinegar and dried fruit was valuable as it was considered anti-scorbutic. Flour, sugar, and pulses were carried, but they attracted weevils. The medical profession of the day knew that there was something in lemons that prevented scurvy and as early as the 17th century used the fruit (calling them limes) in concentrated liquid form from Europe and Africa as a fresh food substitute — giving all English sailors the nickname "limeys." But in the early 19th century, the British West Indian colonies obtained a monopoly as the sole suppliers of lemons for the navy. But these were the real limes, which had none of the anti-scorbutic elements to prevent scurvy that the true lemons did. Until this was corrected, especially when crews were iced in for the winter, scurvy was rampant.

Infamous both in history and literature for its Dickensian squalor, the slums of London's Whitechapel area were home to rat catchers, thieves, prostitutes, pickpockets, murderers, and their victims.[14] Its warrens were so ideally suited to crime that in 1888, Jack the Ripper could disembowel prostitutes with complete equamity. As horrific as those still unsolved murders were, more than forty years before, another murderer also stalked Whitechapel and he inadvertently killed everyone in the Franklin expedition. Stephan Goldner, like many immigrants to London then and now, gravitated to Whitechapel as soon as he arrived from Eastern Europe. The slum was close to the docks; people minded their own business, the authorities never ventured by, and the derelicts around provided a ready source of cheap labour. Goldner set up shop at 137 Houndsditch Road — the current site of the Nag's Head pub. He then drew up an impressive business portfolio with the royal coat of arms on its cover and a list of company branches in every major city — including Montreal. Armed with this and no doubt a smooth line of patter, he tendered to the navy victualling department for the Franklin expedition. The contract was to supply them with 29,500 cans of boiled mutton, beef, and vegetables within the specified 59 days. Delivery was no problem, he told them, and underbidding his competitors, Goldner was awarded the contract on April 1 for £3,800.

The deaths of 22 Canadians by food poisoning in 2008 linked to consuming processed meat is an example how difficult it is even today to regulate and inspect food-processing plants. In 1845, with refrigeration and public health authorities far in the future, it was impossible. Goldner must have scoured Whitechapel's alleys to buy the cheapest meat and vegetables possible — as it was springtime, both animals and vegetables would have been gristle and half grown anyway. Setting up a makeshift abattoir with the cheap labour available in Whitechapel, he had the carcasses chopped up, mixing bone, hair, and yard dirt, and thrown into pots. The stew was boiled for a minimum interval — with the resulting salmonella and *Clostridium perfringens*[15] bacterium explosion, allowing the spores to breed in their billions.

Unaware of the pathogenic bacteria cocktail mix he had created, he then had the meat and vegetables poured into one-pound cans. These were of his own design as he couldn't afford the skilled labour, time, and expense that proper canning demanded. Cans first appeared in 1810, but would not be mass-produced until the introduction of lighter materials. In 1845, tinsmiths fashioned each one by hand from wrought iron in an expensive, laborious process. Not having the time or money for this, Goldner jerry-built the cans himself, taking shortcuts and substituting materials. When found on Beechey Island in 1986, the cans were shown to contain high degrees of arsenic. He had added the poison to the lead to make it softer to solder the seams together. In his defence, Goldner would have been unaware of the effects as until the Pharmacy Act of 1868, arsenic was easily available and used in the metallurgical, medical (to treat syphilis), cosmetic, and food industries. In an era when acid was added to vinegar to make it sharp, chalk to milk to make it whiter, and arsenite of copper to vegetables to make them greener — to say nothing of crushed bone to flour, what Goldner did was not illegal — or uncommon. If the *Clostridium* in the food didn't kill the user, the arsenic certainly would. While Goldner is guilty of mass murder, the naval inspectors must take some blame for being so easily duped, asking no questions, and performing no inspections of his premises at 137 Houndsditch Road. To ensure that the navy inspectors didn't look too closely at what must have been already bursting cans, Goldner did not deliver the order to Deptford until May 17, two days before the scheduled departure. By then no one had time to question his handiwork, which was exactly what he was counting on.

For such an auspicious feat, Barrow had insisted that all 23 officers and 110 of the crew were to be Englishmen. Class-consciousness in early Victorian Britain extended to its heroes. A first for any polar expedition, most officers posed for daguerreotype images before they left — in full dress uniforms and gold fringed epaulettes. The composition of the 133 men was more suited a victory parade than an Arctic exploration.[16] Previous expedition leaders — Parry, Back, Ross, and even Frobisher — had been knighted after their voyages, not before. Knighted in 1829, Franklin had been awarded an honorary degree from Oxford University. Crozier was not quite British — but as Northern Irish and Presbyterian, he was close enough.

The selection of the crew was unusual for a Discovery Service operation, as the actual labour rested on very few — there was one officer for every four men. There were eight stewards (four of whom were cabin boys) to cater to them — Franklin had two to look after him alone. Although there was little need for protection from Native populations, a contingent of 14 Royal Marines was taken along. While splendid for ceremonial duties in their red coats and shiny buttons, they were extra mouths to feed. Alarmingly, in light of future events, there was only one sailmaker and a single engineer for the adapted steam engines.

Franklin and Crozier had their pick of officers as 30 years after the Napoleonic Wars, there still too many on half-pay, their careers frozen.[17] Franklin would have preferred that all the officers have had previous Arctic experience, but couldn't convince many who did to join. For those who had been to the Arctic, half-pay and no prospect of promotion was preferable to three years of bone-chilling claustrophobia in nine-month darkness — with the eventual prospect of being crushed to death by ice.

On the other hand, the enthusiasm of the ordinary seaman to sign on had to be his belly and his pocket. Press-ganged from their homes and occupations to fight the French, after 1815 they would all have been dumped on the street without pay or prospects. Hardtack (slowly baked biscuit) and salt beef or pork three times daily with a rum and tobacco ration was preferable to the scraps and cold gruel they were used to when not on ship. In Victorian England, when unskilled laborers were lucky to earn £20 annually, Discovery Service pay for an ordinary seaman was £60 each year he was away — with £10 in advance, no doubt causing the gin shops and brothels in Deptford to do very well before the two ships set out. Besides, until they were confirmed as dead, their families could live comfortably on the £60 paid to them by the navy. There was also the prospect that they could better themselves. While officers could make use of the library or write home, the ordinary seaman was illiterate and would be bored. Franklin was very concerned about the educational and religious welfare of his men — each ship had a library of 1,200 books, pens, ink, paper, and slates for classes. Besides prayer books, each ship also had an organ for psalms.

On May 19, 1845, having been feted by all, the flotilla moved down the Thames. Painted black with a wide, yellow horizontal strip along them, low in the water because of the coal on deck, the *Erebus* and *Terror* were drawn by steam tugs until they got to the open sea. Accompanying them was the new steam frigate *Rattler* and the rented transport ship *Baretto Junior*. By the first week of July, they saw the ice cliffs of Greenland and then put in at the Danish whaling station of Disko Bay. Here the supplies from the *Baretto Junior* were unloaded onto the two ships, the last of the cattle were butchered, and four men were sent home as being unfit. On July 12, the two ships set out across Baffin Bay, to be last sighted by British whalers at the end of July. Franklin was ebullient and told one of the whaling captains that he had enough supplies five or six years. It was the mildest Arctic winter on record and the ships made good time to Lancaster Sound.

In contradiction to his orders to go south and probably because with the imminent winter Cape Walker was already impenetrable by ice, Franklin sailed up Wellington Channel, hoping no doubt for that mythical open polar sea that would lead to the Orient. He then circumnavigated Cornwallis Island before wintering between Devon and Beechey Islands, the latter named for his colleague on the *Trent*. Then the two ships were made snug. They were dismasted until only their stumps remained, the upper decks housed with awnings, and snow was packed against the sides for insulation. With the fear of fire ever present, holes were cut in the ice for water. From November to February — the months of complete darkness, the men got their first taste of life in the Arctic. Within the holds, oil lamps and candles gave off enough light for reading and the Sylvester Heating apparatus ensured that the officer's cabins and crew quarters were warm. On Beechey Island there remain stone walls and tent locations, evidence of a small community, and signs that there was a storehouse, shooting range for the marines, carpenter's shop, a forge, and an observatory — astronomer John Herschel was a friend of Franklin's and this might have been at his request. What is more foreboding are the three graves[18] and empty Goldner tins of canned meat.

The party, now 126 men, probably left Beechey Island in late August or early September, 1846, and there are signs of a hurried departure — possibly another warmer-than-usual summer had made for an ice-free sea as no record was left behind on the cairn that had been built at the top of Beechey Island for this purpose. To his relief and possibly because of the warm weather, Franklin discovered that Peel Sound between

Prince of Wales and Somerset Islands and Franklin Strait was navigable. Hoping that this led to Queen Maud's Gulf, Franklin must have thought that it would not be long before he would see Point Turnagain once more. Rejoicing in their good fortune, that September the crews of the two ships must have made all speed down Peel Sound. The fact the strait was closing in behind them as it choked with ice must have caused some urgency. But the full extent of Peel Sound was unknown when Franklin had set out in 1845 — Parry had mapped it as a bay — and there were no maps available as to where it led. There is nothing more inconsistent than the Arctic climate and the good fortune earlier of ice-free water now cruelly enmeshed them with each passing day.

With King William Land ahead, Franklin was at a key point in his journey: he needed another safe haven to winter in — and fast. Did he realize that he was faced with a Hobson's choice — that whatever he did would doom him? He had Ross's maps, which indicated that east of Cape Felix in "Poctes Bay" there was a natural harbour. Natives had told Ross this was ice-free most of the year — and Barrow had believed this to be true. There is speculation that had he made for Tennant Islands and hugged the continental side of King William Land, Franklin would have entered James Ross Strait and then Rae Strait. The sheltered water south of the future Gjoa Haven would be ideal for wintering. Invigorated, in the spring of 1847, the expedition would have then gone past the Adelaide Peninsula, around Victoria Island into the Beaufort Sea. It was not to be. Unlike the two ships that did use this route Amundsen's *Gjøa* (47 tons) and the RCMP's *St. Roch* (8 tons), the *Erebus* and *Terror* were too large for coastal sailing — with the false keel they drew 17 feet.[19] Neither Franklin nor the Admiralty were aware that King William Land was an island — it would not be until 1854 when Dr. John Rae mapped it as such (and thus renamed King William Island). Above all, Franklin was a deep-sea sailor and by now his judgment was probably affected by the effects of botulism and scurvy. Whatever the reasons, he aimed for the Victoria Strait, hoping to make Queen Maud Gulf before the ice closed in around his ships. Even if by some miracle he had made the gulf and Dease Strait before becoming immobile, there was nowhere he could have wintered. Captain Richard Collinson inadvertently discovered the only safe harbour in the region in 1852 when he put his ship *Enterprise* into Cambridge Bay to save it from a similar fate. Caught somewhere off the northernmost tip of King William Island, Franklin's ships would be trapped by the ice flow coming down the McClintock Channel. This time there was no Beechey Island to protect the ships and they were running out of coal.

The winter of 1846–47, the second for the 126 men must have been unimaginable. Confined to their ships as the winds howled perpetually around and the ice ground against the metal plates, cracking sometimes like artillery shot, the men must have been close to insanity. The propellers that were to push the ships out must have by now become incapacitated — in any case the remaining coal supplies were needed to heat the ships, cook the food, and melt the water in the tanks. How much coal remained after leaving Greenland two years before is estimated at as little as six tons per ship.[20] With at least another year's voyage ahead, desperate rationing measures must have been in effect. Meals were taken cold by now — there was no longer heat to bake biscuit or make soups and tea. Only prolonged boiling could kill off the toxins in Goldner's cans and there was little enough coal for that. Nor was it understood that after three years, the only anti-scorbutic they had, the daily ration of lime juice had been degraded — that its "shelf life" rendered it useless.

Already weakened by scurvy from the two-year diet of salted meat, now with heart, kidney, and respiratory problems from the arsenic, the men's immune systems must have succumbed easily to the botulism from the *Clostridium* bacteria multiplied in their millions. With every porthole and crack caulked shut, the ships' interior was airless and damp. Crowded into a fetid, common area to eat, sleep, and defecate, driven mad by the darkness and claustrophobia, with water to wash a forgotten luxury, the 126 men passed their infections around, killing officer and seaman democratically. The only hope for salvation were passing Inuit hunters, but after Franklin's experience in 1826 with the "Esquimaux" who robbed him, all contact with them must have been rebuffed.

On May 24, 1847, in the almost 24-hour daylight, a party commanded by Lieutenant Graham Gore travelled across the ice to Point Victory on the shore of King William Island. Gore had been on the *Terror* in 1836 when it was almost crushed by ice, and knowing the fate that inevitably awaited them, was probably glad to get on dry land. Four days later, he deposited a written record of their progress sealed in an airtight tin in a cairn. Printed in several languages it was a form letter that stated:

> Whoever finds this paper is requested to forward it to the Secretary of the Admiralty, London, *with a note of the time and place at which it was found or*, if more convenient, to deliver it for that purpose to the British Consul at the nearest Port.

The date is auspicious as it was the young Queen Victoria's birthday and Gore had been sent out to look for open sea in the strait that led to Queen Maud Gulf. On the document, Gore added, "All Well" and that Franklin was in command. Then he returned to the ships with the news that there was ice as far as could be seen. There would be no breaking out this year. This must have caused the 61-year-old Franklin to fall into a quick decline — if this was the height of summer, what would the upcoming winter hold? But true to his amiable nature, he promoted Gore to commander — only Franklin had the authority to do so. Franklin, the man who had brought them there, died on June 11, 1847, one imagines of broken heart more than anything else — and the hopes and spirit of the whole expedition must have died with him.

Another winter passed as the ships, trapped in the ice, drifted south at about a mile a month. The end of the oil and candles meant pitch blackness from November to March and even with the most miserly use, the six tons of coal, along with the books and furniture must have long since disappeared, adding bone-chilling temperatures to those in the ship's holds. The scurvy, with its accompanying diseases, accounted for the deaths of 21 men that winter — the young Gore among them.

On April 25th, 1848, Captain Crozier ordered the abandonment of the ships. Crozier had been a midshipman on Parry's *Hecla* and remembering the fate of its companion ship, *Fury*, which had been crushed by ice. In their third winter of grinding ice, the ships must have been coming apart and it was only a matter of time before they sank. Also, something was killing the men, reducing their numbers to 105. Crozier understood that there would be fewer each day they remained on board awaiting a rescue that was not going to come. Weak from malnutrition and scurvy, the survivors were going to drag their sick comrades and the remaining food south, aiming for Chantry Inlet and the mouth of the Back River. Here they could row upriver and hope to make the nearest HBC post, Fort Resolution. When he had explored the area in 1833, Back had commented on the plentiful fresh game on the river and that would certainly cure their scurvy. Whatever they did, at least they would be out of the malodorous ships holds.

From the evidence found over the years, Crozier must have planned the trek with naval precision. First, everything useful was assembled ashore at Victory Point on King William Island — stoves, all the clothing, canvas for tents, all remaining provisions, tools, weapons — and the boats. These last were put on sleds made by the carpenters with lumber from the now deserted ships. A Lieutenant Irving was sent to find the cairn where less than a year earlier, Gore had left the "All Well" message. Irving died almost immediately after doing this and his death seems to have panicked Crozier. Almost half of his officers had died or were dying — what was killing them so quickly? Could it be the diet from Goldner's tinned food — now frozen and thawed three times? After dictating a terse message on Gore's paper as to where the ships were abandoned, latitude and longitude of where they were, Franklin's death, and the number of survivors, Crozier then rambled off about Lieutenant Irving and finding Gore's cairn. The message ends with the information that they were leaving for Back River the next day. Then it was returned to the cairn. That he had a whole winter to prepare a detailed account of what had befallen them after Franklin's death and chose not to do so, is surprising.

Little is really known of how the remainder of the Franklin expedition spent their last days.[21] Dragging the sleds filling up with a growing number of the dying, over the low hummocks on King William Island, the emaciated men never had a chance. Crozier must have known it was futile. They weren't going to make it to the Back River before winter set in and if they did, the survivors would not have the strength to row upriver. It must have been, wrote Hugh Wallace, "like a travelling hospital in which the attendants were fast becoming patients." The shallow graves found on King William Island are testimony to death by disease, exhaustion, blistering sun in the day, and the swiftly cooling nights — to say nothing of the toxins in Goldner's cans. In 1859, the skeleton of one of the stewards was found on the edge of King William Island, 80 miles from Victory Point. An abandoned boat was found on Erebus Bay, but bits of copper and cutlery, buttons, and a skeleton here and there are all that remain of their desperate race in search of an overland rescue. There were those who attempted to return to the deserted ships, making it as far as Erebus Bay. Of the *Erebus* and *Terror*, there is no trace. Inuit legends tell of the abandoned ships encased in the ice seen as far as O'Reilly Island before they disappeared.

In attempting to sail through the Northwest Passage, Franklin's crews ended up walking to the shores of the continent. The use of steam resulted in his men dragging sledges, reliance on canned foods led to a

Library and Archives Canada/PA-147732.

Skulls of members of the Franklin expedition discovered on King William Island, Northwest Territories, 1945.

desperate search for fresh meat. The attempt to carry a whole community in miniature, cocooned from the local environment, resulted in the survival of not one member of that community. The aim of the expedition to train officers and men for naval service elsewhere ended in their being unavailable for the Crimean War. The preservation of service discipline resulted in the survivors eating the flesh of their comrades.[22] If there were scientific surveys accomplished, none reached London. The technological innovations that were meant to push the two ships through the ice were the very reasons they failed to do so — the screws powered by makeshift locomotive engines warped and rusted, and the fake keels added too much weight. Over-reliance on coal supplies for power, heating, and cooking led ultimately to disaster. The Franklin expedition proved that reliance on the latest technology, massive expenditure from the public purse, and overconfidence by its creator (Barrow), who knew nothing of the Arctic, could only lead to disaster.

Following the disappearance of Franklin's two ships, a series of expeditions were sent out to search for him. The British government offered a reward of £10,000 to anyone who ascertained the fate of Franklin and his party. The search was kept alive by the press and Lady Franklin and financed by private and public donors, the HBC, and British Parliament. Several expeditions set out for the Arctic — the Admiralty alone launched 14 expeditions from 1847 to 1854. In 1848, the Admiralty sent out three search parties: Sir James Clark Ross through Lancaster Sound, Captain Henry Kellett through the Bering Strait, and John Richardson overland from the Mackenzie River. The HBC financed its own expedition under the grand old man of explorations, the redoubtable John Ross. Beechey Island, that Gibraltar of the North and site of Franklin's winter quarters, would play a major role. In May 1850, there were 11 search vessels at anchor off it. Besides financing her own expedition under Charles Forsyth, Lady Franklin also appealed to the United States and the first American expedition went out in 1851. Every captain must have realized that if they could find Franklin, claim the reward — and also discover the Northwest Passage, so much the better.

In January 1850, in a pincer movement, the Admiralty sent Richard Collinson in *Enterprise* and Robert McClure in *Investigator* through the Bering Strait, and Horatio Austin in *Resolute* and the professional whaler William Penny through Lancaster Sound. Ironically, the contract to supply the ships with provisions had again been given to Goldner.

McClure has been condemned by historians for being arrogant and greedy — motivated more by the reward money for discovering the Northwest Passage than finding Franklin. But before he could be the first to sail through, the *Investigator* was halted by pack ice and McClure retreated south to winter in the Prince of Wales Strait. Once freed, he attempted the passage again, but yet again faced heavy ice. With winter coming, he navigated his ship along the north coast of Banks Island into a large bay that he named Bay of Mercy as a winter anchorage. Had he not erred on the side of caution, McClure might have gone down in history the first person to complete the Northwest Passage, beating Roald Amundsen by about 50 years.

Now concerned about McClure and Collinson, as well as Franklin, the Admiralty mounted its largest expedition in 1852. The Nova Scotia–born Sir Edward Belcher was chosen to lead it — probably the worst choice possible. A former subordinate of Beechey's, he had a reputation as the most foul-tempered, pigheaded officer in the service. Nevertheless he was given command of: *Assistance*, *Resolute*, two screw steamers *Pioneer* and *Intrepid*, and the *North Star*. Leaving the last at Beechey Island, Belcher took *Assistance* and *Pioneer* up Wellington Channel and sent *Resolute* (Captain Henry Kellett) and *Intrepid* (Captain Francis McClintock) as far as Melville Island where they wintered. This time in contrast with Franklin, Kellett's and McClintock's crews made lengthy sledge journeys and food caches were established. McClintock is regarded as the father of the man-hauling sledge, a British institution in polar exploration rather than the use of dogs. Realizing that the large crews of naval ships were idle for much of the time, he devised a system for hauling provisions with six men and an officer to each sledge. Later sails to aid in downwind travel and flags to encourage team spirit were added. It allowed for longer overland exploration from the ships and would be adopted by the Royal Navy to be used by Ernest Shackleton in his 1914 Antarctic expedition. With McClintock's sledges, Lieutenant George Frederick Mecham from the *Resolute* travelled from Ramsay Island at the bottom of the Prince of Wales Strait to Beechey Island by sled — a journey of 1,157 miles — in 70 days.

By now, McClure's crew on the *Investigator* was in critical condition. Living off Goldner's toxic cans of meat meant that scurvy, botulism, and arsenic poisoning affected several crewmen, killing three. Yet again, conditions in the ship's fetid hold bred *Clostridium* spores to which the men's weakened immune systems had no defence. But unlike Franklin, McClure was fortunate. *Resolute* was within reach and travelling by dog sled in early March one of its crew, a Lieutenant Bedford Pim, crossed the Viscount Melville Sound ice and located the *Investigator*. McClure put his lieutenant, Samuel Gurney Cresswell, in charge of transporting six invalids 160 miles to the *Resolute*, which he accomplished without loss of life. Seeing their desperate state, Captain Kellett advised McClure to abandon his ship and begin evacuating all of his crew to the *Resolute*.[23] Then Kellett sent Cresswell with additional ill men to Beechey Island where they could find a ship home. Upon reaching London, Cresswell had become the first British officer to safely negotiate the Northwest passage.

The return of Austin and Penny to London with complaints about Goldner's provision caused a parliamentary inquiry into Admiralty contracts with the Whitechapel merchant.

Preserved Meats (Navy). Return to an Order of the Honourable The House of Commons, dated 5 February 1852; — *for,*

Returns "showing the Date and Terms of all Contracts for Preserved Meat for the Use of Her Majesty's Navy with *Goldner*; also the Quantities issued since the commencement of the above Contracts; specifying the Quantities fit for Use, as well as the Quantities either Condemned or returned into Store as unfit for use, from any of Her Majesty's Stores or Ships, whether at Home or Abroad:

"Complaints when first made; and whether, after such Complaints, further Contracts were entered into with the same Parties:

"Whether these Meats were issued to the Arctic Voyagers:

"Whether Captain *Austin's* Stores were examined and found bad; and if so, were they served from *Goldner's* Contract:

"Of the Quantity of Cases, if any, the Contractor has been allowed to withdraw from her Majesty's Stores after having supplied the same, stating how long such Cases had been in Store:

"And the Contract Prices of Beef and Pork for the Years 1848, 1849, 1850, and 1851."

Admiralty, 12 February 1852. J.H. Hay, Chief Clerk, *Ordered, by* The House of Commons, *to be Printed*, 13 *February* 1852.

A Select Committee was called and various naval provisioners who, having lost contracts because of Goldner, were quite pleased to testify as to how improper cooking and canning might have killed all of Franklin's men. But in the end, Goldner was betrayed by his private secretary Mr. Richie, a Uriah Heep character who told of the purchase of cheap meat, inadequate boiling, and the use of arsenic in the canning. Apparently Richie had gone into the provisioning business himself and now sought to endear himself to the Naval Victualling Board. Having committed mass manslaughter, there is no record of Goldner being prosecuted and his neighbourhood of Whitechapel allowed for a convenient disappearance.

With Belcher's ships locked in the ice and sure to be running out of food, in 1853, the navy hired the supply ship *Breadalbane* to ferry supplies. Proving that the Arctic was as vicious as ever, on August 21, 1853, the *Breadalbane* was holed by ice off Beechey Island and sank within 15 minutes. The 21-man crew was rescued by the accompanying ship, the *Phoenix*.

But by now British Parliament, public, and press had other matters to consider than Franklin's fate. A religious quarrel between Russian Orthodox monks and French Catholic priests over who had precedence in the shrines in Jerusalem and Nazareth was exaggerated into reports that the Turks were violating the rights of Christians in the "Holy Places" of Palestine were being played up in the press. Professing to be their guardians, the Russians seized the excuse to invade the decrepit Ottoman Empire. Alarmed that the czar would take Constantinople and thus threaten the trade routes to India, the British agreed to join the French and Turks in ousting the Russians from the region. Egged on by the press and public, in June 1853, the British and French fleets were dispatched to the Dardanelles.

By the year's end, polar exploration had been overshadowed by war. Franklin had been gone eight years and the British public and press had tired of it, becoming more engrossed in the war of words between the Turks, French, Austrians, and Russians. In January 1854, the Anglo-French fleet entered the Black Sea and the first shots were fired in the Crimean War. Trying to live down the loss of four ships, the Admiralty — its officers, especially — seized on the war as a crusade to protect the Holy Land against the Turks and Russians. Although the ensuing Crimean War was marked by gross incompetence in sanitation and medical care (ten thousand Allied soldiers died of disease before the first shot was fired), it offered infinitely more opportunities than exploration did for career advancement and decorations. Needing all its ships for the Black Sea, the Admiralty declared that if they had not heard from Belcher by March, it would end the search and strike all of Franklin's party off the active list. On March 31, Franklin and the crews were pronounced officially dead.[24]

With the summer of 1854, Belcher's ships were still held in the ice, and against the advice of his officers, he ordered them to be abandoned.

All crews (263 men) returned home on very crowded ships, including the *North Star.* Along with McClure and Kellett, Belcher was relieved of his sword and court-martialed. However, he argued in self defence that with the loss of the *Breadalbane,* the five ships' crews would have been running out of food and the two steamers out of coal. He was acquitted — many believed because of his social standing — and had his sword returned to him in silence. The hero of the hour was Cresswell, as on his return, Parry declared that he was the first person to traverse the Northwest Passage.

That same winter, the HBC had sent its chief medical officer, Dr. John Rae from York Factory, overland to look for Franklin. Unlike other HBC expeditions, this had no commercial purpose, but was entirely for humanitarian (and publicity) purposes. Rae was the perfect choice because he had learned to live off the land and befriend the Inuit. Rae did not endear himself to the Admiralty when he called the Royal Naval expeditions that came to Canada without thought of their survival or learning from the indigenous people, "These self-sufficient donkeys…."

He was convinced that the navy was searching in the wrong area and made for the isthmus of Boothia Peninsula. Rae kept hearing stories from the Inuit that a party of white men had perished somewhere to the west of the Back River. He questioned the Inuit hunters and also bought from them spoons, buttons, inscribed silverware, and Franklin's Royal Hanoverian Order.[25] At Repulse Bay he was visited by more Inuit and he was able to identify the site which the Inuit spoke as the near the Montreal Islands at the mouth of the Great Fish River. In the spring of 1850, they had seen about 40 white men dragging a boat near the north shore of King William Island. After a two-month cross-examination to ensure the accuracy of his findings, the doctor came to his own conclusion about where the Franklin survivors had met their deaths. But with the onset of winter, he had to make a difficult choice: should he wait until next summer to get to their graves or go to London immediately with the news? He decided on the latter — a decision that would haunt and damn him forever. Rae returned to York Factory on August 31, 1854, and sailed for England on September 20.

He arrived in London on October 25, and sent a confidential report to the Admiralty. Smarting from Belcher's fiasco and no doubt jealous of the HBC, the Admiralty immediately made public Rae's findings. The news of Franklin's death coincided with reports from Crimea. On almost the same day, the *London Times* correspondent William Howard Russell told of a militarily insignificant, but emotionally explosive incident that had taken place in the Battle of Balaclava — the Charge of the Light Brigade. The shock of both tragedies arriving simultaneously devastated the British public — like many of her subjects, Queen Victoria wept at the news. A bumbling failure in another time or culture, Franklin was now elevated to heroic status. Or was it (like Scott and Shackleton later) that the British admired those who failed in their search for the Holy Grail and died doing so? It was this outpouring of grief that led to the erection of the Franklin's statue at Waterloo Place, a plaque in Westminister Abbey, and a monument in The Chapel of St. Peter and St. Paul in the Old Royal Naval College in Greenwich. Alfred Lord Tennyson,[26] better known for his poem on the fate of the Light Brigade, would personally compose Franklin's epitaph:

> Not here: the white North has thy bones;
> and thou,
> Heroic sailor-soul
> Art passing on thine happier voyage now,
> Toward no earthly pole.

Lady Franklin declined a widow's pension or to believe Rae, arguing that as he had not been to the site itself, but was relying on the word of "savages," he was not entitled to the reward money. Rae claimed that he had no idea of the reward. But there was worse to come. The Inuit stated that the last survivors had resorted to cannibalism. Awash with grief and admiration for Franklin's men, the nation refused to even consider the possibility. That officers and men of the Royal Navy should be accused of such a deed was unthinkable in Victorian England. Rae would not receive the reward until July 1856. He was given £8,000 and £2,000 was divided among his men.

With the completion of the Suez Canal in 1869 and the construction of the Canadian Pacific Railway across the continent, the British government lost interest in finding a Northwest Passage. This was especially so when the Canadian Pacific began a government-subsidized shipping line on both oceans that connected Liverpool with Hong Kong via Montreal and Vancouver.[27] The Atlantic and Pacific oceans were now linked by railway — the failure of a sea route, wrote Sir William Van Horne, the engineer who built that link, had led to the completion of a land one.

Three years after Confederation, on June 23, 1870, a British order-in-council formally transferred the territories of the HBC (Rupert's Land) to the new government in Ottawa. As Rupert's Land became Canadian territory, the Hudson's Bay Company was given licence to continue operation as an independent, private, commercial company and not an instrument of British government. But as the limits of former HBC empire had never been legally defined or even explored, no one knew what the extent of the territories were or the status of the islands north of the mainland. With the aim of annexing them before the United States or any European power did, on June 29, 1871, the British North America Act transferred all remaining "North-western territory" to Canada.

Three years later, the British Colonial Office received a couple of inquiries concerning the legal status of the Cumberland Gulf area on Baffin Island. The first was from an Englishman who wanted to fish commercially in the area and the second came from a Lieutenant William A. Mintzer of the U.S. Navy Corps of Engineers who wished to mine graphite in that region — there were suspicions that this was under Washington's auspices. Without waiting for permission or a reply, Mintzer began mining in Cumberland Sound, extracting graphite and mica. Fearing that "this yankee adventurer," as the Colonial Office labelled him, would soon be flying the Stars and Stripes over the Cumberland Peninsula, the colonial minister Lord Carnarvon asked the Admiralty if Britain had ever taken possession of the Cumberland region. The Admiralty was able to show that in 1818, Captain Ross had done so.

Fearing more such inquiries, Lord Dufferin, the governor general of Canada, asked if the northern boundaries of Canada had ever been legally defined. What alarmed him and the Colonial Office was that Mintzer's assessment of the mineral potential in the Cumberland area was published the *New York Times*. While the Canadian government appeared sanguine over the issue (evidently still grappling with the immensity of the HBC land transfer), to keep the Americans at bay, the British government was preparing to transfer its Arctic possessions to Canada.

The concerns of the Colonial Office were that no one really knew how far north the territories extended and could the British legally claim sovereignty over them? How would the United States react to their transfer to Canada? It ran contrary to the Monroe Doctrine and — as the Admiralty pointed out — if legitimacy was dependant on previous exploration, the Royal Navy had gone no farther north than Smith Sound at 78° 30' N — but by 1874, American ships had been beyond the 82° parallel. It was also in the interests of the British government to make its claim to the Arctic as vague as possible, as the Colonial Office felt that Britain had a historic right to parts of Greenland.

It is said that there was not a single year in Queen Victoria's long reign in which somewhere in the world her soldiers were not fighting. Continual warfare became a way of life for the British public and its military, who accepted it as the price of empire and world leadership. Until the Crimean War (1854–56), the wars were localized, requiring little in the way of logistics, lives, or public expenditures. But the Crimean War was followed immediately by the Indian Mutiny (1857–59), war in China (1859–61), the Northwest Frontier of India (1855–63), parts of Africa (1863–68), Red River in Canada (1870–73), and so on until the Boer War itself. The constant logistics of moving whole armies by sea around the Cape of Good Hope to Lucknow or Peking or Ashanti land taxed the navy's resources — as it did the Treasury, leaving no ships, men, or money for more Arctic exploration. Fortunately, beginning in 1874, the Empire was at peace — for the next four years at least — which allowed for the last important British Arctic expedition to be mounted.

As a young man, Captain George Nares had been part of Captain Kellett's crew looking for the *Investigator*. In May 1875, with Commander

A.H. Markham as second-in-command and in company with *Discovery*, Nares sailed up the channel between Ellesmere Island and Greenland. The mission's purpose was twofold: find the elusive polar sea once and for all and confirm British (now Canadian) sovereignty as far as the North Pole. Unlike Franklin and Belcher's expeditions, the Arctic Expedition of 1875 was a modest affair. *Alert* was an obsolete naval sloop that with a strengthened hull and more powerful engines had been converted into an exploration vessel.

Nares reached 82° N latitude and wintered in Cape Sheridan (exactly where Peary would in 1905) with *Discovery* kept to the south as a precaution. Having been trained by Mecham in the value of man-hauling sledges, he then had the crews break up into parties for overland exploration. While a sledging party from the *Discovery* explored Greenland, Markham took a sledge party to 83° 26' N on Ellesmere Island, the highest latitude reached by anyone until then. Lieutenant Pelham Aldrich led a sledging

Thomas Mitchell / Library and Archives Canada/C-052514.

G.S. Nares expedition fast to the floe in Franklin Pierce Bay, waiting for the ice to open a water channel on August 9, 1875, in Cape Prescott, Northwest Territories.

party along the island's coastline, hampered by undulating hummocks of coastal ice that made travel dangerous. Incredibly, Aldrich reached Alert Point, naming many of the features he saw on the way — Ward Hunt Island for George Ward Hunt, First Lord of the Admiralty; Cape Hecla after Parry's ship; and Disraeli Fiord after the British prime minister Benjamin Disraeli. A deterioration in the lime juice (which been used instead of lemon juice) carried by the sledging parties led them to be deci-mated by scurvy and Nares abandoning all plans for a second winter. He was fortunate to return home with only one death and was later rewarded with a knighthood. He took the *Alert* to study the ocean currents in the Straits of Magellan in South America. It would not be until 1881 that a United States expedition to Ellesmere Island would reach Lady Franklin Bay and winter at Fort Conger. By then it was firmly Canadian territory.

In Ottawa, to the frustration of the Colonial Office, the Canadian Parliament kept deferring the matter of how the Arctic territories could be included in the country's boundaries. Annexing territories to one day create provinces out of them (with the accompanying religious and lin-guistic baggage) was a controversial issue. Power to extend the limits of the country came from the British North American Act of 1867 and 1870, but because the boundaries of Rupert's Land and the Northwest Territory were unknown, only an imperial act could annex them for Canada. At the same time, the vague terminology used to delineate the country's limits was becoming a problem in the Yukon/Alaska region, as well. Mired in confusion and legal doubt, the matter would languish for three years as correspondence was passed between the Colonial Office in London and the offices of the governor general and prime minister in Canada. Seen from this perspective, the British government had little idea of what it was transferring to Canada and Ottawa even less an idea of what it was receiving.

In May 1878, both sides in the House of Commons in Ottawa agreed that an act of Parliament should be passed defining the boundaries of the country. Wiser minds prevailed on both sides of the Atlantic for fear that if the procedure for an act was used, it would be held up in Parliament, ques-tions would be asked, doubts raised, and the whole project dropped. An order-in-council, it was agreed, would be sufficient to annex the territories.

In February 1880, Prime Minister Macdonald asked the British government for such. Composed in early July and approved by the council in a record three days, the order-in-council to annex all British territories in the Arctic came into effect on September 1, 1880.

As Canada's entire claim to title to the Arctic rests on it, the document is reproduced here:

> At the Court at Osborne House, Isle of Wight,
> the 31st Day of July, 1880.
> Present:
> The Queen's Most Excellent Majesty,
> Lord President,
> Lord Steward,
> Lord Chamberlain.

> Whereas it is expedient that all British territories and possessions in North America, and the islands adjacent to such territories and possessions which are not already included in the Dominion of Canada, should (with the exception of the Colony of Newfoundland and its dependencies) be annexed to and form part of the said Dominion.

> And whereas, the Senate and Commons of Canada in Parliament assembled, have, in and by an Address, dated May 3, 1878, represented to Her Majesty "That it is desirable that the Parliament of Canada, on the transfer of the before-mentioned territories being completed, should have authority to legislate for their future welfare and good government, and the power to make all needful rules and regulations respecting them, the same as in the case of the other territories (of the Dominion); and that the Parliament of Canada expressed its willingness to assume the duties and obligations consequent thereon;"

> And whereas, Her Majesty is graciously pleased to accede to the desire expressed in and by the said Address:

Now, therefore, it is hereby ordered and declared by Her Majesty, by and with the advice of Her Most Honourable Privy Council, as follows:

From and after September 1, 1880, all British territories and possessions in North America, not already included within the Dominion of Canada, and all islands adjacent to any of such territories or possessions, shall (with the exception of the Colony of Newfoundland and its dependencies) become and be annexed to and form part of the said Dominion of Canada; and become and be subject to the laws for the time being in force in the said Dominion, in so far as such laws may be applicable thereto.

— (sgd) C.L. Peel.

The British Foreign Minister Lord Kimberley sent the approved order to the Governor General the Marquis of Lorne in a dispatch dated August 16 and it was published in *The Canada Gazette* on October 9.

The attempts by the Royal Navy at finding a Northwest Passage to the Orient had profound effects on Canada. Franklin's disaster stimulated a detailed survey of the Arctic that would never have occurred had he been successful. The overland efforts of the HBC notwithstanding, it was the Lords of the Admiralty who were responsible for opening up and mapping the vastness of the North, which in due course would be handed voluntarily over to Canada. Franklin-bashing by contemporary authors has been the theme over the years and with each new exhumation of a member of his crew or discovery of an abandoned ship, the exercise is reiterated. His reliance on self-sufficiency and technology, on ceremonial trappings and canned food contributed to his doom. But as Lady Franklin pointed out to the Admiralty, dead men argue nothing for themselves.[28] Isolated and shunned by the government and press once the Crimean War began, she defended her husband's reputation for the remainder of her life and was responsible in 1866 for getting the wording on his statue at Waterloo Place to state that he had discovered the Northwest Passage. The tragedy of losing her husband was compounded when her adopted son Joseph-Rene Bellot was also lost in the one of the search parties when he fell down a crevasse.

The arrogance of the Admiralty and the British nation post Waterloo in thinking it was entitled to an open polar sea that would facilitate a Northwest Passage is as much to blame. The loss of the *Erebus* and *Terror* began a chain of events that involved much of the Royal Navy's resources between the Napoleonic and Crimean Wars. Consider the mathematical acceleration: with two ships lost, four were sent to find them with a fifth sent to find two of the four. Eight ships were sent in the Austin phase of the search and, by 1854, there were 22 expeditions private and naval with 33 ship winterings. Ships were now searching for ships that were searching for Franklin who had been searching for the Northwest Passage.[29] But because of this, one half of the Canadian Arctic, including three possible Northwest Passages, had been mapped out in the search for Franklin. More importantly with exploration, mapping, planting of flags, and building of cairns, Britain could legitimately lay claim to the Arctic — and pass it to Canada.

It would not be until October 2, 1895, with the Colonial Boundaries Act, that the Canadian government asserted some sovereignty over its Arctic windfall, accepting the islands and territories transferred to it in 1880. A Dominion order-in-council was passed, creating the four districts of Ungava, the Yukon, Mackenzie, and Franklin, and police posts were set up. Two years later, a second order-in-council gave the Yukon and Mackenzie districts all islands up to 20 miles from their coasts and the remainder to Franklin. But as to sending troops to assert Canada's sovereignty — that belongs to another chapter.

2

All That Glitters

Critical of the British officers who did not "acclimatize" to changing conditions, Sir George Simpson — now the governor of the Hudson's Bay Company — took every opportunity to do so himself. The "Emperor of the North," as he was called, Simpson also adapted to the new realities, investing in canals, steamboats, and in the Grand Trunk Railway.[1] Reinventing the HBC, he moved its operations from York Factory to Vancouver. Coinciding with the popularity of silk hats in Europe, over-hunting east of the Rockies had driven the beaver to near extinction. In 1821, when the Colonial Office forced the HBC to merge with its rival North West Company, it gave the new company the exclusive right to trade west of the Rockies, therefore defining the future boundaries of Canada:

> ... all such parts of North America to the northward and the westward of the lands and territories belonging to the United States of America as shall not form part of any of our provinces in North America, or to any European government, state or power.

Based on Vancouver Island, the HBC traded in salmon, lumber, furs, and soon coal as far away as California, Hawaii, and China. The riches of the Pacific Northwest were untapped and its rivers gave access to the Pacific Ocean. But in moving to the region, Simpson encountered the Russians to the north and Americans in the south. From the 49th parallel to the Bering Straits, the Pacific coast was the fault line where three European empires — Spain, Russia, and Britain — collided. Britain's claim dated back to 1579, when Sir Francis Drake explored the area — but the Spanish took actual possession of it by building a fort at Nootka Sound. By 1789, with their New World empire disintegrating, the Spanish signed the Nootka Sound Convention[2] (negotiated by George Vancouver) and left the Pacific Northwest to the British and the Russians. While the Russians acquiesced to the HBC's advances, the Americans did not. Using cutthroat and sometimes violent methods, the Yankee traders pushed ceaselessly north of the 49th parallel, heedless of the effects they had on the indigenous people (like selling them alcohol).

The Russian-American Company (RAC), based in Sitka, had been granted a monopoly by Czar Paul I in 1799 to trade in sea otter fur. Like the HBC in Rupert's Land, the RAC was the instrument of its government in North America and connected with a vast trade network in Europe. Unlike the HBC, it ruthlessly suppressed the indigenous population both in the Aleutian Islands and North American mainland by using Cossacks. Despite this, by 1820, the RAC was marginally profitable and all attempts by the imperial Russian government to make its *Rossiyskaya Imperiya* pay off failed. The problems were numerous: its supply line stretched as far back as the Black Sea, which meant that every petty official along the way took his due, it was too far from St. Petersburg to effectively govern and worst of all, the czar couldn't resist meddling in its affairs — at one point he replaced the governors with naval officers. More importantly, the Russians were dependent on American trading ships for provisioning and transporting the pelts to Canton, China.

As the sea otter population on the coast dwindled, the Russians and their Tlingit (an indigenous people off the Pacific Northwest Coast) intermediaries began venturing inland. With the Russian port of St. Michael on the Bering Strait 70 miles from the mouth of the Yukon River, the RAC travelled up it to barter with the Natives for other furs. Its base at Nulato, some 300 miles up the river from its isthmus, was one of Russia's deepest inland incursions, second only to Fort Ross in Sonoma, California. From here, their Tlingit middlemen could extend their reach for furs with the inland tribes. This worried Simpson, who saw the new HBC territory around Fort Yukon being depleted.

When the czar attempted to extend Russian America south to the 51st parallel in 1821, both the American and British governments protested.

Tripartite negotiations between Russia, Britain, and the United States culminated in two treaties being signed in St. Petersburg. The 1824 United States–Russian treaty was characterized by its clear objectives and language: the parallel 54° 40' N was established as the boundary between the Russian and American territories and no American settlement could be established north of it or the Russian settlement south of it. It also granted American merchants the right to trade in Russian America for a period of 10 years.

At first glance, the Anglo-Russian treaty the following year seems curiously done. The diplomats who drew it up obviously had no idea of the topography of the region for the treaty gave the coast of the Alaskan panhandle to Russia and the interior to Britain. The demarcation line between British North America and Russian America began at the same 54° 40' N parallel at Prince of Wales Island, and then moved north along the Portland Channel to the 56th degree of north latitude. From here it followed the summit of the mountains parallel to the coast until the 141st degree of west longitude from where it extended "… in its prolongation as far as the Frozen Ocean." Although the complex boundary lines would not be firmly established until 1903, the arrangement suited both fur-trading monopolies well. It effectively blocked the American commercial interests out of the northern Pacific coast and the Yukon. For if the Russians controlled the coastline and the British the interior, the Yankee traders had access to neither.

As strange as the arrangement may seem today, it should be remembered that before the use of steam or the internal combustion engine, all trade on the Pacific Northwest was completely dependent on a network of water routes. It took seven years for the HBC to send or receive trade goods overland by sled and porter between Montreal and its Forts Selkirk and Yukon.[3] Thus, control of rivers like the Yukon, Teslin, Pelly, Porcupine, Liard, and especially the Stikine were essential to conducting trade. The HBC lost Fort Yukon, which was on the Russian side of the border, but consolidated its presence in New Caledonia (it would not be named British Columbia until 1858) by erecting forts at strategic river locations: Fort Vancouver on the Columbia River (1826), Fort Langley on the Fraser (1827), Fort Halkett on the Liard (1829), Fort Simpson on the

Nass (1831), and Fort McLoughlin near Bella Coola (1833). It also leased Fort Wrangell at the mouth of the Stikine River from the Russians, abandoning it in 1849 after all the sea otter and beaver stocks in the area were wiped out. Simultaneously, a number of abandoned North West Company forts in the Yukon were reactivated to control river junctures there — both measures giving the HBC the option of shipping to the Pacific, Bering Strait, or Beaufort Sea. The Russians even contracted with their former rivals for provisioning and shipping their own furs to Canton.

The United States was another story. Apart from the occasional Royal Navy vessel, the only British power in the region was the HBC, and Simpson was aware that it would take little for Washington to seize all of New Caledonia (the future British Columbia) and the Yukon. In 1845, James Polk had been elected president on the platform of "Fifty-four-forty or fight!" Polk, who had bullied the Mexicans to annex Texas and California, now sabre-rattled for a war in the Pacific Northwest that would allow the United States to claim territory up to the 54° latitude. The HBC received reports that American settlers who had immigrated across the border were ready to set up their own local government and proclaim independence. But reluctant to fight both the Mexicans and Canadians simultaneously, Congress persuaded Polk to back down and the State Department negotiated the Oregon Treaty with the British in 1846, which made the 49th parallel the official United States–Canada border from the Lake of the Woods to the Pacific Ocean — excluding Vancouver Island, where the HBC were established.

His treasury in desperate circumstances after the Crimean War, in 1859, Czar Alexander II offered to sell his North American territories either to Britain or the United States. He hoped for a bidding war to get a good price, but the United States became occupied with the Civil War and the British (who could have seized all Russian territory during the Crimean War) refused to negotiate. Unlike Britain and France, from the very beginning of the Civil War, the czar had thrown his support behind the Union. Alexander II had emancipated the serfs in his own country and championed President Abraham Lincoln's Emancipation Proclamation. With the war's end, in December 1866, Baron Eduard de Stoeckl, the Russian ambassador to Washington, broached the issue. He had an ally in Secretary of State William Henry Seward, who had wanted this in 1859. About to be impeached, the unfortunate President Andrew Johnson did not need another contentious issue. But after an all-night session, the terms were negotiated and the treaty signed at 4:00 a.m. on March 30, 1867. The United States purchased 586,412 square miles (1.5 million square kilometres) of Russian America for $7.2 million in gold. A new American company, Hutchinson, Kohl & Company, was formed to take over all of the assets of the RAC.[4] The Aleut name of "Alaska" was chosen for the former Russian colony and 250 United States soldiers, commanded by General Lovell Rousseau, were sent to Sitka for the formal handover ceremony on October 18, 1867. They were the first North American military force in the Pacific Northwest until 1869 when Fort Wrangell was rebuilt as an army base.

With Alaska and the panhandle now part of the United States, the HBC's outlets on the Yukon, Porcupine, and Stikine Rivers were effectively strangled. The United States controlled all access to northern British Columbia and the Yukon with the right to levy duty on Canadian goods passing up or downriver. The unsatisfactory alternative for the HBC was to have its trade goods from Montreal portaged overland to the Mackenzie District. Governor Simpson died in 1860 and his company underwent major changes in the coming years — its stock was traded publicly and in 1870, Rupert's Land was transferred to the Canadian government.

The following year, the Treaty of Washington was signed to settle outstanding differences between the United States and Britain arising from the Civil War. While the chief point was payment to the United States for damage done by Confederate cruisers, Prime Minister Sir John A. Macdonald was invited to be one of the five British commissioners because other issues affected Canada. For the United States and Canada, the new owners of the Pacific Northwest, it was no longer only furs but mineral rights that were important, or more precisely, access to them.

Reflecting the growing stature of the United States on the world stage, the British (and the German Kaiser, who was asked to arbitrate) awarded the Americans several concessions, like free navigation of the St. Lawrence River, opening of Canadian fisheries to American fishermen, and San Juan Island in the Portland Channel on the Pacific coast.

Compensation for the damage by the Fenians to Canadian property was ignored, causing Macdonald to complain bitterly that the other four commissioners had sacrificed Canadian interests for Britain's. But he did sign the treaty and defended it in Parliament as necessary "for the sake of peace, and for the sake of the great Empire of which we form a part." However, one point was a minor victory for Canada in that freedom of navigation was granted on the Yukon, Porcupine, and Stikine rivers. This had been at the behest of Donald Alexander Smith, the chief commissioner of the HBC — and future builder of the Canadian Pacific Railway. Insignificant to the commissioners in Washington as it might have been, it had far-reaching consequences both for the HBC (which could now use steamers to bring in supplies on the Yukon and Porcupine rivers) — and the Yukon gold rush.

Frederick Schwatka could have stepped out of the popular fiction of the day. A former U.S. Cavalry officer who had been at the Battle of Little Big Horn, he was also a lawyer, a medical doctor, and an explorer. In 1880, on behalf of the American Geographical Society, Schwatka searched for and found remnants of the Franklin expedition. But while in the Arctic he named landmarks after American presidents Hayes and Sherman. Three years later, he was asked by the United States government to determine the position of the 141st meridian — the demarcation line between Alaska and Canada. Schwatka rafted down the Yukon River from head to mouth to do so — his line was about 12 miles off. What concerned Ottawa more was that he also named or renamed topographical landmarks along the way: Lake Lindeman after the secretary of the Bremen Geographical Society, Lake Bennett after the editor of the *New York Herald*, and the Chilkoot Pass after a French geographer. All but the last have remained on maps today. There was no question in either Ottawa or Washington that both countries claimed the Lynn Canal/White Pass area and beyond, and in November 1892 they agreed to conduct a joint survey of the Alaska panhandle. This led to 11 survey parties — four American and seven Canadian — working their way through the coastal mountains, all producing maps that supported their own country's interpretation of the 1825 St. Petersburg Treaty. Whether there was gold discovered in the Yukon or not, the conflicting surveys ensured future mistrust and bitterness — sadly not for Russia and Britain, the two countries that had drawn up the treaty, but for Canada and the United States.

In 1895, the term "Northwest Territories" meant the void on the map of Canada between the provinces of Ontario and British Columbia. Encompassing what would be the present provinces of Alberta, Manitoba, Saskatchewan, the Yukon, and the Northwest Territories, it was vaguely administered from Regina. The Canadian government's response to the growing interest in the Yukon region was to have Thomas White, the minister of the interior, send an expedition from the Geological Survey of Canada in 1887. Dr. George Mercer Dawson and William Ogilvie were told to determine the 141st meridian, survey the Alaska/Yukon boundary, and report back on the mineral potential in the region. Dawson had been hired by the International Boundary Commission to survey the

George Mercer Dawson, assistant director of the Geological Survey of Canada. His colleague William Ogilvie named Dawson City after him.

W.J. Topley/Library and Archives Canada/PA-026689.

49th parallel, and, although frail in health and hunchbacked (he was called "Little Giant") he painstakingly travelled thousands of miles by boat, portage, and on foot through British Columbia and the Yukon, curious about the minerals in the area. William Ogilvie had trained as a surveyor under Robert Sparks of the well-known Ottawa family. The pair examined the upper Yukon basin and reported that there were gold deposits in the region, predicting that a gold rush would occur soon. Dawson's findings were published in the annual report of the Geological Survey of Canada for 1887–1888, which for the politicians in Ottawa was the first hint of what was to come.

There had always been rumours of gold in the Pacific Northwest — for many years both HBC and RAC factors had written of it to London and St. Petersburg. Not wanting an invasion of foreign (i.e., American) prospectors, both companies had cautiously suppressed the news. But as the gold strikes became frequent and moved northward, it was more difficult to do so. In 1842, gold was discovered in the Queen Charlotte Islands and in 1858 on the Fraser River. Compared with the United States, where only American citizens were allowed to mine for gold, Canadians were more accommodating — anyone could mine for the precious metal in Canada provided they paid a tax or royalty to the government to do so. As the author Pierre Berton pointed out, if the Klondike's gold had been across the border, no Canadian could have mined it. But as the richest strikes were in Canada, much of the gold ended up in the United States.

None of this concerned an increasing number of American prospectors inadvertently crossing the 49th parallel as there were successive gold strikes at Cariboo Lake (1860), on the Stikine River (1861), and Vancouver Island (1871). It was these prospectors who took steamboats from St. Michael, Alaska, up the Yukon River to Circle City[5] (the miners believed that it was on the Arctic Circle), where they unloaded their supplies for gold mining camps in the nearby bush. They were not amateurs escaping the humdrum of urban office and factory jobs, family life, or farming — most had worked on earlier strikes in Nevada, California,

Colorado, and even Australia. They were gypsies who lived by the unwritten code of the prospector and whose most precious foodstuff was fermented yeast used to make bread or "sourdough." Completely mobile and self-sufficient, with allegiance to no one except themselves — all they owned was what they carried, allowing them to "stampede" to the next strike. Now they were coming to the Yukon.

The Alaska Commercial Company had built Fort Reliance in 1874, eight miles from the mouth of the Thron-diuck River — the salmon stream referred to as "Hammer-Water" by the locals because its mouth was so shallow that they hammered stakes across it to spread their nets and catch fish. More a collection of cabins than a fort, Reliance was a point of reference so that the Sixtymile and Fortymile rivers were named for their distance from it. Coarse gold was discovered at the mouth of the Fortymile River in 1886, the strike attracting prospectors from Circle City who were unaware that they had crossed an international boundary to get there. The town of Fortymile soon had a population of over 1,000 people who somehow kept six saloons, doctors, blacksmiths, a watch-maker, a dressmaker, a library, a theatre, and the territory's first post office in business. Fortymile might have been in Canada, but as writer Pierre Berton wrote, "It was really an American town, getting its supplies from the United States without customs payments and sending out mail with U.S. stamps."[6] Without government authorities in the region, the miners drew up their own mining laws on the rules of staking and protecting claims and arbitrated local matters by councils.

The public in eastern Canada likely first heard of the Yukon because of the Church Missionary Society. A British couple, Bishop William and Nina Bompas, ran the mission at Fortymile and in 1896; she went on a speaking tour of eastern Canada to raise funds for their church. She lectured in Montreal, Ottawa, and Toronto, publicizing the plight of the Native people on the Yukon River and the effect that the invasion of debauched (as she painted the stampeders) gold-hungry foreigners was having on them. It wasn't just that game had disappeared along the rivers or that the landscape was altered due to placer mining and the frequency of forest fires, but worst of all, that the miners brewed *hootchi-noo* — a concoction of molasses, sugar, and dried fruit fermented with

H.J. Woodside/Library and Archives Canada/PA-016944.

Working a claim on Bonanza Creek, Yukon, 1899. Most of the "stampeders" were Americans who were barely aware where Alaska ended and Canada began.

sourdough — selling it to the Native peoples, causing a general licentiousness in the town.

Her words fell on deaf ears as far as the federal government was concerned. No treaty was signed to protect the Natives and nor were they given their own reservation for fear that gold might be discovered on it. The unofficial opinion seemed to be that there were too few in the territory to worry about. The Han, for example, who lived in the area of the Klondike were all but wiped out by the diseases introduced by the gold rush.[7]

And it wasn't only in the goldfields. When Franklin named the island at the mouth of the Mackenzie River after Herschel, he was amazed at the large number of Inuit in the region. The Victorian fashion for women's corsets had made baleen valuable, causing American whalers to pursue their quarry to the Beaufort Sea, especially where the water opened earlier off the Mackenzie River's mouth — making for a longer whaling season. Joining the Americans to ashore to winter at Herschel Island were Scottish whalers, both establishing stations to trade with the Inuit.

Because two whaling fleets had been caught in the polar pack ice in 1871 and 1876, the United States government established relief stations along the north coast of Alaska. What should have worried the Canadian government was that the whalers were followed by American revenue cutters from Point Barrow, Alaska, who also called at Herschel Island.[8]

Missionaries complained about the effect the Americans had upon the Inuit population, trading whisky with the Natives for "furs, walrus ivory bones and their young girls." By 1893, Bishop Bompas had written to everyone in authority — from the Department of the Interior, the Church Missionary Society and the North-West Mounted Police, to Thomas Mayne Daly, the superintendent-general of Indian Affairs, warning of the effect that the influx of whites had on what had been an isolated, morally unaware society. As to the whalers and miners, they considered the missionaries "whiners and complainers" who did not understand the traditions of the frontier.[9]

The North-West Mounted Police (NWMP) had been created in 1873 to make the prairies safe for the settlers expected from Europe and to demonstrate sovereignty to the Americans. When neither the revolt by the Mètis nor the American annexation occurred, the government in Ottawa wondered at the future role of the mounted police and considered disbanding them. But the complaints from the Yukon now gave the NWMP a purpose and a unit was sent to the Yukon. In 1894, Inspector Charles Constantine was instructed to travel to Fortymile and set up a post with three officers, 20 constables, and a collector of customs. The last would be responsible for levying customs duties on all goods that came down the Yukon River and tax the gold that went out. Fort Constantine was the first Canadian government presence in the Yukon, and the duties of the NWMP in the 200,000 square miles of unexplored wilderness extended to far more than ordinary policing. The Mounties would be responsible for keeping law and order, handling the mail, maintaining the registry of claims, collecting royalties on gold being mined, and monitoring miners' movements into the interior. They were also the territory's magistrates, customs inspectors, and prison wardens. Incredible as it may seem, the size of the force was considered sufficient for the job. There were few inhabitants to police and fewer entry points into the region.

The misdeeds of American miners and whalers in the far-off Yukon would have been lost in Ottawa in the spring of 1896 when all attention was on the election contest being waged between Wilfrid Laurier and Charles Tupper. Similarly, the news that Laurier had been elected prime minister on June 23 would have been of little significance to the small party making its way along Rabbit Creek, a tributary of the Thron-diuck River. "Siwash" George Washington Carmack, his wife, Kate, and daughter, along with Skookum Jim and Tagish Charlie, were looking for logs to sell in Fortymile. Both men had worked for Ogilvie as guides and porters. A former U.S. Navy cook, Carmack had been his interpreter. From the Dakl'aweidi clan of Tagish, Skookum Jim got his nickname (which means "strong" in Chinook trade jargon) for carrying 156 pounds of bacon over the Chilkoot Pass for Ogilvie, double the load most prospectors could carry. Although the actual story has since been mythologized, it seems that where the creek forked, Jim was cleaning a saucepan when he saw a glint in the water. After the celebratory dance and whoops, they discovered that there was even more gold in the creek that fed into the fork.

On August 16, none of them could have had any idea what they were setting in motion. For after that, everything changed — for them, the North, and Canada. After staking their claims, they went to Fortymile to register them. The experienced prospectors who heard their story doubted it — the valley was too wide for gold and as Carmack was the only white man in the group and mistrusted by the miners because of his affiliation with the Natives, they had difficulty in getting anyone to believe them. Fortunately, their former employer William Ogilvie was on hand to confirm that the dust they had in a cartridge case was "new" and so the frenzy began. With this, everyone at Fortymile must have run or poled upriver to Rabbit Creek (now renamed Bonanza Creek and its tributary Eldorado) and, overnight, sluice boxes cut across both creeks as the best claims were staked.

At the swamp where the Thron-diuck River (mispronounced "Klondike" by the prospectors) joined the Yukon River, a tent village grew overnight, which William Ogilvie would name "Dawson City" after his colleague George Mercer Dawson. On September 5, the little steamer *Alice* arrived at Dawson City from St. Michael, Alaska, 1,600 miles downriver, bringing with it food and supplies. It was the first and — as the river was beginning to freeze over — would be the only steamboat until the next summer. With stampeders pouring into Dawson through the winter, Ogilvie and Constantine became alarmed — it wasn't only the deteriorating food situation, but that the majority of prospectors were American. Vigilante governments were running the mining communities on the American side of the border and in Skagway, Alaska, a gangster named Soapy Smith was operating with impunity. In January 1897, both Ogilvie and Constantine warned Ottawa about the situation. With the Yukon River frozen, their letters were carried by hand and dog sled to the nearest railhead and took two months to reach the office of the minister of the interior. In the time-honoured tradition of Ottawa's bureaucracy, Ogilvie's report was filed away before its import could be realized. Fortunately, Constantine's warning was heeded and the NWMP made plans to dispatch 19 more constables to the Yukon.

That winter, Dawson became the City of Gold — and nothing else. The irony was that as miners brought in increasingly large amounts of nuggets and dust, there was nothing they could buy with them. It was not that there was no salt, whisky, sourdough, or nails for sluice boxes and cabins, but worse, the food had run out. In vain, they hunted for game in the surrounding hills, but by then the caribou had migrated and the Arctic hare had disappeared. So desperate was the need for fresh meat that sled dogs were killed and eaten and, as with the Franklin expedition, scurvy and starvation set in. Inspector Constantine, who made Fort Herchmer in Dawson City the new NWMP headquarters, posted a notice that read:

> I, having carefully looked over the present distressing
> situation regarding the supply of food for the winter,
> find that the stock on hand is not sufficient to meet the
> wants of the people and can see but one way out of the

difficulty, and that is an immediate move down-river, of
all those who are now unsupplied, to Fort Yukon, where
there is a large stock of provisions.

There were steamboats from St. Michael with supplies caught in the
ice at the former HBC post of Fort Yukon, so the starving men began
trekking downriver. A curious sight unfolded along the Yukon River as
the exodus of ravenous miners escaping Dawson were met by the equally
wild-eyed going upriver to stake their claims. The starving either bought
all their food or in some cases robbed them of it. Although the river
would be free of ice in May, the food shortage worsened as each steamboat to Dawson brought even more hopefuls.

The outside world knew none of this until July 14, when the *Excelsior*
arrived in San Francisco and the *Portland* arrived in Seattle, and the
miners staggered off the ships with an estimated $800,000 worth of gold
— and the Yukon gold rush was on. Newspapers worldwide picked up
the story of the unwashed, ragged millionaires who could barely carry
their sacks of gold dust to the bank. The Hearst newspaper chain — soon
to be a byword for "yellow journalism" in the Spanish-American War
— needed little excuse to print exaggerated accounts of the rush and
even the most respected newspaper in the British Empire, *The Times*
of London, ran a lengthy piece on July 26 about the discoveries of gold
in the Yukon — and then sent its own correspondent to the scene. The
Department of State in Washington was concerned enough that on July
26 the United States military commander in California, General Rufus
Shafter, was asked to provide a full company of infantry to establish a
post at Circle City "to protect American interests."

At Canadian and American ports on the Pacific coast, a whole industry sprang up around the rush. Who really struck it rich were the chambers
of commerce in Canadian and United States west coast ports, merchants
who outfitted potential prospectors, shipping lines that put every vessel
safe and unsafe to sea — and glue factories that made large profits by selling their worn-out horses to those who had never packed one, let alone
understood the terrain they would have to negotiate. Besides pickaxes,
pans, tents, saddles, shotguns, and sled dogs selling briskly, there were

other more imaginative goods and services like bogus maps of the Yukon goldfields, steam-powered sleds, amphibious boat sleds, clairvoyants who promised that they could tell exactly where the gold was, ingeniously designed "ice bicycles" (bicycles with a forward ski and X-ray machines that their inventors claimed could see through rock to the seams of the precious metal). Bicycle clubs were going to bicycle there, a carrier pigeon service between Seattle and Dawson City was planned, and when an aeronaut from Kalamazoo, Michigan, offered to take passengers to Dawson by balloon, customers offered huge sums of money to accompany him. Given the number of crazy schemes to get there, it was apparent that no one really knew where the Yukon was, its topography, or the distances involved to get to Dawson City from the coast.

Although Washington, London, and Ottawa issued warnings against going to the Yukon, thousands of Canadians, Americans, Australians, and Europeans deserted jobs, homes, and families and travelled to the Klondike. Famed author Jack London was a typical example — a man down on his luck who saw the Klondike gold rush as "his ticket out of poverty." Family fortunes and savings accounts were emptied and that summer every small town from Winnipeg to Victoria was affected by the sudden loss of manpower. The reason why so many did this, with so little knowledge of the journey they were embarking on, must be taken in context with the era. At the end of the 19th century, the British Empire had enjoyed an unparalleled eight decades of peace. The Afghan, African, and Sudanese wars at the edges of the Empire had no effect on the home front and few could recall a time when Queen Victoria and *Pax Britannia* did not reign. Bored with prolonged peace, there was a pent-up appetite in the male population of the English-speaking world for adventure. The explosion in literacy in the late 19th century had created a generation raised on serialized cowboy pulp fiction with camping in the wilderness and "hot lead from six guns" and this — before the new century dawned — was the last frontier.

More serious was the lingering economic depression that began in 1873 and 14 years later showed no signs of ending. The year before the gold-laden ships docked, the banks in San Francisco had failed, which resulted in a domino effect that led to bank failures elsewhere, causing the Great Panic. Especially hard hit by the economic turmoil were the urban middle class and white-collar professionals who lost their savings — and their faith in the work ethic. Gold was immutable and if the newspapers were to be believed, all it took to become a millionaire in the Yukon was to apply a pickaxe to the ground or pan to a creek and the gold came leaping out. It was instant wealth for little investment in time and energy. As Robert Service would write in "The Spell of the Yukon" — for the stampeder, it wasn't the gold so much as finding it that mattered.

When the Children's Crusade got to the waterfront at Marseilles in 1214, they expected the sea to open for them as it had for Moses so they could walk to the Holy Land. Those who disembarked at ports in Alaska and British Columbia were just as naive — and as doomed in their quest. For the wealthy that had the fare, there was comparatively luxurious passage on a steamer from St. Michael up the Yukon River to Dawson Then there was the Stikine River route, which involved taking a ship to Wrangell and then going up the Stikine River into Canadian territory to Glenora and Telegraph Creek — where before the transatlantic cable was laid, a telegraph line had been planned to Russia. The would-be prospectors then trekked overland for 150 miles to Teslin Lake where they had to build their own small boats and scows with lumber from the nearby forest. These were then precariously navigated through the rapids to the Yukon River and Dawson City. The third route was the Valdez Trail: by sea to Valdez, up the Copper River Valley, and across the Scolai Pass to White River by dog team, hand sled, and pack horse. Then it was by scow on the White and Yukon Rivers to Dawson City. The Dalton Trail — which the present-day Haines Highway follows, had been carved out by one Jack Dalton and all travellers with horses paid him a toll to use it. The fifth route was the most famous — and familiar to history. This was the Chilkoot Pass from the town of Dyea, adjacent to Skagway, where thousands of prospectors climbed to the summit, hauling sleds and packs on their backs to reach Lake Lindeman, which was connected with Lake Bennett. It is estimated that approximately 25,000 men came over the

Chilkoot Pass and a town of tent stores, saloons, and carpenter shops had grown up at Lake Bennett with a transient population of 5,000 men who worked on their boats, scows, and rafts.

From the politically powerful Manitoba family, Clifford Sifton had come to national prominence (and Prime Minister Laurier's favour) for negotiating the complex Manitoba Schools Question and then tackling the Crow's Nest Pass Agreement. As thorny as both those issues were, they did not prepare him for the Gordian knot that was the Yukon. Remembered more today for his successful immigration policies than the hard line he took with the United States, Sifton was chosen by Laurier in November 1896 to be his minister for the interior and superintendent-general of Indian affairs. His mandate was to establish civil government in the Yukon, regulate and tax the gold mining, and the issue that complicated both of the other two — assert Canadian sovereignty over the disputed territory. Besides the $15 registration fee and $100 annual assessment imposed, a 10 percent on claims with an output of $500 or less monthly and 20 percent royalty on every claim yielding above that amount was levied, something guaranteed to be unpopular with the miners. Additionally, the government reserved every alternate claim in any new goldfield that may be found. Sifton's philosophy was that taxes stimulated local economic development, and collecting them enforced civil authority.

To the Victorians, there was nothing that the building of a railway could not solve whether in the Andes, Africa, or Alaska, and by 1895, several American and British speculators had lobbied both Washington and Ottawa for opportunities to open up the interior of the Yukon with ribbons of steel. Encouraged and financed by the government of British Columbia, a syndicate of Michael J. Heney, Erastus Hawkins, John Hislop, and Samuel Graves attracted enough investors to consider a railway to Dawson City through the White Pass (named for the minister of the interior who had sent out the Dawson-Ogilvie survey party). The bill to incorporate the White Pass and Yukon Railway was introduced in the House of Commons on May 21, 1897. It asked no money from the Canadian taxpayer — which alone aroused the suspicions of Opposition members. Also, on the order paper presented in the House (and no doubt the company letterhead, as well) His Highness Francis, Duke of Teck, was shown as a board member. As he was an impoverished member of the British royal family, the Ottawa *Colonist* newspaper speculated that the Liberal government might be planning to let the duke rule the Yukon through the railway company. Despite both these suspicions, the bill passed on June 29, 1897, and the White Pass and Yukon Railway Company began hiring men and buying rails, locomotives, horses, and dynamite.

With an overwhelming number of the Yukon inhabitants being American, the federal government felt it had to assert its authority and an order-in-council on August 16, created the Yukon Judicial District within the Northwest Territories. It was to be run by a commissioner appointed by Ottawa and the legislation ensured, among other things, that only British subjects could serve on a jury in the Yukon. A veteran NWMP officer, Major J.M. Walsh, was taken out of retirement, appointed commissioner of the Yukon, and would arrive there in October. One of Walsh's assistants was Thomas Dufferin "Duff" Pattullo, the future premier of British Columbia.

The Regina-based government of the Northwest Territories was not unaware of the Yukon's potential as a tax base. In October, without informing Sifton, Frederick Haultain, the president (or premier) of the Northwest Territories Executive Council, sent his agent to Dawson City to impose an annual licence fee of $2,000 on each drinking establishment. Given the free spending, thirsty miners, and the multiplying number of saloons, a "sin tax" was a money-making guarantee. Sifton was furious at this and began measures to take the Yukon region out of the Northwest Territories and put it under the authority of the Department of the Interior. Haultain (who would be the only premier of the Northwest Territories before it was divided into the provinces of Alberta, Manitoba, and Saskatchewan) accused Sifton of overruling the self-governing rights of a territory and appealed to the prime minister. But his Conservative loyalties had not enamored Haultain to Laurier and the Yukon Territory Act in June 1898, which gave Ottawa complete control of the Yukon, was a direct result of the liquor tax spat.

With all entry points to the Canadian goldfields only accessible through Alaska, the Laurier government was harassed by merchants in Vancouver and Victoria for a route that was as Canadian as possible. Because the mines were in Canadian territory, goods purchased in Canada did not have to bear duties. But although the Canadian stampeders were travelling from one part of their country to another, they were penalized for buying their supplies in Canada by being charged customs duties of up to 30 percent when they passed through Alaskan territory. Those who attempted to move their Canadian goods under bond (a guarantee that goods would not be used or sold while passing through United States territory) were robbed by unscrupulous American customs officials who imposed "inspection fees" upon them that equaled the duty charges. As a result, 90 percent of the Canadian stampeders bought their mining equipment and provisions from American companies.

The only all-Canadian route to Dawson City was the overland Edmonton Trail. It began at Edmonton and followed much of the present-day Alaska Highway, entering the Yukon Valley at the headwaters of the Pelly River. It took two years to reach Dawson City this way and those who had tried it had either turned back or died along the way and are buried beside it. One party began with 75 horses and arrived in Dawson two years later with only three remaining. To reconnoitre this in September 1897, an NWMP expedition commanded by Inspector J.D. Moodie left Edmonton. Nineteen months later, after innumerable hardships, Moodie's party staggered into Tagish proving that the Edmonton Trail was impractical.

Sifton sent W.T. Jennings, a civil engineer, to assess all coastal passes for the best rail route to the Yukon and then travelled to the Yukon himself to survey the situation. In what was the largest federal government party to enter the territory, on October 8, 1897, the minister, accompanied by the commissioner Major Walsh, Mr. Justice J. McGuire as registrar, two mining inspectors, William Ogilvie, 10 constables, and a dog driver with several teams of huskies arrived at Skagway. They hoped to reach Dawson City before the river froze, but made it as far as Little Salmon. To ensure that duties were paid and all traffic was counted, Sifton had customs officers stationed on the river at Tagish. On the way home, the minister met Jennings at Wrangell and the engineer reported that a 165-mile railway between a port on the Stikine River to Teslin Lake could be built and in operation by September 1898, for a cost of $4 million. It would be an all-Canadian route except for the U.S. Army base at Wrangell. Upon his return to Ottawa, Sifton touted what became known as the "Stikine Trail," to be the preferred way to Dawson City. He planned a steamboat line up the Stikine River, passing Wrangell to Telegraph Creek and then a railway to Teslin Lake and a second steamboat on to Dawson.

The HBC had just built a trading station at Galbraith's Post on Teslin Lake and the Canadian Development Company (CDC) ran a sawmill and shipyard near it. In anticipation of Sifton's projected railway, a small steamer called the *Anglian* was built by the CDC, the steamer machinery hauled over from Telegraph Creek by superhuman effort.

By October, the Yukon River had frozen over and both the United States and Canadian governments were increasingly concerned that the food supply in Dawson City would run out, resulting in looting and anarchy — and there were signs that both were proliferating. On November 25, much of Dawson City burned when one dance hall girl threw a lamp at another. Despite the presence at Circle City of a detachment of the Eighth U.S. Infantry, commanded by Captain Patrick Henry Ray, steamers were still being held up and robbed of food — and the governor of Alaska petitioned Washington to send more soldiers to maintain law and order. In December 1897, Congress appropriated $200,000 to mount a relief expedition to the Yukon with food, and more troops were deployed to Dyea near Skagway to reinforce the 14th U.S. Infantry regiment stationed there. There were fears in Ottawa that once in the Yukon, the American relief expedition of army personnel would remain.

Constructing a railway between Telegraph Creek and Teslin Lake proved more difficult than Sifton had thought — and not only because of the terrain. The minister was a strong advocate for a Canadian northern railway — as the Canadian Pacific Railway had bound eastern Canada to the Pacific coast, so too would a railway with the Yukon. Parliament was on its Christmas break when he contracted with two railway promoters, Sir William Mackenzie and Sir Donald Mann on January 26, 1898, to build a narrow-gauge railway between Telegraph Creek and Camp Victoria on the shores of Lake Teslin. Selling thousands of tickets to Dawson City, Mackenzie and Mann sent a construction crew of 400 men to lay the track. When the members returned from their break on

February 8th, they were presented with the Yukon Railway Bill — its immediate passing essential because (they were warned) of "the imminent breakdown of law and order in the Yukon."

If Samuel Benfield Steele had been an American citizen there would have been several books, movies, and television series about him. The third person to join the NWMP in 1873, by the time he replaced Constantine, Steele had played a major role in or witnessed all the great milestones in the country's history — negotiating with Sitting Bull in 1877, the North-West Rebellion in 1885, and witnessing the last spike at Craigellachie months later. In January 1898, NWMP Commissioner L.W. Herchmer cabled Steele in British Columbia, ordering him to catch the first train to Vancouver and report for duty in the Yukon to deal with the "temporary emergency." Bluff, gruff, and fearless,[10] Steele took charge of the Chilkoot Pass and imposed his own rules: no miners could enter Canadian territory without a year's worth of provisions and every stampeder on the Yukon River had to be registered by his constables. Unfortunately, Steele reported to two masters — Major Walsh, the Yukon commissioner, and Sifton in Ottawa.

The latter cabled Steele in February and ordered him to move the Yukon customs posts from their position in Canadian territory to the summits of White and Chilkoot passes — a border area still under contention between Ottawa and Washington. His order coincided with the U.S. battleship *Maine* being sunk in Havana harbour on February 15 — an incident that ignited a patriotic frenzy in the United States aimed at Spain and all European powers that still had colonies in the New World. Why the minister was intent on goading the United States to act precipitately is explained by events in Ottawa. The Commons were overwhelmingly Liberal and the Yukon Railway Bill passed with a single, dissenting voice from the Opposition. N.C. Wallace, the member of North York, pointed out that there had been no breakdown of law and order when gold was discovered in British Columbia and he thought that the NWMP were capable of ensuring that anarchy did not break out in the Yukon. But, as a safeguard he added, the federal government should send a military force to discourage the United States from annexing the Yukon. He gave no reason why he thought this, but warned, "They wanted to get a military foothold, they wanted to get some sort of possession of our Canadian territory. We know what their dealings with Canadian and British people have been. They get a foothold here and a foothold there, and once they get possession, it's extremely hard to dislodge them."[11] Sifton arose and refuted the claim that the United States had designs on the Yukon or that Canadian sovereignty was in peril. But to prevent the impending breakdown in law and order caused by the food shortage and the threat posed by the overwhelming number of Americans in the territory, he considered a railway essential. Without the Teslin railway in operation next winter, the minister foretold dire consequences:

> We would have to face the fact that 200 or 300 of our officers would be surrounded by starving thousands of armed men, of alien men, not citizens of Canada, but citizens of foreign countries, and these men would have possession of the Yukon district instead of the Government of Canada.[12]

It was the fear that the Yukon Railway Bill would not get through the senate (which had been well-packed by former Prime Minister Sir John A. Macdonald with Conservative cronies) that made Laurier first contemplate sending troops to the Yukon. Soon rumours were circulating in Ottawa that a force was being prepared. On March 10, when a member of parliament asked for clarification, Laurier announced:

> In view of the very large influx of people who are expected to crowd into the Yukon, it has been thought advisable to have a sufficient force there to maintain law and order. This could not be done unless the Mounted Police, which is practically a military body, were largely increased. But we have thought it well to follow the practice that has obtained in other countries and since we have a small permanent force to employ it....

The prime minister's fears proved correct — the railway bill came to an embarrassing halt in the Upper House. In the haste to get the bill through, the Conservative senate smelled Liberal chicanery — irked that Mackenzie and Mann were being given a commercial monopoly for five years and 25,000 acres of land. They refused to pass the land-appropriation bill and although miles of corduroy road had already been hacked out by June, the project was cancelled. Sir Charles Tupper, the leader of the Opposition who had originally advocated the Stikine route "to secure the trade of the Yukon to Canada," now opposed the bill.[13]

The 17 miles of railroad that Mackenzie and Mann had laid down before the contract was voided cost the Liberal government $328,000, or about $20,000 per mile. Unfortunately, no one told the thousands of stampeders who had made it to Telegraph Creek that the railway was cancelled, and they had to drag their belongings through the bush to Teslin Lake, discarding most of the contents on the way, and putting the poor horses out of their misery.

Sifton was said to be furious by the bill failing to get through. "I spent an immense amount of time and trouble," he said, "in working out a solution which would have cost the country nothing at all, and after a year or two, blundering people will find out that the course suggested was the right one."[14] He was right as the idea for a railway to the Yukon did not die. On May 27, 1898, men, locomotives, and building material were put ashore at Skagway to begin the White Pass and Yukon Railway. Had Henry Graves et al. known what lay ahead might they have changed their minds?

The failure to get the railway built on the Stikine Trail caused Sifton to begin negotiating the historically infamous "Treaty 8." The largest land settlement between the Dominion of Canada and the First Nations, Treaty 8 covered a land mass of 840,000 kilometres that was home to 39 First Nations communities. Signed on June 21, 1899, by Commissioner David Laird, representing the Department of Indian Affairs and the Cree, Beaver, and Chipewyan nations, it opened up First Nations lands in northern Alberta, northeastern British Columbia, northwestern Saskatchewan, and much of the Northwest Territories to mining development, that is, the search for gold. It also guaranteed safe passage — an all-Canadian route — for stampeders going to the goldfields.

The United States government, mobilizing for war against Spain, protested Steele's moving of the customs posts — as Sifton had hoped they would. The U.S. Collector of Customs in Alaska informed the NWMP of this on March 14, 1898. The next day, Steele received a message from Colonel Thomas M. Anderson, the commanding officer of the 14th U.S. Infantry regiment at Dyea:

> I have before me copies of three notices said to have been posted at or near Lake Lindemann, the 12th instant. One of these gives warning that all goods on which duties are not paid will be seized and sold, within the next fourteen days. This purports to have been signed by your Collector of Customs and dated March 12, 1898. With all respect I must renew my request that you will explain why you find it necessary to exercise civil and military authority over American territory or a territory which is at least in question. I respectfully ask a suspension of extreme measures until this boundary question has been settled.

Walsh had seen and defused a similar situation when Chief Sitting Bull and the whole Sioux nation crossed the United States–Canadian border in 1876–77. He understood how precarious the situation in the Yukon was for Canada, which had no means of enforcing its claims. He warned Sifton, "I do not think you appreciate how thoroughly this district is in the hands of a foreign element. It would be the easiest thing in the world for a few bold men to take possession of this country." Walsh was not alone in thinking that the overwhelming number of Americans in the Yukon might seize control, establish a provisional government, and then ask Washington to intervene on their behalf. There were also rumours that a group of Americans calling themselves the "Order of the Midnight Sun" were planning to liberate the Yukon from "British tyranny." Was it just a bunch of boys whooping it up in the Malemute Saloon? Laurier couldn't take that chance.

If Sifton had intended the exchange to ratchet up the matter, he succeeded, for the prime minister now consulted with the Department of Militia and Defence. Sending troops to maintain law and order was unprecedented in Canada's short history — but there was no discussion of it in the House. As the leader of the Opposition, Tupper was wise not to raise a fuss. When he was high commissioner in London from 1884 to 1885, he had called for the deployment of Canadian troops against the Mahdi in the Sudan.[15] Public opinion was completely in favour of the government's decision to send in the army, as the Ottawa newspaper, *The Evening Citizen*, would editorialize on May 11: " We were given to understand that famine and rebellion were lurking among the fastness and along the trails and that if troops could not be hurried into the Klondike on short notice, the richest mining districts of the world might pass under the control of an alien population."[16] Laurier may not have believed that the United States was going to use the relief expedition to annex the Yukon, but many of his advisors did. A military force — as opposed to the mounted police — was a potent symbol of sovereignty. It demonstrated that the Canadian government was prepared to use as much force as necessary to maintain its civil authority in the Yukon.

The military clout available to the federal government was the Permanent Force and the militia. The Militia Act of 1868 had given Canada political control over its troops and after 1871, besides a general officer commanding (GOC), the only British troops in the country were the garrisons at Halifax and Esquimalt. The tiny core of the Permanent Force existed to train the part-time militia and there was little need for any more. Both Sir John A. Macdonald and Laurier agreed that Canadian security was not threatened by the distant wars that periodically flared up in the British Empire and with all of the western hemisphere protected by the Monroe Doctrine, there was no need for a navy. Citizen armies were cheaper than standing ones and Canadians could be expected to flock to the colours in time of crisis — as they did. During the North-West Rebellion of 1884–85, except for the GOC Major-General Frederick Middleton and his staff, all were Canadian and of the 6,000 officers and men in the expedition, only 363 were regulars.

As expected, when word spread about the federal government sending a military force to the Yukon, the office of the adjutant general was flooded with volunteers who wished to enlist. But the minister for the militia and defence, Frederick William Borden, a cousin of the future prime minister, Sir Robert Laird Borden, knew that with a departure in early May, there wouldn't be time to train civilians to the standards of the Active Militia and the whole Yukon Field Force had to come from Canada's tiny Permanent Army. Accordingly, all of the three Permanent Force units — the Royal Canadian Dragoons, the Royal Canadian Artillery, and the Royal Regiment of Canadian Infantry were ordered to supply men from their sub-units at Fredericton, Quebec City, St. Jean, Kingston, Toronto, London, and Winnipeg to the Yukon Field Force in Ottawa.

Order-in-council No. 596 was signed on March 21 for 200 volunteers from the Permanent Force — this was a quarter of its strength — to be dispatched to the abandoned HBC post of Fort Selkirk, 320 kilometres upriver from Dawson City. At the confluence of the Yukon and Pelly rivers, the fort had a checkered past. The local Chilkats had pillaged and burned it in 1852 and when Frederick Schwatka had visited the site in 1883, all that remained of the HBC's presence were the basalt rock chimneys. Five years later, two NWMP constables set up a post at Fort Selkirk to monitor traffic on the river. But the federal government had plans for Fort Selkirk as the future capital of the territory.

It was only when the troops were already on their way to the Yukon, that Borden informed the House: "It was intended to increase the mounted police force, but on further consideration it was thought that it would better serve the objects in view to send a detachment of the permanent force…."[17] When asked about the expense, the minister was ready. The cost of establishing a garrison would be $200,000 for the first year and probably $50,000 less for succeeding years. Sending a comparable number of NWMP constables would be prohibitively expensive — police pay was higher than that of soldiers — this was a bargain.

In the 1884–85 campaign, the British military had criticized Adolphe Caron, the Canadian minister of militia and defence, for appointing officers to the Permanent Force on the basis of patronage, regional influence, and social connections. Patronage to ensure officer positions in the militia was a sacred ministerial perk. Connected with political constituencies, it bought local loyalties at a minimal cost and even the Opposition and newspapers accepted it as standard practice. It was only when Caron left office in 1892 that the system could begin to change. Middleton's successor as GOC, Major-General Ivor Herbert, worked strenuously to reform the Canadian military — expanding headquarters' staff, sending officers to England on training courses, and popularizing the force in Quebec. Unfortunately for Herbert, when the United States threatened war over the British Guiana–Venezuela boundary dispute in 1895, he publicly criticized the Canadian government for not having a mobilization plan in case of American invasion. Interfering in Canadian politics meant that neither he nor his successor, General W.J. Gascoigne, would complete their terms as GOC of the Permanent Force and at the Imperial Conference in 1897 the new Prime Minister Laurier must have accepted another British GOC with reluctance.

But the patronage tradition had created a shortage of competent, trained officers. Major T.D.B. Evans of the Royal Canadian Dragoons (RCD) "B Squadron," Winnipeg had been promoted to replace one such patronage officer, whose gross lack of skills had led to a mutiny in the squadron. At the age of 21, Evans had been commissioned into the 43rd Ottawa and Carleton Rifles of the Volunteer Militia in 1881. He earned certificates from the schools of Cavalry and Artillery before seeing action with the Active Militia in 1885 at Batoche. In 1888, drafted into the Permanent Force with the rank of lieutenant, he was sent to the School of Musketry in England and selected to lead the Canadian cavalry contingent to London for Queen Victoria's Jubilee. Considered the "outstanding Canadian soldier of his generation," Evans had just been appointed as honorary aide-de-camp to the Governor General Lord Aberdeen. He was given command of the combined Yukon Field Force of infantry, artillery, and cavalry and promoted to the rank of lieutenant-colonel.

The B Squadron also contributed Captain E.W.E. Gardiner, who had been commissioned from the ranks as his adjutant and Sergeant-Major D.D. Young as his regimental sergeant-major. Major Aime Talbot of the 9th "Voltigeurs de Québec" Volunteer Battalion was made paymaster, Surgeon-Major G. LaF. Foster of the 68th Kentville Battalion the medical

Larss & Duclos/Library and Archives Canada/C-001339.

The Yukon Field Force Drilling, 1900. Laurier's government believed that the United States was going to annex the Yukon and a Canadian military force — instead of mounted police — was a potent symbol of sovereignty.

officer and, completing the headquarters section was Major D.C. Bliss of the Reserve of Officers as quartermaster. Bliss, who had seen action during the North-West campaign, had been employed by the Department of the Militia as a civil servant. Foster had just graduated as a doctor from McGill University had joined the Active Militia in 1897. Captain L.G. Bennett from the Engineer Reserve at Halifax (there was no Corps of Engineers then) and Lieutenant Louis Leduc of the 65th Volunteer Battalion were granted permanent commissions. The main body was composed of three officers and 130 men from the Royal Regiment of the Canadian Infantry, three officers and 46 gunners from the Canadian Artillery, one officer from the RCD's A Squadron in Toronto, and 15 men from B Squadron in Winnipeg.

—*—

The North-West Rebellion had been a summer campaign, but this time the soldiers were going to garrison duties near the Arctic Circle. That Canadian soldiers had never been so far in the North presented the military with unique problems. Not only were there no standard operating procedures in place for the climate or terrain, but also going to an area where the supply chain was precarious meant that the force would have to carry all its own stores with them. They had to be self-sufficient and outfitted for the Arctic winter. The Canadian Army's first quartermaster-general, Colonel Percy Lake, was aware that nothing from uniforms to medical supplies, tobacco, or ammunition could be replaced locally. Contracts were put out for suitable clothing, footwear, and food to civilian outfitters and suppliers, the uncustomary speed brought questioning in the House by the Opposition. Soon the men were being measured for the basic uniform of scarlet infantry frock with dark blue trousers tucked into boots and a tan, felt hat. For the hot Yukon summer and marching to Fort Selkirk, duck or canvas fatigue dress and the ubiquitous wedge cap were issued. Winter clothing included caribou-skin parkas and mukluks, a fur cap, a dark-grey pea jacket with detachable fur collar, knee-length woollen stockings, and buckskin-covered woollen mitts.

The 12 officers and 191 men would be armed with brand new Lee-Enfield rifles,[18] two Maxim (machine) guns, and two obsolete seven-pound field guns that were to be dismantled for the journey. Hardly the weapons for policing rowdy stampeders, the seven-pounders were more likely for a show of sovereignty. Rations consisted of 40,000 kilograms of tinned meat, 20,000 kilograms of hardtack biscuits, and 63,000 kilograms of flour. Each rifle had to have 300 rounds of ammunition with 25,000 rounds for the Maxim guns and 200 rounds for each of the two seven-pounders. All members of the force were put through medical examinations and sworn in for a three-year term of service.

On May 4, Borden elaborated:

> At first, I believe, it was intended to increase the mounted police force, but on further consideration it was thought that it would better serve the objects in view to send a detachment from the permanent force … which would

have a decided moral effect upon the scattered population throughout the district, and if necessity demanded
would be ready to assist in enforcing law and maintaining order there…. In addition to the 200 members of the
force, there will be a very few men who will go up as arti-
ficers and boatmen to assist in carrying the expedition.

After Sifton's recommendation, the troops had to be sent to the Yukon
by the Stikine River route: by ship to Wrangell, overland to Glenora, and
then by boat from Teslin Lake, and down the Teslin and Lawes rivers to
Fort Selkirk. Major Walsh objected to the concentration of troops at the
isolated Fort Selkirk and lobbied for them to be quartered in Dawson
City where they would be needed. But the government saw Selkirk as
more central to the gold strikes, with the added advantage that it was not
located on the swampy plain of Dawson City. The Stikine Trail was not
an all-Canadian route — only the torturous Edmonton Trail was — and
they would have to change from ocean-going steamer to river steamer
at the Alaskan port of Wrangell and pass through U.S. Customs where
the weapons would be held in bond. But the Laurier government could
hardly ask Washington for permission to float a foreign army (however
symbolic) down 1,600 miles of the Yukon River from St. Michael to
Dawson City — particularly as the reason for sending it was that it feared
a United States military relief expedition in the Yukon. What if they were
marooned in American territory when the river froze? The Stikine route
meant the least amount of time spent in American territory. Once in the
Yukon the troops were to remain in barracks at Fort Selkirk and with a
detachment sent to Dawson City.

The federal government dispatching a military force to the Klondike
was a godsend to certain interested civilians in Ottawa. The stampeders
were suffering hardships on the trail because they lacked any form of
collective organization. But by attaching themselves to the Yukon Field

Force, the transport and provisioning problems for these civilians were solved. Eleven administrative staff from Sifton's department were asked to accompany the force to sort out clerical details in the territory. That her husband's aide-de-camp was leading the force was an unexpected gift to Lady Aberdeen, the wife of the governor general. She had founded the Victorian Order of Nurses (VON) the year before and read an appeal from a Reverend Robert Dickey of Skagway, calling for trained nurses to go to the Klondike. In late March, four members of the VON were attached to the force. Their mission was to provide medical services to the troops and miners. They were Georgia Powell from Bouctouche, New Brunswick; Amy Scott from England; Rachel Hanna from Port Carling, Ontario; and Margaret Payson from Weymouth, Nova Scotia. The work of Florence Nightingale in the Crimean War notwithstanding, the public, press, medical profession, and military were still coming to terms with the concept of females who were not camp followers involved in military campaigns — let alone going to the remote Yukon. The expedition guaranteed favourable publicity for Lady Aberdeen's nurses and as president of the National Council for Women of Canada, with chapters in cities across the country and soon of the Women's National Health Association, Laurier appreciated that Lady Aberdeen was a national figure.

The Toronto *Globe*, the forerunner of the the *Globe and Mail*, managed to get one of its reporters, a Miss Faith Fenton, onto the expedition list. Fenton, whose real name was Alice Freeman, was a schoolteacher, but since teaching was so poorly paid, she freelance-wrote for magazines like *The Ladies' Home Journal*. As journalism was considered so disreputable a profession, especially for females, Freeman wrote under the Fenton name in order to keep her teaching job. She managed to keep her journalistic life secret until 1893, when the school found out she had interviewed members of the nascent suffragette movement. Freeman resigned from teaching to become Faith Fenton, a full-time journalist and convinced the *Globe* to hire her for the adventure.

Posted to the Yukon, the NWMP's Inspector Cortlandt Starnes (the future commissioner of the Royal Canadian Mounted Police, from 1923 to 1931) managed to have his wife Marie sent with the force. Although a request by a British scientific party was refused, two Roman Catholic priests were accepted — their only connection being that one was a personal friend of the prime minister.

The news of Commodore George Dewey engaging the Spanish fleet at Manila Bay on May 1 filled the headlines as the force's final preparations were being made at the Cartier Drill Hall in Ottawa. The enthusiasm for military spectacle and adventure spilled across the border and the men and officers were lionized by Ottawa society. Both the prime minister and governor general took a personal interest in the expedition, but none more so than Lady Aberdeen, who kept her four nurses in the spotlight with a dinner at Rideau Hall followed by an exhibition of their uniforms to be worn in the Klondike. The nurses were sent three weeks ahead of the force in a private railcar so that they could enjoy a fortnight's publicity tour/vacation along the way. In Winnipeg, they were presented with fitted coon coats by the Hudson's Bay store and were also guests of honour at a reception hosted by the local National Women's Council at the Hotel Manitoba. The nurses' annual salary was $300, which the governor general had sent along, plus $600 in a bank transfer to Dawson to help them to set up in the district.

In Ottawa, on the evening before the men left, Borden hosted a farewell dinner for the officers, and on the morning of May 6, 1898, just before they entrained, the officers were treated to breakfast by the prime minister and governor general.[19] They marched from the Drill Hall to Union Station through streets lined by a cheering crowd and the band played "The Girl I Left Behind Me." A special Canadian Pacific Railway train took them across the continent. When they overnighted at Winnipeg to pick up the additional 16 men from the Royal Canadian Dragoons, the newspapers thought they were the "finest lot of men ever seen in Her Majesty's uniform here" and local merchants lavished them with unlimited supplies of " the soothing weed," and a "fountain of beer that never ran dry."

And although the force had seen no action, the citizens of Vancouver treated their entry into their city on May 11 as a triumphant procession. The men were put up in a former theatre and the officers in a hotel. Here, the civilians — the 11 clerks, and six women joined them.

On May 14, the Yukon Field Force and 60 tons of supplies were put aboard the Canadian Pacific steamship *Islander* at Vancouver on its scheduled run to the Alaskan goldfields. The first operational hardship suffered by the force occurred then — it was discovered that civilians were ensconced in the bunks reserved for the force. Colonel Evans took charge of the matter, ordering all of them to sleep on the bridge and assigned their bunks to the officers and females in the party. The U.S. Army unit at Wrangell welcomed their Canadian counterparts with all hospitality they could muster while the arms and supplies were cleared through U.S. Customs. A pair of chartered sternwheelers, *Strathcona* and *Stikine Chief*, took them upriver to Glenora on May 19. While the force began training for the journey ahead, an advance party consisting of a construction crew, accompanied by three of the nurses, left on June 1 to build the log cabin barracks at the fort.

The Hudson's Bay Company had been contracted by Ottawa to have a sufficient number of mules and horses waiting at Glenora to carry the forces' 60 tons of supplies in one lift. But there only 141 pack animals waiting and Major Bliss had to press the HBC to find another 170 animals — an exercise that must have taken all his skill because every other party going to Dawson City wanted animals, as well. Whatever they got must have made the poor stampeders envious — each mule was loaded up to 200 pounds. The main body left Telegraph Creek for Teslin Lake on June 9. Only the nurses rode — sharing a horse between three, alternating between riding and walking. Wearing brown duck suits with bloomers, gaiters tucked into hobnail boots, they made sure of mosquito netting over their heads. Rachel Hanna recorded in her diary:

> Up at two in the morning, breakfast at three, tent down and everything packed by four and on the trail before five. Our lunch consisted of two hard biscuits and a cup of water from the nearest spring. We had dinner when the last of the men came in, sometimes eight or nine sometimes as late as eleven. The trail is bad, bad for people and very bad for pack animals … from mountain to swamp and bog we went — bogs into whose cold mossy depths we would sink to our knees, and under which the ice still remains; swamps where we trampled

down bushes and shrubs to make a footing for ourselves and where the mules stuck many times, often as many as twenty all down at once, sometimes having to be unpacked to be taken out, our baggage dumped in the mud and where the mosquitoes held high revelry.

The mosquitoes were so thick; Sergeant Bateman's red coat was brown with them. We had to stuff the openings in our gauntlets with paper and not stopping for lunch, hold a piece of food inside our veils and eat as we walked.

On the other hand, the author Pierre Berton would paint what historians have since thought an exaggerated picture of the force making for Teslin Lake: "... the most outlandish sight of all: two hundred and three uniformed soldiers in scarlet jackets and white helmets marching as best they could in close order ... trudging in step through the mud holes and over rocks and stumps, performing barrack square evolutions ... and dragging their Maxim guns along with them."[20] There is no evidence that they marched in formation or wore their dress uniform along the trail.

The advance group arrived at Teslin Lake on July 1 where the little steamer *Anglian* was being prepared to take them to Fort Selkirk. It was scheduled to return by August 18 for the other nurses and remainder of supplies. The main body arrived on July 10, and tents were pitched in Camp Victoria. Now the military rations of corned beef and hardtack could be supplemented with local fish and game — salmon varying in weight from 10 to 15 pounds were speared with a bayonet fixed to a pole. The men were put to work building boats and scows and when the *Anglian* did not return on schedule, the force pushed off from Camp Victoria on August 29 in a convoy of five pilot boats and four scows, the men rowing by day and camping on shore at night.

The Yukon Field Force arrived at Fort Selkirk on September 11 without a single causality, a feat in itself, given the unknown terrain and modes of transport used. The barracks rooms, mess, cookhouse, a storehouse, sergeants' mess and officers' mess, and hospital — the average size was 20 by 24 feet, by 10 feet high. Fronting on the river were the orderly room, cells, and commanding officers' quarters. At the rear of the barracks were wash houses, the coal shed, dog kennel, latrines, and a storehouse (90 by 27 feet) built of poles and roofed for the storage of the 2,200 pounds of fresh beef purchased by the force.[21]

For some of the men and women, their time at the fort was short-lived. As soon as they heard that there was a typhoid epidemic raging in the goldfields, two of the nurses left immediately for Dawson. Steele had replaced Constantine on June 24 as the beleaguered NWMP welcomed the 70 more constables — making a total of 239 policemen in the territory. It wouldn't be enough for the expected tsunami of stampeders, and on September 3, Sifton sent a message to Evans to send half of his men to Dawson. Although as the minister of the interior, Sifton was not authorized to do this, by the time his instructions had arrived at Fort Selkirk, Major Walsh at Steele's insistence had asked that a detachment of the force be stationed at Dawson City as auxiliary police. Captains Burstall and Ogilvie, with 50 other ranks, and one Maxim gun, moved to Dawson City by river steamer on October 1. They were to mount guard at the commissioner's office and residence, escort the gold shipments a few times a month from the diggings to the banks, escort prisoners on work detail, and help in collecting the government royalties.

The Dawson City that the soldiers entered that summer had been a swamp less than two years before. Now with a population exploding almost by the hour — from 2,000 miners in 1897 to 18,000 and rising, it was the most populous city east of Winnipeg, larger than Vancouver and Victoria and comparable in population to Seattle. The NWMP calculated that more than 28,000 men had passed their post at Tagish that summer with another 5,000 arriving on the steamboats up the Yukon. To better patrol the river system, in 1899, the NWMP bought three launches, the *Gladys*, the *Jessie*, and the *Tagish*. A larger river steam ship called *Vidette* was bought in 1902 for $3,000 to transport supplies, equipment, and men to NWMP posts up and down the rivers. But it was becoming impossible to estimate the total number of stampeders, for most were in town a few hours before leaving to prospect in the creeks or giving up and returning home.

It might have been a city in name only, but Dawson had eight dance halls, five churches, two newspapers, two hospitals, one skating rink, a Masonic Temple, a Salvation Army citadel, and a free reading room or public library. There were also prostitutes — of a sturdy kind as the slight ones did not survive the trip — and the VON nurses would record that "… ladies of the night plied their trade from one-room cabins facing onto lane ways between the main streets. Business was brisk." There was electric lighting in one hotel and even a local telephone system and a cinema that advertised, Edison's latest "projectorscope," showing life size pictures of the sinking of the USS *Maine* and Battle of Manila Bay.

But Dawson lacked a sewage system, a cemetery, and a garbage dump, and its muddy streets sucked in horses, pulled wagons down up to their axles, and unwary pedestrians to their knees. What it did have in abundance was a plague of mosquitoes, a putrid stench — and typhoid. On October 14, a fire started by fighting dancehall girls burned 11 buildings on Front Street before it was contained. Firefighting in a log-cabin city filled with alcohol and caches of dynamite, where it was impossible to tell the difference between looters and shopkeepers desperately trying to save what they had brought thousands of miles, and where the river — the only source of water — had frozen over was an impossible task. But it did prompt the commissioner to order a fire engine and train men to use it.

For the former lawman Wyatt Earp who arrived that summer, Dawson City was more law-abiding than any American frontier community. Under Steele's benevolent dictatorship, it came as a shock to the Americans that handguns were forbidden, but liquor was not (except to minors), that all bars, saloons, and gambling parlours closed over the weekend, that prostitutes were tolerated, and that those who broke the law were punished by being made to chop firewood or returned to United States territory.

Sifton's prophetic warning — that there would be thousands of starving, alien men milling about — had some truth. While no one actually died of starvation, many, like Jack London, would contract scurvy. The author would lose all his teeth and for the remainder of his life London's face was marked with the experience.[22] The stampeders who continued to pour in discovered that all the best claims had been staked and what food there was sold at highly inflated prices. Those who had the best properties were mining them for millions of dollars. The year of the most gold production in the Yukon would be 1900 when more than $22 million was taken out of the ground. But for the thousands of disillusioned, gaunt, ragged scarecrows who had arrived too late, all there was to do was walk up and down Front Street, reuniting with those they had met on the trail, pointing out the few who had struck it rich, selling what they had left. Rarely did they bother to pan for gold. All they could think of now was a ticket out. It was as though having survived the journey was enough for one lifetime and finding the mother lode no longer mattered. There was also adventure and gold to be had elsewhere — the Spanish-American War continued and in South Africa the Boer republics were demanding the removal of British forces. For the non-patriotic, there were rumours of a gold strike in Nome, Alaska.

As to the bulk of the Yukon Field Force at Fort Selkirk, what they actually did through the long winter provoked comment in Ottawa — and when asked, Borden admitted that he did not know. After the close of river navigation, mail service was provided by dog and horse teams. In 1899, a total of 75 dog teams served Dawson in the winter months. But it was not until August 1, 1899, that Colonel Evans replied with a full report. There were classes in flag signalling, topography, and stretcher bearing, and weekly tactical exercises in the surrounding countryside. Besides the routine garrison drill and duties, there was a barrack guard of five men and a regimental fire piquet of four. The Regimental Amusement Committee put on hockey matches and snowshoe-racing competitions in the winter. And in the summer there were cricket, football, and rounders matches, and the fort's gardens supplied fresh fruit and vegetables. On May 24, 1898, to celebrate Her Majesty's birthday, the whole Yukon Field Force paraded in scarlet and blue frocks, white helmets with brass spikes. A highlight of the report must have been the role that the Yukon Field Force played in the October 14 fire; an account of it appears in the history of The Royal Canadian Regiment:

> One morning in mid-October, as the men of the Dawson detachment were settling into their new routine, the bugles of the main guard sounded the alarm and the troops, tumbling out into the dark of a bitterly cold dawn, saw a great glare in the sky and knew that Dawson City was on fire. A carouse in the Monte Carlo theatre had resulted in an upset oil lamp, so the story later ran, and a score of buildings were blazing fiercely. For a time, despite the efforts of the Mounted Police, the Yukon Field Force detachment, and of the civilian population, the fire spread rapidly, the danger being intensified when certain of the civilian salvage crews discovered whiskey in a blazing saloon, dragged a half dozen barrels to the street, stove in the tops, and invited all so inclined to drink as much as they wanted. Meanwhile the flames swept on. Dynamite was used without effect, but eventually a fire-engine, released by the Yukon Commissioner from a warehouse where it lay in bond, supplied streams of water which brought the fire under control. Blocks of the town lay in ashes by this time; the remaining blocks would also have burned but for the work the police and the troops accomplished.[23]

The force's assistance in fighting the town's fires was repeated on April 15, 1899, and on January 10, 1900. The newspapers denounced the causes of these fires as "Dawson's curse" — drunken dancehall girls fighting — but they burned much of the city. When the recently hired municipal firemen went on strike, the soldiers dousing fires on April 15 must have been particularly welcome. There was little else for the force to do. The expected crisis with the Americans had not occurred and by the summer of 1899, the gold rush had ended, the population of Dawson was in decline, and the NWMP had the remaining miners under control.

Major-General Edward Thomas Henry Hutton arrived in Canada in June 1898, as the new GOC of the Permanent Force. Having served in the Sudanese campaign, Hutton had been influenced by General Wolseley's zeal to modernize the British Army. When posted to New South Wales, Australia, in 1894, he attempted to modernize the state's military — quarrelling with the premier, who did not want to spend the funds that this would entail. Hutton was returned to England in 1896 and then sent to Canada after the Imperial Conference. Given another opportunity to pursue his reforms with colonial troops, he attempted to create a "national army" free from political patronage. It would be an integrated force of regulars and militia that could be mobilized for the defence of Canada (and the Empire) at short notice. Borden agreed, and with the Boer crisis, it was an idea whose time had come. But to do so, Hutton needed the Yukon Field Force returned home. They were the seasoned instructors and, as he pointed out, 24.4 percent of the regular army. He noted in his Annual Report:

> With reduced number of Permanent troops now available, it is found to be impossible to satisfactorily carry out the instructional system for officers and N.C. officers of the Active Militia at the various schools of instruction. It is even difficult to carry out the ordinary routine duties appertaining to troops in barracks. I have already represented that officers and men at the various schools of instruction are overworked.[24]

William Ogilvie, the Ottawa surveyor who had laid out the town site of Dawson City, succeeded Walsh as the Yukon Commissioner in July 1898, and was of the same opinion. He wrote to Ottawa:

> We do not deem it necessary here to have any more of the militia in attendance, and I would respectfully submit that neither the Council nor myself consider the

presence of the militia in the country necessary at all …
As for a rebellion, the time for that is past and gone. Last
spring there was undoubtedly a crowd of discontented
people here who hung about Dawson, waiting for something to turn up. They did not get what they expected,
nor did they get what in some instances they might have
got with perfect propriety. This exasperated them to such
a degree that a little more would have raised a rebellion.

The period of service for the volunteers would soon expire and a deci-
sion to withdraw or extend the force had to be made in early 1899. In typical
Canadian fashion, a compromise was reached. The government agreed in
July 1899 that the force might be halved, and on September 8, 100 soldiers
left for Ottawa. The government also had a change of heart about making
Fort Selkirk the administrative capital of the territory. The White Pass and
Yukon Railway arrived at the town of Closeleigh, joining the Canadian gov-
ernment telegraph service already there. Across the river from Closeleigh,
a new town grew up called Whitehorse, so named from the whitecaps
or "white horses" of the rapids and it was chosen as the capital instead.
Forgotten, too, was Sifton's Stikine Trail — this time with permission from
Washington to cross United States territory, the troops went home via Lake
Bennett, the White Pass, and Skagway — the journey taking them 10 days.

On October 5, except for a caretaker unit of nine men, the 88 remaining soldiers abandoned Fort Selkirk and took up duties in Dawson. Far
away in South Africa, Boer farmers attacked British forces and a week
later laid siege to Kimberley and Mafeking. Laurier's government, pressured by imperial sentiment in Ontario, announced that it would send a
volunteer infantry contingent to South Africa. All of the men would be
recruited from the militia with the officers and junior officers from the
Permanent Force. Three of the Yukon Field Force, Burstall and Leduc,
who had left in September and Evans, who had left in November (by dog
team to Skagway) were among the first contingent to sail to South Africa.

As to the remainder of the force (now called the Yukon Garrison),
through the winter of 1899–1900 it occupied itself with guard duty of
the gold shipments, picquets, and fighting Dawson's fires. Although

Americans still outnumbered Canadians, the rush was clearly over — the government census returns for 1900 showed that there were only 5,404 men, women, and infants in Dawson City, of which 1,712 were British, but 3,361 American.[25] In the House, the Opposition found its voice and now accused the government of wasting money by sending the force in the first place, as the Mounted Police could easily have handled the situation. Three of the men died of natural causes at Fort Selkirk and one at Dawson. Little is known of them except that one, Jerry Corcoran, died of drink. Subsequent oral histories of First Nations in the area at the time mention there were a lot of drinking and fighting among the soldiers.[26]

In March 1900, leader of the Opposition, Charles Tupper, questioned whether it had been necessary to send the force in the first place. He said the Yukon had turned out to be one of the most orderly places in the Dominion. Laurier replied that the reason for this tranquility, even at the height of the gold rush, was "… largely due to the care taken by the government to provide such a police and military force as to check the possibility of any demonstration."[27] But he acknowledged there was the possibility of the force being withdrawn soon. Borden defended the government's decision, saying that the force had been sent in anticipation of the huge influx of people into the territory and the military presence had provided stability in the region:

> It is true there has been good order in that country, but there has been good order because the Government had taken the precaution of sending the Mounted Police there and sending the militia there to see good order was preserved.[28]

Borden presented a report on the status of garrison to the Cabinet in May. He noted that if it were to be retained in the Yukon, the minimum number of men required would be 88. Few, if any, of those presently serving, he informed them, wished to remain in the Yukon and if the garrison was to be retained, the government would have to replace them. The minister admitted that there was no longer any justification for keeping the force in the Yukon. The threat to Canadian sovereignty had never materialized and the much-reduced population was peaceful. Considering this, the government resolved to withdraw the remainder of the troops by the summer of 1900 — as soon as the rivers were open for navigation. Not only were they needed for service in South Africa, but also to replace the British garrisons at Halifax and Esquimalt. With typhoid and scurvy no longer threats in Dawson, the decision was made to withdraw the nurses, as well, with the municipality taking over the hospital.

On receipt of instructions, the Yukon Garrison packed to leave. On June 25, with the exception of Corporal Edward Lester, the men embarked on the SS *Columbian* for Whitehorse, marched over the pass to Skagway and arrived in Vancouver on July 5. Five of the force bought their release locally — and two deserted in Vancouver. The rifles, Maxim guns, and ammunition were left with the NWMP and the two seven-pounders can still be seen at the RCMP office at Dawson City. Lester, the medical sergeant at Fort Selkirk, was required by the NWMP as a witness in a murder trial and it would not be until July 31, 1901, that he would return home — the last of the Yukon Field Force. Thus, the first foray of the Canadian military in the North ended. Pleased to get so many of the militia back, the GOC praised them: "A soldier-like spirit and zealous attention to duty characterized all ranks of this Force during its two years service in the Yukon."[29]

Today, Fort Selkirk is a historic site co-owned and co-managed by the Yukon government and the Selkirk First Nation, due to the fact that the parade square had been built around a First Nations burial site. The only remnant of the Yukon Field Force is the reconstructed Big Jonathan House — formerly the barracks — and the marks in the basalt cliffs that the soldiers had used for target practice. The four soldiers who died are commemorated along with Evans in the names of five mountain peaks near the fort.

The Boer War followed by the carnage on the Western Front made Canadians look everywhere else but the North. The Yukon Field Force disappeared into history — there were no battle honours, casualty lists,

or newsreels to commemorate it. As to the men and women of the force
— many served in South Africa and in the Canadian Expeditionary Force
that was sent to the Western Front. Colonel Evans distinguished himself
in South Africa as second-in-command of the 2nd Battalion, Canadian
Mounted Rifles. In August 1900, Evans was confirmed in command of
the unit, renamed the 1st Battalion, Canadian Mounted Rifles. Under his
leadership, the Canadians took a key hill at Leliefontein on November
7, 1900, preventing the Boers from trapping a British force. In 1902, he
was put in command of the 2nd Regiment, Canadian Mountain Rifles
and led them in action at Harts River on March 31, 1902. He was made a
Companion of the Order of the Bath and his future looked bright. Sadly,
Evans would die of overwork and exhaustion in 1908.

Several former force soldiers distinguished themselves in promotion and
decorations.[30] Sergeant William Rhoades commanded the 5th Canadian
Mounted Rifles and earned the Distinguished Service Order (DSO), the
Military Cross (MC), and the Croix de Guerre. Corporal Michael Docherty
commanded Lord Strathcona's Horse in 1917–18 and was awarded a DSO.
Bombardier William Kruger won an MC and retired as a lieutenant-colonel.
Captain J.H.C. Ogilvie went to South Africa and distinguished himself at
Paardeberg and Israel's Poort. When his regiment returned home, Ogilvie
remained accepting a commission in the South African Constabulary with
the rank of major. He died of wounds received at Klipgat in December
1901. Captains Henry Burstall and Percy Thacker both reached the rank of
major-general in the First World War, with Burstall knighted for his services in command of the Canadian artillery. On May 22, 1921, Lieutenant-
General Sir Henry Burstall, KCB, KCMG, ADC, dedicated The Royal
Canadian Horse Artillery Monument in Kingston, Ontario.

Major-General Hutton, like his predecessors, blundered into
Canadian politics by attacking the sacred cow of patronage. The GOC's
public speeches so embarrassed the Laurier government that he was also
returned home before serving out his term. But it was just in time for
the Boer War, where Hutton commanded a brigade of mounted infantry,

The Right Honourable Clifford Sifton, Member of Parliament (Brandon, Manitoba). He had negotiated the Manitoba Schools Question for Prime Minister Laurier, but nothing prepared him for the complexities of the Yukon.

Dawson Main Street, 1898. Dawson was overnight the largest city west of Winnipeg — with starvation, scurvy, and thousands of Americans. Ottawa was prompted to act in response to the possibility that the United States might send in troops.

Ascending Summit of Chilkoot Pass, 1898. More than 25,000 men came over the Chilkoot Pass and at its summit, Steele imposed Canadian sovereignty and his own rules: every "stampeder" had to be registered by his constables.

HMS Alert *at 82° N in Lincoln Bay, September 1875.*

Winter quarters of HMS Discovery, *frozen in September 6, 1875, during the G.S. Nares expedition to the Arctic from 1875 to 1876.*

Library and Archives Canada/PA-202182.

Above: *The historic Royal Canadian Mounted Police marine patrol vessel* St. Roch. *The first vessel to sail the Northwest Passage from west to east (1940–42), the first to complete the Northwest Passage in one season (1944), and first to circumnavigate North America.*

Right: *Captain Joseph-Elzéar Bernier, C.G.S. Arctic expedition, 1923.*

Indian and Northern Affairs/Library and Archives Canada/PA-118126.

Left: *Lieutenant-Colonel Samuel Benfield Steele; a true Canadian hero.*

Below: *RCAF Kittyhawks of 111 (F) Squadron at Kodiak, Alaska, 1942–43. Their commanding officer, Gordon McGregor, would become the first president of Air Canada.*

Signing of the Canada-United States agreement on the construction and maintenance of the Alaska Highway, March 18, 1942, Ottawa, Ontario. (L–R): Honourable Jay Pierrepont Moffat, Right Honourable W.L. Mackenzie King, Colonel O.M. Biggar.

Canadian troops disembark in the Aleutian Islands. The mission took place between August and September 1943, at Kiska, Alaska. They arrived unaware that the Japanese had already left.

Golf ball geodesic radome — the weather-tight dome covering the AN/FPS-19 radar antenna was designed by Richard Buckminster Fuller who would do the same for the U.S. Pavilion at Expo 67, now the Montreal Biosphere.

In August 1952, a cairn was unveiled dedicated to the memory of the seven RCAF servicemen and two civilian observers who perished in the 1950 plane crash at Alert.

which included Australian, New Zealand, and Canadian units, one of which was Colonel Evan's Canadian Mounted Rifles.

One of the long-serving British officers who remained in Canada was the quartermaster-general who had outfitted the force in record time, Colonel Percy Lake. Eventually promoted to major-general and knighted, Lake would become the First Chief of the General Staff of the Canadian Army. He created a General Staff and drew up plans for mobilization, which became essential in 1914. Best of all, he kept his opinions on patronage to himself.

Faith Fenton, the Toronto *Globe* correspondent, sent home breathless stories like "Up the Stikine: Incidents of a Slow and Perilous Journey." She would marry Dr. J.N.E Brown, who was working for Commissioner Ogilvie and later to be the Dawson district medical officer. The couple would later settle in Toronto where Faith entertained all with her Yukon experiences.

Of the four VON nurses, Margaret Payson, married a wealthy miner, worked in the Dawson City post office, and "kept cats and dogs to her heart's content." Amy Scott and Georgia Powell served in field hospitals in South Africa, and Rachel Hanna became matron of St. Andrew's Hospital in Atlin, British Columbia, and then at age 48 accompanied the 1st Canadian Contingent to France in 1914.

William Ogilvie is remembered for his reputation as a bon vivant in boomtown Dawson and the building that was his office is preserved as a National Historic Site. In recognition of Ogilvie's surveying the Yukon and serving as its commissioner, in 1966, the government of Canada named a range of mountains north of Dawson City after him. They also contain the headwaters of the Ogilvie River.

Sam Steele, "The Lion of the Yukon," inevitably clashed with Sifton's system of patronage where wealthy Liberal supporters were rewarded with mining contracts and he was transferred out of the Yukon in September 1899. Much loved by the citizens of Dawson, the entire population assembled at his farewell to thank Steele, the miners demonstrating their gratitude by presenting him with a bag of gold dust. Steele went on to command Lord Strathcona's Horse in South Africa and the 2nd Canadian Division in the First World War. With the exception of a plaque at his birthplace at Purbrook, Ontario, there is no monument to him. As Charlotte Gray has pointed out, "Canada doesn't do heroes; we are better at recalling their clay feet."[31]

Bishop Bompas died in 1906, still railing against the authorities in Ottawa. With Fortymile now abandoned, he moved to Carcross where, no longer a bishop, he built a boarding school for Native children and translated the Bible into Native languages. Buried in Carcross, in death (as in life,) Bompas was mourned more by the First Nations than the whites.

The missionary would have been pleased to know that Canadian law and order finally arrived at Herschel Island. In 1903, Sergeant Francis J. Fitzgerald and Constable F.D. Sutherland set up a NWMP post on Herschel Island, the northernmost point of Canadian sovereignty. Their job was to prevent the debauchery that the missionaries claimed the whalers were inflicting on the locals and to collect duties on whales killed in Canadian waters. Unfortunately, Ottawa had given them no material support and without food or coal, they had to rely on the charity of the American whalers for both. By 1903, the whaling industry was in decline — the whales had been driven to near extinction — and women's fashions no longer dictated the use of corsets. By then it was too late for the island's Native population. Captain Howard, one of the whaling captains, would tell the *Dawson Daily News*: "The Huskies in this region are diminishing very rapidly, measles cleaning out a whole band.... The Indians at this point are also decreasing, consumption and indigestion being the principal causes."

Neither Dyea nor Skagway developed into the gateways of the interior that they might have been with Canadian incorporation. Skagway achieved some fame in 2008 as the childhood home of presidential candidate Sarah Palin, who recalled that she and her brother would be sent to Whitehorse to take advantage of the free medical coverage.

The population of the Yukon declined in direct relation to the production of gold. From an all-time high of 40,000 people in 1898–99, it dropped to 27, 219 in 1901, and to 4,157 in 1921. Gold production, which was an estimated $22,275,000 in 1900, reached $ 3,594,000 in 1910 and $ 625,000 in 1925.[32] With the exodus of the stampeders and despite the best efforts of Ogilvie and the business community, the frontier society succumbed to the morality of middle-class southern Canada. In 1901, restrictions were imposed on the gambling halls, the sale of liquor in dancehalls was forbidden, and prostitutes were barred from Dawson City.

The Canadian Pacific steamship *Islander* that the Yukon Field Force had embarked on at Vancouver hit an iceberg in the Lynn Canal off Douglas Island on August 14, 1901. Reportedly carrying $6 million in gold from Skagway, it sank within 15 minutes, taking 40 lives with it. Salvage operations brought it to the surface in 1934 but much of the reported gold shipment was said to be missing.

Although only 175 kilometres in length, the narrow-gauge White Pass and Yukon Railway was one of the most difficult engineering feats in history. It wasn't only that its engineers had to blast their way through or around mountains or cement-hard permafrost, or that its 35,000 workers were either on strike or deserted to join the gold rush, there was the almost insurmountable tangle of Ottawa bureaucracy to contend with, as well. Through it all, the summit of White Pass was reached in February 1899, Carcross on July 29, 1900, and Whitehorse on June 8, 1900. By this time, the gold rush had ended, but the railway continued on, carrying passengers and freight until 1982, when it was shut down with the collapse of the lead-zinc mining boom. Ironically, the son of the Duke of Teck, Prince Alexander, did rule the Dominion of Canada — in a vice-regal way. During the First World War when the family was forced to give up the Teck name as too Germanic, King George V made Alexander the Earl of Athlone and in 1940, he would become the 16th governor general of Canada.

For Clifford Sifton, the day of the sourdough had ended. He promoted large-scale, capital-intensive, more efficient mining that almost eliminated the one-man pickaxe-and-pan operation. In January 1898, the minister brought in new regulations that encouraged corporate control of the creeks by "concessions," or large companies. As minister of the interior from 1896 to 1905, he kept the territory under tight federal control, resisting all pleas from the stampeders to come and see what harm his policies were doing. In the Yukon's future was hydraulic mining using high pressure hoses that pumped water against hillsides and dredges — giant machines that floated their way up the creeks, eating into their gravel for gold.

One of the hardliners in the Cabinet, Sifton pressed the prime minister not to give in to American intransigence on the boundary issue. In 1903, Laurier appointed him the agent in charge of preparing the case for the Alaska Boundary Tribunal, sending him to London as counsel. Echoes of the annexation scare during the Yukon Gold Rush and Canadian participation in the Boer War had created nationalism in English Canada even as the bellicose Theodore Roosevelt was elected president of the United States. The vaguely worded Anglo-Russian Treaty of 1825, with its ambiguous boundary line that followed the summit of the mountains 16 kilometres inland from the Pacific coast, returned to haunt both Britain and the United States. Acting for Canada, the British government had traditionally held that the treaty specified that the boundary intersected the Lynn Canal 88 kilometres south of Skagway, putting that port and Dyea within Canada. In an effort not to sour bilateral relations, President McKinley had once proposed that Canada be given a permanent lease of a port near Haines, but Ottawa rejected that compromise as insufficient. With Dyea and Skagway so close to one another, Canadians hoped that even one port could be given to the dominion as its door to the interior. But the mood in Washington was such that many Americans thought the boundary should be as high as Lake Bennett. It was no longer a case of gold-hungry prospectors inadvertently crossing the border. In this new century, for any commercial company whether American or Canadian, whether railway, telegraph, mining, or shipping, the legalities of the agreed-upon border were essential.

With growing mistrust on both the Canadian and U.S. sides, the Anglo-American joint high commission, which had been considering the boundary dispute, ceased to meet after February 1899. To Roosevelt, it was a test of the United States' growing strength on the world stage. He knew that the British, faced with growing German militarism in Europe, needed American support. For the Canadians, recent events during the gold rush had demonstrated that if the interior of the Yukon was ever to develop ports like Skagway, then Juneau and Dyea had to be in Canadian territory.

—*—

On January 24, 1903, U.S. Secretary of State John Hay and the British Ambassador to Washington Michael Henry Herbert created a joint commission to establish the Alaskan border. A six-member tribunal — "six impartial jurists of repute" — three Americans and three British would meet in London to review the boundary question. Roosevelt appointed Secretary of War Elihu Root, Senator Henry Cabot Lodge, and Senator George Turner — all three who had made their views on the matter public. Britain appointed its chief justice, Lord Richard E. Webster Alverstone, and two Canadian lawyers, Sir Louis Jette and John Douglas Armour (Allen B. Aylesworth replaced Armour who died in July 1903). Appointed chairman of the commission, Alverstone had arbitrated in the Bering Sea dispute in 1893 and again in the boundary case between British Guiana and Venezuela in 1898. Root, Lodge, and Turner had been instructed by the president to get full acceptance of the American claim. Anything less, Roosevelt told Lord Alverstone, guaranteed that the United States would declare war on Canada — and thus the whole British Empire.

The Canadian argument was that because of the ignorance of the diplomats of the day — in many cases the mountains mentioned by the Anglo-Russian Treaty of 1825 were actually on offshore islands — the western border of Canada was the Pacific Ocean. The United States maintained that the entire coastline with the offshore islands was American territory.

The negotiations ended on October 20, 1903, with Lord Alverstone agreeing that the boundary line should be around the headland of the contended inlets — that the ports of Dyea, Skagway, and Juneau were in United States territory and agreed to the equal division of the four islands at the mouth of the Portland Channel. The final vote was thus four to two. The Canadian commissioners Jette and Aylesworth voted against the decision and refused to put their signatures to the document. As soon as the results were known, Sifton cabled Laurier, asking for instructions. As Canada had no control over its foreign policy, what the prime minister could have done was debatable. Laurier commented that it was "… one of those concessions which have made British diplomacy odious to Canadian people." Unwilling to compromise over this or any issue, Sifton would resign from the Cabinet and later the Liberal Party within two years.

The Canadian government — indeed the whole nation — felt shortchanged and the imperial family connection that Canadians had gone to war for in South Africa was now questioned. The boundary dispute convinced the nation that it needed greater control over its own foreign affairs. The Toronto correspondent of the London *Daily Mail*, attempting to convey the feeling in Toronto, cabled his newspaper, stating: "Canadians are becoming weary of negotiating with Washington through London and of the solemn and elaborate farces called arbitration which for one hundred and twenty years have been robbing Canada to enrich the United States. 'We should dicker for ourselves,' said a Toronto newspaper today; and the sentiment in echoed everywhere." One of the results of the United States victory on the Alaskan boundary was the defeat in 1911 of the Reciprocity Pact and of the Liberals. The rejection of free trade with the United States secured Robert Borden's victory.

That Canada had the weaker claim in the Alaskan boundary issue has been accepted by modern jurists and as it did not control its own foreign affairs, the idea that it could have obtained better terms by direct negotiation between Ottawa and Washington rather than by arbitration by Britain is unlikely.

As for the Yukon, Canada and the world was so altered by the Great War that when that ended, it distracted itself with flappers, Model T Fords, and the Jazz Age. For the thousands of stampeders whose search for gold had begun it all, Robert Service captured their plight in "The Spell of the Yukon."

> I wanted the gold and I sought it:
> I scrabed and I mucked like a slave.
> Was it famine or scurvy — I fought it:

I hurled my youth into a grave.
I wanted the gold and I got it:
came out with a fortune last fall.
Yet somehow life's not what I thought it:
and somehow the gold isn't all.

3

Exploration and Aircraft

The decade before the First World War was one of prosperity and peace — at least in North America, allowing the governments of both Sir Wilfrid Laurier and Robert Borden to indulge in a series of minor forays into the eastern Arctic. Politicians, commercial interests, concerned individuals, and scientists called for government-sponsored expeditions that would set up permanent stations in the Arctic to enforce fisheries regulations, investigate ice conditions for commercial shipping and establish Canadian sovereignty. The last was especially critical as other foreign nationals were interested in its waters and territories, as well.

American and Scottish whaling ships had been operating off Baffin Island since 1820 and had followed the whales into Hudson Bay since 1860, where they set up stations and traded with the Inuit. In the absence of any tangible authority, the whalers were unaware that the bay, its natural resources, or Natives belonged to any one country or that there should be restrictions and revenue paid on the number of whales killed. For them, no one owned the Arctic and its resources. As all of the New World had once been, it was a no man's land to be exploited albeit only in the short summer months.

Nations have traditionally relied on their military to protect their national sovereignty and secure their natural resources and much of the complacency about the North that characterized Sir John A. Macdonald's government occurred because there were no such means available to Ottawa for enforcing Canadian claims in the Arctic. In this the era of "gunboat diplomacy," Canada had no gunboat to send. For the Laurier government to find, equip, transport, and maintain even 200 men during the Yukon gold rush had been a major operation and, given the number of flashpoints for a possible war in Europe like the Morocco Crisis of 1911 or the ever-deteriorating situation in the Balkans, the GOC was not going to allow that to reoccur. The Permanent Force could not afford another such disruption. Besides, other than the United States, there were no discernible threats to Canada's Arctic possessions. Czarist Russia, the only other major regional power, had ignominiously lost much of its fleet to the Japanese in 1905.

Thus the North became the preserve of government departments other than the military. The nearest that the Dominion had to a navy or a coast guard was the Department of Marine and Fisheries, which was established in 1868 and maintained lighthouses, buoys, harbours, and imposed fisheries regulations. It had a fleet of some 32 ships and some of which, like the CGS (Canadian Government Ship) *Canada*, were armed for fisheries protection. But sending one of them to the Arctic was never contemplated. Instead, funds were given to the Department's tiny meteorological section, which had taken over weather observations from the British Army in 1871.

The Canadian Meteorological Service came into the spotlight with the first International Polar Year of 1882–83. The brainchild of the Austro-Hungarian explorer Karl Weyprecht, the International Polar Year was a scientific program to establish a network of stations in the Arctic not for purposes of sovereignty, but to study its geology, flora, and fauna, and take weather and ice measurements. Three such meteorological stations were set up on Canadian soil with Canada and Great Britain jointly managing one at Fort Rae, Great Slave Lake, while the United States naval officer Lieutenant Adophus Greely built Fort Conger at northern Ellesmere Island, and the German government set up at Baffin Island.

With the completion of the transcontinental railway, farmers in Western Canada began lobbying for a railway to Hudson Bay from where a shipping route could take their grain to Europe. In 1884, a parliamentary committee recommended that meteorological observation stations similar to those of the Polar Year be erected around Hudson Bay to study ice conditions, which would allow for a shipping season in the summer. The Hudson's Bay Company had been operating in those waters for over 200 years and its records would have given the government a history of ice conditions. When the Select Committee of the House of Commons consulted it in 1884, its officials said that Inuit from Baffin Island could only cross to the mainland trading posts on the south side of Hudson Strait about once every ten years because of the open water.

Funds were provided by Parliament to charter the *Neptune*, a Newfoundland sealing ship of 465 tons, strengthened for ice navigation and with auxiliary power. Captained by Andrew Robertson Gordon, RN, a deputy director of the Meteorological Service, through the summer of 1884, the *Neptune* dropped off three-man observer teams at Point Burwell at the mouth of the Hudson Strait, Ashe Inlet, Stupart Bay, Nottingham Island, and Diggs Island. The scientists were to observe and record weather, tides, ice movements, and geology — anything that would help the government decide whether a shipping season was feasible. There was no thought of maintaining permanent stations in Hudson Bay and when the study concluded in 1887, Gordon's recommendations were that there could be a short shipping season through the Hudson Straits and that the proposed railway terminate at Fort Churchill rather than the Nelson River estuary, which was unsuited to traffic.

For the Victorians, the "holy grail" had been the quest to be the first person to find the source of the Nile. For the Edwardians, it was the race to either one of the geographic poles. Expeditions from a number of countries attempted to reach 90° N (which was on shifting pack ice in the middle of the Arctic Ocean) by ship or, tragically, once by hydrogen balloon. In 1893, the Norwegian explorer Fridtjof Nansen reached latitude 86° 14' before being forced to turn back. But Hansen's partner, Otto Sverdrup, would spend five seasons, from 1898 to 1902, exploring Ellesmere Island to use as a base to conquer the Pole. Unaware that Ottawa regarded this as sovereign Canadian territory, Sverdrup would name islands after Axel Heiberg and the brothers Ellef and Amund Ringnes — all Norwegian brewers who had financed his expedition. He then attempted to interest King Oscar II of Sweden in establishing a national claim over Ellesmere and Devon Islands and when the king showed no interest, he began lobbying the new Norwegian government when that country separated from Sweden in 1905. They were even less interested and the landmarks that he had explored and named on Sverdrup Island and around much of Ellesmere Island like Nansen Sound, Norwegian Bay, and Bjorne Peninsula remained part of Canada.

Since their transfer in 1880, the sovereignty of the Arctic islands — from Prince Patrick Island to Ellesmere Island (known since 1954 as the Queen Elizabeth Islands) had been in question. Uninhabited, they could be claimed by the Norwegians, Danes — and Americans. Inuit hunters from the Thule region of Greenland had hunted muskox on Ellesmere Island for centuries. When Ottawa informed Copenhagen that its Inuit were no longer to do so, the Danish government responded that as far as they (and the hunters) were concerned, Ellesmere Island was *terra nullius* — no man's land. This time it wasn't a case of opening a two-man RCMP post on Ellesmere Island and flying the Red Ensign as had been at Pangnirtung, Baffin Island, in 1923, or Devon Island in 1924. J.B. Harkin of the Department of the Interior wrote:

> To securely establish Canada's title, occupation and administration are necessary. Therefore, next spring (1921) an expedition should be sent north to locate permanent police posts. This should be followed by the transfer of some Canadian Eskimos to the island.[1]

To exercise Canadian sovereignty over all Arctic Islands the government then passed P.C. 1146 in July 1926, a regulatory act that designated all northern lands between the 60 and 141 meridians as a special Arctic Islands preserve that would allow the RCMP to arrest hunters from Greenland. The Norwegian government then began pressing its claim to all that Svedrup had discovered in the Arctic. Ottawa was repeatedly asked for a statement on Canada's position concerning his discoveries. When the Department of External Affairs failed to respond to any inquiries, on March 26, 1928, the Norwegian government notified Canada of its intention to affirm its rights to possession under international law. The elderly Otto Svedrup prevented a diplomatic row when he wrote on April 22, 1929, that the Norwegian governments' rights would be "definitely relinquished should I at any time so desire." He proposed that Mr.

E. Bordewick, the Canadian Pacific agent in Oslo, "arrange suitable compensation from Canada" to pay for his expedition's four-year effort. After lengthy negotiations, the Canadian government made an *ex gratia* payment of $67,000 to Sverdrup and the Norwegian government affirmed that they "… do not as far as they are concerned claim sovereignty over the Sverdrup Islands but formally recognize the sovereignty of His Britannic Majesty over these islands."[2] Sverdrup died on November 26, 1930, a fortnight after Norway had recognized Canadian sovereignty over his discoveries.[3]

Inuit families from three Baffin Island settlements were relocated to Devon Island in 1934. Canada was not alone in using relocation as a means to asset its sovereignty. In 1925, as Norwegian fishing activity in the area increased, the Danish government relocated its own natives from the south of Greenland to Scoresby Sund on the east coast. The Russians had done the same bringing in Inuit families to Wrangel Island in 1926 — only removing them in 1981 when sovereignty was no longer in question.

Denmark would take steps to protect its sovereignty over eastern Greenland in 1931 by instituting legal proceedings against Norway in the International Court of Justice. The court's decision in 1933 on what was called "The Eastern Greenland Case," referred to effective occupation and a continued display of authority as the basis for sovereignty. Canadian officials in Ottawa could not know that soon relocating a few Eskimo families and posting RCMP constables would be insufficient to display that sovereignty.

Of all those who raced to the Pole, none challenged Canadian sovereignty (or sought the headlines) more than U.S. Navy Rear Admiral Robert Edwin Peary. For him, being the first man to get to the North Pole wasn't for scientific or even nationalistic purposes, but purely for celebrity. Born into genteel poverty, Peary repeatedly told his mother, "I must have fame." Using Fort Conger as a base, from 1886 to 1909, Peary led eight Arctic expeditions through Greenland and Ellesmere Island, one of them four years in duration. What annoyed Canadians who came after was his cavalier attitude to the fragile polar environment. To feed and clothe his large parties, Peary depleted Ellesmere Island of caribou and muskox, forcing its residents to migrate elsewhere. Later explorers to the area complained about the mounds of old tin cans, empty boxes, putrid walrus blubber, and five Eskimo graves that Peary had left behind.

With no less than six railway promoters bidding for the contract to build a railway to Hudson Bay, Louis Henry Davies, Laurier's minister of fisheries asked Dr. William Wakeham to check Gordon's findings, monitor the whaling in Hudson Bay, and assert Canadian sovereignty in the Arctic for the first time. The commander of the Gulf of St. Lawrence fisheries patrol, Wakeham had been appointed by the Privy Council in 1893 to examine Canadian/American boundary waters, a study that would form the basis of the Boundary Waters Treaty with the United States. In June 1897, in the chartered Newfoundland sealing ship *Diana*, he would sail to Cumberland Sound. In a ceremony at Kekerten Island, at a deserted Scottish whaler's base on August 17, he would formally proclaim Canada's sovereignty over Baffin and all of the Arctic islands:

> Landed and hoisted the Union Jack in presence of the agent, a number of our own officers and crew, and the Esquimaux, formally declaring in their presence that the flag was hoisted as an evidence that Baffin's Land with all the territories, islands and dependencies adjacent to it were now, as they always have been since their first discovery and occupation, under the exclusive sovereignty of Great Britain.[4]

The gesture was more symbolic than anything else and with the government's focus on the Yukon between 1897 and 1900; Wakeham's proclamation went unnoticed.

The unfavourable decision in the Alaska boundary dispute in 1903, coupled with the fear that American whalers' activities in Hudson Bay would provoke President Roosevelt into making new territorial claims, pressured the Laurier government into a token response. In the House, W.F. MacLean, the Conservative Member of Parliament for York South, pressed the government on May 12, 1903, into establishing its claim over Hudson Bay the world's largest inland sea; by having it renamed the Canadian Sea. The Acadian nationalist, Senator Pascal Poirier, urged Laurier on October 20 to send an expedition to the Pole and even called for the purchase of part of Greenland from Denmark.

Poirier was a supporter of Captain Joseph-Elzéar Bernier, a former ship's captain who was obsessed with claiming the Arctic for Canada before other nations could. In 1898, in charge of the prison at Quebec City, Bernier asked the government for a ship to get to the North Pole before Peary did. By lecturing across the country on the subject, he gained the support of Lord Strathcona, Governor General Lord Minto, 113 members of Parliament, and thousands of ordinary Canadians. Bernier had raised $70,000 in subscriptions by 1901 and Laurier, despite private misgivings, persuaded Parliament to vote $100,000 for his Arctic exploration. The prime minister was concerned that the race to the Pole was attracting unauthorized visitors to Canadian territory and outlined a plan that would "quietly assume jurisdiction in all directions." Once police posts were established in the Arctic, he planned to send "… a cruiser to patrol the waters and plant our flag at every point." Only when that was done, would it be time to issue a proclamation claiming jurisdiction over the whole of Canada's northern territory.[5]

It wasn't a cruiser, but the veteran *Neptune* that took the 1903 expedition to proclaim Canadian sovereignty in the Arctic. Unique in that its purpose was not meteorological observation, the expedition was exclusively "to show the flag" to Inuit and whaler, to establish the first police detachment in northern Hudson Bay, and inspect the declining whaling industry. Commanded by A.P. Low of the Geological Survey and captained by S.W. Bartlett, who had sailed with Peary, the *Neptune* carried representatives from several government departments including the interior, marine and fisheries, and the NWMP. The following are the instructions that were given to Superintendent J.D. Moodie who commanded the six-man NWMP force onboard:

> The Government of Canada having decided that the time has arrived when some supervision and control should be established over the coast and islands in the northern part of the Dominion, a vessel has been

Geological Survey of Canada / Library and Archives Canada/PA-038265.

Hoisting the flag at Cape Herschel, Ellesmere Island, Northwest Territories, August 11, 1904. A.P. Low expedition.

selected and is now being equipped for the purpose of patrolling, exploring, and establishing the authority of the Government of Canada in the waters and islands of Hudson Bay, and the north thereof.

At the same time, the Fisheries Act was amended so that a licence fee of $50 could be imposed on every ship whaling north of 55°. The expedition wintered at Fullerton Harbour near Chesterfield Inlet. Named by the Royal Navy after the secretary of state, the 4th Earl of Chesterfield, it was a traditional gathering place for the Inuit. Here the NWMP's Division M was established to collect licences and customs duties from whalers. In the summer of 1904, the *Neptune* sailed north to Ellesmere Island and upon landing at Cape Herschel, a ceremony was enacted by Low and Moodie with the flag being raised, the sovereignty of King Edward VII proclaimed for Canada, and the event recorded by the building of a cairn and the leaving of a written proclamation. On the return passage, they went west into Lancaster Sound to Beechey Island where the unfortunate Franklin had once wintered, and then south to Port Leopold where a similar ceremony was repeated on Somerset Island. Low would compile the information gained on the voyage into a book, titled *The Cruise of the Neptune 1903–4*, which for the first time gave the government a survey of its Northern possessions.

William Frederick King had joined the Department of the Interior's Boundary Commission as a young man and been made a sub-assistant astronomer. He gained experience establishing the 49th parallel boundary between Canada and the United States, became chief inspector of surveys by 1886, and in 1890 was Canada's first chief astronomer. He concluded in May 1904 that Canada's claim to the Arctic was "imperfect," especially with regard to the islands. He warned the Laurier government that: "It may possibly be best perfected by exercise of jurisdiction where any settlements exist." While British explorers acting under their sovereign's instructions had discovered most of the Arctic coasts and islands, explorations by Americans and other nationals had neither been undertaken with such official sanction nor followed by the ratification of their claims by their parent governments. The chief astronomer was concerned about the occupation of parts of the Arctic by nationals of other lands —the Americans in particular. He advised the Canadian government to assert, "unequivocally their jurisdiction in these regions." Permanent occupation, King concluded, was the ultimate determinant of sovereignty.

That year it looked as if Bernier had realized his dreams. The government bought the 650-ton sailing vessel, *Gauss* in Kiel, Germany, at a bargain price of $75,000. It had been built for a successfully completed two-year Antarctic expedition and was strengthened against the pressures of pack ice. Bernier sailed her back to Quebec City and renamed her CGS *Arctic*. As fisheries protection officer from 1906 to 1911, he made a series of "sovereignty voyages" with the vessel to the eastern Arctic, hoisting the flag, building cairns, informing the Natives that they were Canadian, and fining whalers who had not taken out licences.

The Northwest Passage, the dream of Frobisher, Ross, and Franklin was successfully crossed in 1906, by the Norwegian explorer Roald

Amundsen, who took three years to complete the journey in the tiny *Gjøa*.[6] Concerned that this would encourage others, Bernier's supporter, Senator Poirier, would initiate the Polar Sector Principle, which decreed that the Arctic should be divided into sectors that bordered on the Arctic Rim states. He introduced a motion in the senate on February 29, 1907:

> A country whose possession today goes up to the Arctic regions will have a right, or should have a right, or has a right, to all the lands that are to be found in the waters between a line extending from its eastern extremity north, and another line extending from the western extremity north. All the lands between the two lines up to the North Pole should belong and do belong to the country whose territory abuts up there … That it be resolved that the Senate is of the opinion that the time has come for Canada to make a formal declaration of possession of the lands and islands situated in the north of the Dominion, and extending to the north pole.

The resolution was not adopted, but on his next voyage, Bernier made for Melville Island on the McClure Strait. Here in 1819, Edward Parry had glimpsed the Beaufort Sea and thought that the Northwest Passage was close to being conquered. On July 1, (Dominion Day) 1909, Bernier and his entire crew wore their most formal uniforms and, with a baby muskox in tow, trekked up to the huge boulder known as Parry's Rock. There they erected a bronze plaque, claiming the entire Arctic Archipelago for Canada. Fittingly, Bernier then etched his own name into the rock with that of Parry.

This Memorial

Is

Erected Today to Commemorate

The taking possession for the

"DOMINION OF CANADA"

Of the whole
"ARCTIC ARCHIPELAGO"
Lying to the North of America
From long. 60° w. to 141° w.
Up to latitude 90° n.
Winter Hbr. Melville Island
C.G.S. Arctic. July 1st, 1909.
J.E. Bernier. Commander

On the return voyage, Bernier collected fisheries licences from whaling ships at Baffin Island and as well as a $50 licence from the American millionaire big-game hunter Harry Whitney, who was in the area to shoot polar bear and muskox. Fearing that this might become a trend, Bernier would later write to Laurier. "Now that we have taken possession of our Arctic archipelago, it might be advisable at this session of Parliament to pass a game law regulating hunting in this region."

When he returned home, Bernier heard that on April 6, 1909, Peary had finally arrived at 90°— to the puzzlement of his Inuit guides who couldn't understand what all the hardship had been about.[7]

In Ottawa, Laurier's last year in office was taken up in heated debate getting the Naval Service Act passed to create the Department of Naval Service. One of its first initiatives was to send Captain Irving B. Miles to Hudson Bay. If the Liberals were returned to power, Laurier promised that the Hudson Bay Railway would connect The Pas with a port on the bay. Miles conducted hydrographic surveys of both Churchill and Port Nelson and "was outspoken in his praise for the former," while condemning the latter for the shallow water, strong current, and storms. Somehow this was lost on the incoming Conservative government of Robert Borden. Also needing western support, in 1912, his government first extended the boundaries of the province of Manitoba to include both Churchill and Port Nelson and then, in 1913, construction was begun on a port — in the estuary of the Nelson River.

With the change in government in Ottawa, even the ceremonial, licence-collecting, and conservation patrols in the Arctic were ended. Bernier begged to be allowed to continue, but was refused. The old sea captain left the government's service to look for gold in Baffin Island, returning to the Arctic in July 1922 on his old ship to take Dr. J.D. Craig, (later surveyor general of Canada) and the Royal Canadian Mounted Police (RCMP) to establish police posts at Craig Harbour on Ellesmere Island and Pond Inlet on Baffin Island. Bernier retired in 1925 and was given a small government pension. He died in 1934 — an unknown evangelist of Canadian sovereignty. As for his ship, the *Arctic* — it was bought by the Hudson's Bay Company and later converted into a lighthouse for use on the St. Lawrence. Almost within sight of Bernier's home, it was left to rot by a wharf in Lévis.

With the world's attention focused on events in Europe and the decline in the whaling industry, further sovereignty expeditions to the Arctic were deemed unnecessary and the last government foray into the Arctic before the war was that of the Manitoba-born Vilhjalmur Stefansson and his Canadian Arctic Expedition of 1913–18. Sponsored by the Geological Survey of Canada, it was scientific in purpose.

Without German colonies or strategic minerals, the Arctic was of no military consequence during the First World War — its isolation and ice ramparts protected it from the ravages that Europe endured. As casualty lists and the issue of conscription dominated the headlines, Canadians looked east rather than north, and securing the Arctic was forgotten.

By 1918, the nation, which two decades before could not raise 200 men, had four divisions on the Western Front, the makings of a navy, and in September of that year, its own air force. The Militia General Order the following year cut the Permanent Force down to 4,000 men and the Canadian Air Board (CAB) chaired by the Honourable A.L. Sifton, the brother of Clifford Sifton, planned to use the nascent Canadian Air Force for non-military duties such as fisheries inspection, mapping, crop-dusting, treaty flights, police support, and fire detection. In coping with the challenges in southern Canada, the Department of Militia and Defence did not acknowledge that the North even existed. The annual Reports of the Department from 1901 to 1922 make not a single reference to the region.[8] But it was two technologies developed during the war that would change the North forever: aircraft and wireless communication.

Postwar, Stefansson would reappear in the corridors of Ottawa to press first Prime Minister Robert Borden and later Arthur Meighen to endorse his campaign to annex Wrangel Island from the new Bolshevik government in the USSR. At the same time, the Danish government was making inquiries as to the sovereignty of Ellesmere Island, much of which had been explored by its citizens from Greenland. With Stefansson's lobbying becoming impossible to ignore, the government set up the Advisory Technical Board on Canadian Sovereignty under Dr. Edouard Deville. Its mandate was to determine if Canadian title to the Arctic islands, the chief of which was Ellesmere Island, should be developed, and if so, how would the Dominion go about it? Raising the flag, building cairns, and telling the locals that they were now subjects of the British king were not enough. The board recommended occupation of Ellesmere Island on a permanent basis– and before a foreign power did so — as the ultimate proof of sovereignty.

Prime Minister Arthur Meighen put Stefansson's plan to acquire Wrangel Island for Canada before the Cabinet and on February 19, 1921, told him that acting on his advice: "… this Government purposes to assert the right of Canada to Wrangel Island…."[9] Meighen was out of power before it could be taken further, but in a Commons debate on May 12, 1922, now leader of the Opposition he said: "The island of Ellesmere … is also one which the government should give some attention. An expedition is about to be launched by a Dane … with the approval of the Danish government designed to make some occupational claim in Ellesmere Island…."

Influenced by Stefansson and the Danish "threat," the Sovereignty Board advised that Ellesmere Island should immediately be seized and occupied. It even hatched a science fiction–type scheme of borrowing a British airship, filling it with supplies and RCMP constables, and then launching it from Scotland to parachute both men and supplies over Ellesmere Island. That the use of airborne troops in winter terrain was more than two decades in the future says much for the imaginative calibre of Ottawa bureaucrats. Interestingly, the Sovereignty Board did not even consider the Department of Militia and Defence at all in this.

Ellesmere Island was visited in 1921 by a Danish expedition and in 1930 by a German expedition led by Dr. H.K. Krüger and his Danish colleague, A.J. Bjare. If permission was asked by either expedition of the Canadian government to do so, no record exists, but the subsequent disappearance of Krüger and Bjare led the RCMP to mount a search and in a 1,400-mile journey, Corporal W.N. Stallworthy covered neighbouring Axel Heiberg Island looking for them. Stallworthy believed that Krüger had gotten lost and crossed Sverdrup Channel to Meighen Island where the pair perished from starvation.

As to Wrangel Island, antagonizing the unpredictable Bolshevik government was hardly wise and the British Foreign Office, which was responsible for Canada's external relations, disavowed any interest in it. That Canadian soldiers had been in Siberia as late as 1919 was not forgotten in Moscow. In Ottawa, Sir Joseph Pope, the first permanent head of the Department of External Affairs who had been involved in the Alaska boundary treaty, advised against endorsing Stefansson's plan to annex it, saying that it was essentially "Asiatic" in location.

Unfazed, Stefansson would send out a small expedition led by the inexperienced Allan Crawford, a young University of Toronto student, and have them occupy the island and raise the British flag over it. With the exception of their female Inuit guide and the expedition's cat, everyone else would die of scurvy and exposure. Then, rapidly losing credibility in Canada, Stefansson would land a group of Americans on Wrangel Island while he attempted to persuade Washington to annex it. This time Bolsheviks acted decisively and sent an icebreaker to the island and threw the Americans into a Siberian prison. Moscow invoked Senator Poirier's sector principle and proclaimed its sovereignty by extending its boundaries to the North Pole.

The decade of the 1920s marked the great record-proving flights across the oceans and over the poles. Because of the increasing number of foreign aviators like Richard Byrd, Floyd Bennett, Lincoln Ellsworth, and Roald Amundsen, who had to fly over Canadian territory to get to the North Pole, Parliament discussed an amendment to the Northwest Territories Act. On June 1, 1925, scientists and explorers who intended to work in the Northwest Territories — which incorporated all of the Canadian Arctic — would have to get licences and permits to do so. The minister of the interior, Charles Stewart, who introduced the amendment in the Parliament, claimed Canadian sovereignty up to the North Pole, specifically the sector between 60° W longitude and 141° W longitude.

The next year, the sector configuration was used once more to create by order-in-council the Arctic Islands Preserve, with laws introduced in 1929 that protected wildlife.

Enforcing all of these sovereignty-defining regulations fell on the RCMP and their lone patrol ship, the *St. Roch*. Named after the Quebec riding of Ernest Lapointe, the minister of justice, the *St. Roch* was launched on May 7, 1928, specifically for the RCMP to patrol the Arctic. The other vessel to figure in any form of a sovereignty patrol was the Hudson Bay steamer *Nascopie*. Here was a vessel with a storied past — and future. In 1916, the HBC had chartered the *Nascopie* to the French government as an armed supply ship to carry wheat from Russia to France and munitions back. But it was on a voyage from Russia to Newfoundland that the *Nascopie* encountered a German submarine north of Murmansk. They exchanged gunfire and it looked as if the submarine was hit and sunk. Later it was confirmed that it didn't sink, but the HBC took great pride in the fact that one of their ships had fought a U-boat.[10] The *Nascopie* was hired in July 1933 by the Department of the Interior to call at police, mission, and meteorological posts in Hudson Bay and Baffin Island and at Robertson Bay, Greenland.

Squadron Leader Robert Logan had been a last-minute addition to Captain Bernier's voyage in 1922. An aerial reconnaissance of ice conditions on Hudson Strait had been suggested in 1919 and the Department of Railways and Canals had asked the Air Board for an ice survey the following summer. Nothing came of it until Bernier's voyage scheduled to depart Quebec City on July 18, 1922, when the Department of the Interior asked that the Air Board send a qualified observer to consider the role of aviation in the Arctic. Logan would later write: "I had known nothing about the proposed expedition before July 6th when I received orders to proceed to Ottawa without delay and to be prepared to stay away for at least 18 months."

A Dominion land surveyor before the war, Robert Logan had learned to fly at his own expense to join the Royal Flying Corps. Said to be an expert in meteorology, navigation, and wireless before he was shot down and captured in 1917, Logan had developed advanced aerial photography techniques. His orders were:

... to obtain as much information as possible regarding flying conditions in the Arctic Archipelago ... and submit suggestions in determining the types of aircraft suitable for use and methods for their employment in various ways in the northern Archipelago.[11]

The first member of the Canadian military to serve in the Arctic, the squadron leader remembered crossing the Circle:

Old time skippers such as Captain Bernier (now 70 years plus) had the habit of joining their passengers in drinking a toast to celebrate the crossing of the Arctic Circle. The Captain called us all to the main cabin and ordered the steward to fetch a bottle of port wine from the supply of medicinal wines in the ship's stores. We sat around the table in the dim light while the Captain poured in each of our cups a modest portion of the red liquid. After he made his little speech we all held up our cups and prepared to drink the toast. The first man to do so nearly choked. And so did the Captain. Instead of port wine the bottle contained cold tea. We learned later that the steward and the cook were in cahoots in using the real wines for "medicinal purposes" and had refilled the bottles of a whole case with tea.[12]

Logan immediately realized the value of aircraft in the North for survey, transport of RCMP personnel, conducting ice and fisheries patrols, starting a caribou industry, and defence. With Dr. Craig, he noted the abundant potential "aerodrome" sites everywhere they went. He saw the role of airships in the Arctic: "In many ways the Arctic is ideal for lighter-than-air craft. The sunlight is practically constant during a long season of the year ... an airship can remain in the air for much longer periods than an airplane and can carry a fairly heavy load."[13] He knew that only the coastlines of the islands in the Arctic had been surveyed and no one had seen their interior or knew the mineral wealth they might contain: "For any extensive aircraft operation a large amount of gasoline ... will be required ... indications of such a supply have been found on Bathurst Island, where analysis shows oil shales yielding 140 gallons of oil to one ton of shale." Logan reported that flying operations in the North were feasible in the summer and ski-equipped aircraft could be used in the winter. But before any major flying operations could begin in the North, he recommended that CAF personnel be sent there to familiarize themselves with climatic conditions, the use of water and air-cooled engines, and skis in the North. He was uncannily prescient in his next statement:

> Much has been said of the possibilities of future hordes of Slavs overrunning Europe.... Aircraft operated from Arctic or sub-Arctic bases that would swoop down and leave trails of destruction throughout the rest of the world.... Whether war with such a country as Russia would ever come or not, should not affect the determination to develop flying in the Canadian Arctic and sub-Arctic regions because Canada if it considers itself worthy to be called a Nation, should have enough pride and spirit to take at last ordinary precautions and be prepared to defend itself in case of any emergency.[14]

At Craig Harbour (named for Dr. Craig) on Ellesmere Island, Logan and the ship's doctor climbed a glacier at the head of a fjord on August 24. They determined by celestial observation that they were 828 nautical miles from the North Pole. The pair celebrated with a lunch of "cold, boiled polar bear meat, raw onion, hardtack and snow.... The menu was not what we would have chosen ... the chief steward and the cook had got so 'high' on Lemon Extract that they could not prepare any lunch for us to take."[15]

The squadron leader had a sense of occasion — or the theatrical. On August 29, 1922, at Craig Harbour, wearing full uniform and in the presence of the Inuit guide Katko and his two children; he planted the flag of the Royal Canadian Air Force. At latitude of 76° 12', it was the farthest

Library and Archives Canada/RE 13080.

Squadron Leader Robert Logan displays a Canadian Air Force Ensign, the first Canadian military flag in the Arctic at Craig Harbour, Ellesmere Island, during the 1922 expedition.

North that the RCAF would reach until 1945. A bronze tablet "Canada NWT" marked the spot.

They arrived back in Quebec City on October 22, and before he was recalled to duty at Camp Borden, Logan spent months in Ottawa writing up his findings. His report on setting up bases for flying in the Arctic was not met with enthusiasm. "It was harder to convince the powers controlling the finances that the results would justify the expense. The general attitude among civil servants and politicians at the time was, 'Who will ever want to fly in the Arctic regions?'"[16]

He had hoped to be sent back to the Arctic to carry out test flights and work on aerial photographic mapping but was told that: "... there was no likelihood of any such experimental work being done in the Arctic for at least several years..." Logan left the RCAF and went on to pioneer aerial survey routes in Central Africa and across the Atlantic, flying with Charles Lindbergh. During the Second World War, he surveyed landing sites in Greenland for the U.S. Army Air Force and lived through the Cold War, seeing what he had prophesied 50 years before come to pass. He was also correct in his assessment of the mood in Ottawa. The government of William Lyon Mackenzie King was disinclined to spend money on air operations in the Arctic to defend Canada — let alone Europe — from the Slavic hordes. But getting votes was something else....

But Logan's recommendation that the Royal Canadian Corps of Signals (RCCS) should be sent to the Yukon by the Department of the Interior to set up communications was acted upon without delay. On his return from the Arctic, he met with O.S. Finnie, the director of the Northwest Territories branch of the Department of the Interior, to establish a radio net in the northwest. Logan's report was seized upon by the Department of the Interior to provide communication in the North — with high-frequency radio rather than telegraph wires. Although the gold rush had ended, mining operations continued in the Yukon, especially a silver strike at Mayo. Various government departments like the Gold Commissioner and the RCMP needed to remain in touch with each other and with Ottawa and the RCCS was seen as the solution.

Of the 4,000-man Permanent Force, the signals element was a fraction — five officers, 14 non-commissioned officers, and 150 men. It was known as the Canadian Signalling Instructional Staff. Based in Ottawa and Camp Borden and employed for wireless communication with the Canadian Air Force, the force was granted by His Majesty the King the title "Royal" on June 15, 1921, thus becoming the Royal Canadian Corps of Signals (RCCS).

The operating costs of the Department of Public Works to run Yukon Telegraph Service had become excessive. Because of the wilderness alone, it ran through the 1,000-mile line from Hazelton, British Columbia, through Yellowknife to Dawson City, it cost $200,000 to maintain. Men had to been stationed every 10 miles to maintain it and many were eaten by bears. By late 1922, the idea of the military taking over communication in the northwest became part of interdepartmental correspondence. Acting Deputy Minister of National Defence G.J. Desbarrats outlined his department's concerns to such a proposal. The DND agreed to undertake the project, but insisted that the Department of the Interior provide the funding. With the signing of a formal inter-department agreement in 1923, the RCCS began planning installation of stations and training of personnel.

In the summer of 1923, Major W.A. Steele and eight signalmen left Vancouver aboard the SS *Princess Louise*. From Skagway they took the White Pass and Yukon Railway to Whitehorse then riverboat to Dawson City and Mayo to set up the first Northwest Territories and Yukon Radio System (NWT&Y) stations. Sergeant Bill Lockhart was chief operator at Mayo and Sergeant Heath was his counterpart at Dawson. The stations used 120-watt transmitters, which were set up in rented accommodation.

The system also handled commercial traffic — with the hope that eventually this would pay for its operation. Until then, it was decided that the operating costs of the army radio system in the North would remain part of the defence budget, but subject of a special vote. Besides Dawson City and Mayo, the Department of the Interior asked for additional stations at Forts Simpson, Smith, and Herschel Island. The last did not open on schedule because the ship carrying the equipment sank in the Bering Sea. The detachment personnel had travelled to Herschel Island via the Mackenzie route and a relief craft with food, clothing, and supplies was dispatched down the Mackenzie — it also sank. This did nothing to deter the four-man detachment at Herschel Island, who, under the command of Lieutenant H.A. Young (later major-general and Canada's Minister of Public Works), built a radio out of "bits and pieces of their personal luggage," and were able to communicate with Dawson City, supplementing their food supplies by hunting and trading with the locals. When it finally arrived in 1925, the replacement station was installed in Aklavik on the Mackenzie Delta rather than Herschel Island. Because of the vital services it provided in the North, from 1920 to the start of rearmament in 1936, the RCCS was the only part of the Permanent Force that actually increased in size. The DND Report for 1924 to 1925 stated:

> The amount of paid traffic (i.e. messages sent by commercial concerns or private individuals) shows a steady increase month by month and reports from the Yukon and Northwest Territories emphasize the importance

that this radio system bears in the everyday life of the inhabitants of that northern country.[17]

It became the one military activity that gave the Canadian government a net profit. Stations were repeating daily news bulletins and weather reports by 1929, transmitted from Edmonton. The only military presence in the North, the NWT&Y system provided vital communications at little expense to the taxpayer. In September 1957, the RCCS (now called RCSIGS) was ordered by the federal government to turn all 28 stations of the NWT&Y Radio System over to the Department of Transport. By now, the NWT&Y had an income of $5 million a year from charges for commercial messages. Fort McMurray went first, while Resolution turned over on March 25, 1959, was the last NWT&Y station to close. The NWT&Y Radio System, including its headquarters in Edmonton, had closed entirely by 1965.

Military aviation, the First World War's other technological leap, would come to the North in 1927. The Liberal government of Mackenzie King needed the support of the prairie-based Progressive Party to remain in power and the Hudson Bay port project was made a priority. The falling price of wheat in the 1920s led to agrarian unrest in Saskatchewan and brought Charles B. Dunning, a one-time penniless British immigrant farmer to power. In 1925, with the price of wheat as low as $1.25 a bushel, shipping it from Port Arthur through the Great Lakes to Montreal then transferring it to a Liverpool-bound ship cost a prohibitive 28 cents. The Churchill-Liverpool route was approximately 1,043 nautical miles shorter than Port Arthur–Liverpool and definitely more economical. Constructing the grain silos and port on the Nelson River estuary had presented severe engineering problems and that site was abandoned by 1924 — allowing the Liberals to point out that Borden's Conservatives had wasted $5,639,000 on it — and Churchill was chosen instead.

King brought Dunning into the Cabinet as his minister for railways and canals and in the spring of 1927, the prime minister announced that the government was going to send an expedition to Hudson Strait to study the patterns of ice movement for the shipping season. The Departments of Railways and Canals, Marine and Fisheries, and National Defence joined to form an interdepartmental committee and planned a yearlong aerial survey of the area. Besides studying the ice conditions, the expedition was to find three locations for direction-finding stations to aid in marine navigation.

At first, the RCAF planned to use kite balloons to do this, but since they cost $45,000, they were rejected for aircraft. The plan was that they would fly from three bases in patterns at a constant altitude, one at either end of the strait with a third in a central location. The crew would take oblique photographs with handheld cameras. With the use of a stereoscope, the ice movement could be interpreted from these photographs and a shipping season could be planned.

For once it was to be a well-funded, organized, and equipped mission, and Norman B. McLean of the Department of Marine and Fisheries was put in charge. His department would provide support personnel like cooks, radio operators, and storekeepers. The RCAF would supply six officers and 12 airmen to operate and maintain six aircraft, the Royal Canadian Corps of Signals would provide the men and radio equipment for air-to-ground communication, and the RCMP would send three constables for security.

While the RCAF had flown in winter conditions, its pilots and machines had never done so in Arctic isolation. An aircraft that was extremely rugged, versatile, with a wide cabin and reliable engine — and immediately available — was needed. Wing Commander E.W. Stedman and Flight Lieutenant Thomas A. Lawrence (both future air vice-marshals) were promoted to the rank of squadron leaders and ordered to evaluate suitable machines. The RCAF usually obtained its aircraft from Canadian Vickers, Fairchild, or Avro, but because of the time factor, none of the companies could oblige. Lawrence was sent to Anthony Fokker's plant at Hasbrouck Heights near Teterboro, New Jersey, to test fly the Fokker Universal. Fokker aircraft had an enviable reputation in the aviation industry at the time and had been used by Richard Byrd, Floyd Bennett, and Amelia Earhart. High-wing monoplanes with steel-tube fuselages covered with fabric, the Universals still had an open cockpit, but an enclosed cabin for the passengers. They were powered by Wright Whirlwind J4-B 200 hp radial engines that gave them a cruising speed of 98 miles per hour, a range of 535 miles, and endurance of four hours. Best of all was that their undercarriages were interchangeable for wheels, skis, or floats. Earlier that year, James Richardson had bought three Fokker Universals for his Western Canada Airways to ferry men, materials, and dynamite from the railhead to the construction site at the port of Churchill and from March 27 to April 17, the three aircraft had performed the first airlift in history.

Lawrence decided that the Universal was suitable and Anthony Fokker and his manager R.B.C. Noorduyn (who would later design the Norseman bush plane) were able to fill the order for six Universals with the Department of Marine and Fisheries paying $16,000 for each. Defects later discovered were that the floats and fittings were liable to break under stress. Also to be taken on the expedition for reconnaissance of landing possible sites was a de Havilland D.H.60X Moth on floats with the lyrical name of *Spirit of the Valley of the Moon*.

The aircraft were flight-tested at Camp Borden, where the pilots and maintenance engineers were put through courses on winter-flying, rigging, first aid, navigation, dog-handling, engine maintenance, and photography. Accompanying them would be Fox news photographer

Library and Archives Canada/RE 13778.

Three Fokker Universals on the Hudson Strait Expedition (1927–28), where the open-cockpit, enclosed-cabin monoplanes proved their worth.

Georges Valiquette who was to make a 16-mm silent film of the whole expedition. On July 17, 44 men, the seven aircraft, lumber for the pre-fabricated buildings, three Fordson tractors, motor launches, and all supplies necessary to sustain a six-month operation left Halifax in three ships, the old icebreaker CSG *Stanley*, a second icebreaker from the Quebec Agency, the CGS *Montcalm* and a chartered freighter, SS *Larch*. Lawrence would later relate that the air force officers were unhappy with the whole expedition. They had been told that whatever the outcome of their task, the grain port at Churchill was going to be built to placate the western grain farmers.[18]

The ships arrived at Port Burwell 10 days later and the Moth was unloaded to scout out locations. The only available maps of the region were from British Admiralty charts that dated from 1837 and were wholly inaccurate. Two Universals were to operate out of each of the bases: Port Burwell was Base A, commanded by Flight Lieutenant F.S. Coghill between the two. The headquarters at Wakeham Bay was Base C with Squadron Leader Lawrence in charge. Base B was at the southernmost corner of Nottingham Island, commanded by Flight Lieutenant A.A. Leitch. Communication was by long-wave wireless with the other bases and short wave with Ottawa. Unfortunately, communication from the aircraft to the bases was by one-way radio and messages had to be sent by Morse code, but until the plane landed, there was no way of knowing if they had arrived.

The Moth was lost on August 26 when it was caught in a storm while moored. The daily observation patrols began on September 29 from Wakeham Bay, October 11 from Nottingham Island, and October 23 from Port Burwell. Through the late summer and autumn, the aircraft flew on pontoons. Navigation was by dead reckoning with land in sight at all times. By the time the ships left on November 11, the buildings had been completed. At Port Burwell, the abandoned Moravian Mission house was refurbished as living quarters. Ice appeared on the bay soon after, and by December 16, the pontoons had been replaced with skis, and the Univerals were flying off a "runway" made on sea ice. Detailed flight reports and aerial photography provided a visual record of ice conditions in the strait and much of the flying was at low level in order to photograph the ice.

Operating single-engined aircraft over a treacherous environment with fog, wind, snow, and dangerous shore ice made accidents inevitable. Besides the emergency rations of bully beef, hardtack, and chocolate, each aircraft carried a primus stove, rubber raft, Arctic sleeping bags, and, at Lawrence's insistence, an Inuit who could help if the aircraft crashed. Aircraft were lost three times. On December 15, Flight Lieutenant Leitch lost his way in a snowstorm as he was returning to Nottingham Island. Not sighting land, he landed on an ice floe to wait the storm out. The engine was drained of oil and that night the crew attempted to sleep through bitter weather. The next day, with emergency equipment onboard the Fokker, the crew warmed their oil, poured it back into the engine, and started up. They made it home with only about a quart of fuel left their tanks. Squadron Leader Lawrence was flying from Wakeham Bay to Nottingham Island on January 8, 1928, when he ran into heavy snow 20 miles east of Cape Digges. He turned back and landed at Suglet Inlet and the next day took off and tried to reach Nottingham Island, but again met snowstorms, so he put down at Deception Bay. Lawrence and his crew camped in the Fokker, living off their survival rations for nine days while storms swept through the area. Finally, on January 16, Flying

A Fokker Universal of the Hudson Strait Expedition (1927–28), readied for an ice patrol at Base B in the Hudson Strait. Engines and oil had to be pre-heated for usage in Arctic temperatures.

Officer B.G. Carr-Harris, flying from Wakeham Bay, found them and landed alongside. They dug Lawrence's plane out of the snow and the next morning both aircraft returned to Wakeham Bay.

The third accident could have been fatal for the crew. On February 17, 1928, Flying Officer A. Lewis took off from Port Burwell with Flight Sergeant N.C. Terry and an Inuit named Bobbie. Close to the southeastern end of Baffin Island, they were en route back to base when the engine began to vibrate and miss. At the same time, visibility deteriorated and Lewis laid on a course, which he thought would get them back to Port Burwell. Eventually he ran out of fuel and touched down on hummocky rough ice, which he thought to be in Ungava Bay. The three men began walking eastward with their emergency kit. After a day they realized that they were actually on an ice floe in the Atlantic off the Labrador coast, and doubled back. For the next seven days they travelled westward, getting across open water with an inflatable raft that was part of their kit. When their emergency rations ran out, they resorted to eating raw meat from walruses that Bobbie shot. Eventually they got to the Labrador coast and for the next four days saw no sign of life. On the fifth day after reaching the coast, they met an Inuit hunter and his wife, and with Bobbie acting as an interpreter, were given food and transportation by dog team back to Port Burwell. It was March 1, 1928, by the time they returned.

In Ottawa, the government was considering whether or not to extend the mission. The Department of Marine and Fisheries pronounced satisfaction with the results obtained so far and informed the Department of National Defence on March 10 that it was unnecessary to continue. All flying ended on August 3, by which time the ice had left the strait. In the eleven months of operations with 227 ice patrols (over 370 hours flying time), 2,285 photographs had been taken.

The plan was for aircrew and aircraft to fly to Ottawa, and fuel caches had been laid down by the Hudson's Bay Company at Cape Smith, Povungnituk, Port Harrison, Great Whale River, Fort George, East Maine River, Rupert House, Moose Factory, Remi Lake, and Trout Mills. But on August 25, when the five remaining Fokkers took off, three made it into the air, but the fourth could not because of engine trouble, and the fifth, piloted by Flight Lieutenant Coghill, crashed with a broken pontoon.

When the other four aircraft were examined, the undercarriage mounts and pontoon fittings on two were very weak. Squadron Leader Lawrence made the decision that all should return home by sea and radioed the SS *Larch* and CGS *Montcalm* for assistance. The Fokkers were disassembled and stowed aboard the ships. Two of the aircraft were put aboard the *Larch* and the other two were flown to Wakeham Bay where they were shipped on the CGS *Canadian Voyageur*. The expedition arrived back in Halifax in October 1928.[19]

Even in the heart of winter, the results demonstrated that the complete Hudson Strait never froze and that ice began in mid-November and cleared completely in August, making a three-month shipping season possible. McLean recommended that Canada acquire two icebreakers to keep the strait open longer and as navigational aids radio stations were located at Cape Hopes Advance and on Nottingham Island in 1928 and on Resolution Island and Churchill in 1929. They also discovered how existing maps of the North were very inaccurate. Much of the coastline had been poorly drawn, there were islands that had not been charted, and those that had been were inaccurately located. The Hudson Bay Railway to Churchill was completed by September 1929, when a token wheat shipment was sent on the *Nascopie* and the first commercial cargo shipment for Britain on August 31, 1931. Unfortunately, the onset of the Depression, coupled with the short shipping season and the high Lloyd's insurance rates — all meant that less than 5 percent of western grain ever went through Churchill and the shipping route has never achieved its full potential.

The expedition was a success for the RCAF in that no lives were lost and that despite the lack of all navigational aids, the pilots were lost only twice. The RCAF learned that although the aircraft's undercarriage had been interchangeable with wheels, pontoons, and skis, there could be no flying in the seasons in between freeze-up in the fall and ice break-up in the spring. However, with permanent bases in the Arctic, air operations were possible. Lawrence also recommended that the ideal aircraft for the Arctic would be a twin-engined amphibious flying boat with air-cooled engines having seven- to nine-hour endurance with a crew of four and a full emergency kit and rations for 16 days. In keeping with government policy at the time, there were no decorations given to anyone, not even who survived the ordeal of being lost.

A competitor of Anthony Fokker was Sherman Fairchild, who specialized in building aircraft for aerial photography. Realizing the unsuitability of the open cockpit and handheld cameras in Fokkers, in 1926, the Fairchild Manufacturing Company of Longeuil, Quebec, began building the FC-2. The high-wing monoplane was specifically designed for surveying and had large windows, an enclosed cockpit, and a heated cabin for the photographer and folding wings so that it could be more easily put under cover in the Arctic. It also had a glass panel in the floor so that that a vertical camera could be used. Using Fairchilds, the RCAF pioneered two long-distance flights to the Arctic Circle in 1930. In the first on July 2, two aircraft under the command of Flying Officer J.C. Uhlman left McMurray, Alberta, to take Lieutenant-Colonel E. Forde of the RCCS and two officials of the Department of Indian Affairs and Agriculture on an inspection tour of posts along the Mackenzie River Valley. They flew as far as Aklavik, Northwest Territories and Herschel Island in the Beaufort Sea. On July 6, Flight Lieutenant F.J. Mawdesley, in a Fairchild 71B with Flight Sergeant H.J. Winney in a Vickers Vedette, left Ottawa to explore water routes in the Northwest Territories. They landed in Aklavik on July 19 and continued on to Great Bear Lake, Coronation Gulf on the Arctic coast, and Fort Reliance on Great Slave Lake. Then they flew east to Chesterfield Inlet and north as far as Repulse Bay on Melville Island. They returned through Churchill, touching down on the Ottawa River on October 1, having flown 15,000 miles and taken more than 3,000 photographs.

In 1936, the RCAF flew Sir James MacBrien, the RCMP commissioner, in a Fairchild 51 on an inspection tour of northern detachments. The trip covered 11,000 miles in one month, the longest single journey by air made in Canada at that time.

During the Depression, the RCAF was reduced to a third of its strength and commercial aviation firms took over much of its mapping, crop dusting, and treaty flights. By 1935, except for the occasional special flight to Aklavik, it concentrated on training for an eventual war. There were no permanent stations built in the North — the RCAF used southern-based

aircraft for specific missions, usually in support of another federal government department. None of the RCAF northern operations involved
sovereignty patrols or (with the exception of Squadron Leader Logan's
gesture), "showing the flag." Given that it did not become completely
independent of the army (the RCAF chief of Air Staff continued to report
to the army's chief of the General Staff) until 1938, this is not surprising.

When military aircraft did overfly northern Canada, they belonged
to the U.S. Army Air Force. In 1934, Washington wanted to demonstrate
that its brand-new Martin B10 all-metal bomber had the range to reinforce Alaska in case of a Japanese attack. Lieutenant-Colonel Henry "Hap"
Arnold was ordered to lead 10 B10s from Minneapolis across Alberta to
Prince George, British Columbia, and then onto Fairbanks, Alaska. There
was already an Exchange of Notes granting reciprocal "blanket" permission for flights of military aircraft over Canada and the United States and
this would be renewed each year until 1939. But as chief of General Staff,
General A.G.L. McNaughton opposed this, fearing that if there was a
Japanese–United States conflict that Canada's only hope was to remain neutral. But External Affairs' Under Secretary of State Oskar Douglas Skeleton
saw it as an opportunity to further Canadian–United States relations at no
cost and convinced the government to allow the over-flight to take place.
Overruled, McNaughton (who, as future events would demonstrate, never
quite mastered the relationship between politics and the military), left the
army to become president of the National Research Council.

For the U.S. Army Air Corps, the flight was the first display of strategic air power and it tendered a proposal that year for a bomber that
would have the range to not only reach American bases as far away as
Hawaii and Panama, but also be used for hemispheric defence.

The militia's sole contribution to the North was the RCCS and its
wireless communications network over the northwest. The radio stations were, unlike the RCAF's flights, the DND's only permanent installations in the North. As for the Royal Canadian Navy, it never ventured
into northern waters at all.

—*—

Between the wars, for most Canadians, their vision of the Arctic came from the silent movie *Nanook of the North*, released in 1922. Considered by modern historians as more "salvage ethnography" than documentary, it had all the clichés that the moviegoer expected: "noble savage" hunters with two or more wives living in igloos and killing walruses with spears. The Inuit featured in the film were from the east coast of Hudson Bay — coincidentally the same families who would be relocated to the high Arctic by the government 30 years later. But when it was distributed, it was paired with Harold Lloyd's movie *Grandma's Boy* — a box-office success. *Nanook* was such a hit in the 1920s that ice cream in Germany was sold as "Nanuks," as "Esquimaux" in France, and "Eskimo Pies" in Britain. The movie gave the world their first images of the Canadian Arctic and its Natives.[20]

That year, Vilhjalmur Stefansson's book *The Friendly Arctic* was also published, a revelation to all who read it. Stefansson wrote that the North should not be regarded as some bleak, frozen wasteland, but with the advent of long-range aircraft, tankers, and submarines, it was poised to become the future crossroads of the world — the strategic and commercial equivalent of the Mediterranean Sea. Stefansson died in 1962 — just as it was about to begin.

4

Sovereignty and Mackenzie King

The Second World War changed the Canadian North/Arctic with the ferocity and the transience of the Yukon gold rush.[1] Unlike the 1914–18 conflict, this time geography and developments in aviation and radio put the Arctic on the periphery of military strategy. It was about sovereignty — in this instance, that of the northern part of the western hemisphere. This time three arms of the Canadian military were involved, either in the Norwegian or the Alaskan polar regions. RCN escorts fought their way through the Barents Sea in the Murmansk convoys, Canadian soldiers landed in Spitsbergen, Norway, in OPERATION GAUNTLET, on Kiska, the Aleutians in GREENLIGHT FORCE, and the RCAF squadrons flew in defence of Nome, Alaska.

In the Canadian North, where airfields and highways were thrown up almost overnight, the battle over sovereignty was against a friend and neighbour, the United States. Between 1941 and 1945, the temporary influx of American airmen, soldiers, and construction battalions far outnumbered the local inhabitants in Labrador, northern British Columbia, and the Yukon. Canadians, who since the British had bequeathed their Arctic possessions to them, never had the wealth or interest in developing the North, now watched, in askance, as the United States military literally and metaphorically bulldozed its way through Northern Canada. Grateful that the airfields, highways, and pipelines that sprang up brought victory over the Axis closer, Canadians allowed the United States to change their North forever. In contrast to the cautious Ottawa bureaucrats who weighed the postwar benefits of such developments with a view of eventual ownership, the United States military charged in with a "can-do" exuberance, the detritus of which can still be seen in the North today.

Because of a shrinking world, the North increasingly became part (a minor part) of Allied global strategic military planning. Traditional Canadian fears of American annexation were replaced by pragmatic acceptance of the uneven partnership that was born at Ogdensburg, New York, and continues to this day. The sequence of events that led to the United States impinging on Canadian sovereignty began in 1930 with the planning of the Alaska Highway.

Automobile clubs, chambers of commerce, and tourism promoters in Alaska, the Yukon, and British Columbia had lobbied since 1921 for a paved highway from Seattle through British Columbia to Alaska, and the idea had been first considered by the Hoover administration. A Canadian delegation of federal and provincial public works officials twice met with their United States counterparts in 1930 to plan the route. The cost was estimated at US$2 million for the Alaskan section (the Yukon border to Fairbanks) and US$12 million for the Canadian section (Hazelton, British Columbia, to the Yukon border). Ottawa could see no value in paying for a highway that would be of little use to Canadians. The Yukon and White Pass Railway, complemented by the picturesque sternwheelers on the rivers and an increasing number of bush pilots were sufficient for the declining population in the Yukon. Besides, the federal government was then expensively involved in the building of the Trans Canada Airway — the chain of airfields and radio and navigational aids from the Maritimes to British Columbia.

The Depression stalled further talks on the Alaska Highway until the United States War Department revived the idea in 1934 as being of some military significance, but nothing occurred. In the summer of 1936, as Germany reoccupied the Rhineland and Italian troops invaded Ethiopia, President Roosevelt enunciated his "Good Neighbor" policy at Chautauqua, New York: "Our closest neighbours are good neighbours. If there are remote nations that wish us not good but ill, they know that we are strong; they know that we can and will defend ourselves and defend our neighborhood." He invited Prime Minister Mackenzie King to Washington to discuss neutrality in the Pacific and also to build a highway through British Columbia to Alaska.

King, who had never cared much for Roosevelt's "New Deal," was leery of both proposals. Canada was content, he said, to be protected by its geography, its British Commonwealth ties, and the Monroe Doctrine. A supporter of British Prime Minister Neville Chamberlain's appeasement of Hitler, what King (who met the German chancellor in Berlin on June 29, 1937), feared more than the Germans or Japanese was a second conscription crisis that would result from the mobilization of more men into the Canadian military. His pre-war policies were centred on national unity and isolationism in that order. King said that at best, Canada would act as a bridge between the two great Anglo-Saxon nations, Britain and the United States.

Decisively re-elected that November, FDR entered his second term determined to campaign for collective security on the North American continent to counter a Japanese threat to Alaska. In July 1937, when Japan attacked China, Roosevelt again pressed for construction of an Alaska Highway, exasperated that King had done nothing to encourage it. Due to visit Alaska in the fall, he arranged to stop over in Victoria on September 30 (the president would not go to Ottawa until 1943), knowing that British Columbia Premier T.D. Pattullo (who had as a young man worked in the Yukon gold rush) was a fervent supporter of the highway.

Canadians on the west coast felt isolated from Ottawa not only by the Rockies, but also the knowledge that because of the deteriorating European situation, the east would get the few defence dollars that came available. The current thinking was that the battlefields of France were Canada's first line of defence, not the North or Pacific coast. As late as 1940, when H.D.G. "Harry" Crerar was chief of the General Staff, continental defence was a minor concern, second to putting more Canadian divisions into Britain. Anglo- and Euro-centred by tradition and training, to counter the supposed Japanese threat to British Columbia, the Canadian military counted on the United States fleet in Hawaii and the British military base at Singapore. King at one time had considered buying two Royal Navy destroyers for British Columbia's protection, but never followed through.

When the Japanese sank the USS *Panay* in Nanking harbour on December 12, 1937, Roosevelt asked both the British and Canadians for naval consultations, especially on coastal defences from Seattle to

Alaska. King demurred, but did allow two RCN officers — one of them Commodore Percy Nelles — to confer with their American counterparts at the Canadian Embassy in Washington. At the meetings, the Canadians were taken aback by a request from the United States War Department to use airfields in British Columbia to reinforce Alaska.

In early January 1938, what in a more cynical era might suspiciously be regarded as "plants," articles appeared in Canadian newspapers head-lined: CANADIAN DEFENCE WEAKNESS "MENACE" TO U.S. SECURITY[2] and JOINT COASTAL DEFENCE PLAN ENVISAGED.[3] Primarily at the urging of Anthony J. Dimond, the Alaskan delegate in the United States House of Representatives, the Alaska Highway Bill was approved in May, and although no funds were allocated, the president could now appoint a commission to survey the best routes for the construction of the high-way. A similar commission was also appointed by Ottawa and after aerial reconnaissance and ground studies, a number of routes were suggested.

That August, both King and FDR jointly wielded a giant pair of scis-sors to cut the ribbon and dedicate the Thousand Islands Bridge over the St. Lawrence River. While the Canadian prime minister chatted ami-ably to media about the symbolic significance of the bridge between the two nations, FDR took the opportunity to proclaim, "… the people of the United States will not stand idly by if domination of Canadian soil is threatened by any other empire." While Canadian and United States newspapers would cheer his speech calling it the "Roosevelt Doctrine," the Nazis would laugh it off as "electioneering talk" and *Time* magazine would tartly ask: "Invasion by whom? Polar bears?"

It took the Munich Crisis in September to frighten the prime minister for the first time and he told the Cabinet that if Britain was, "… worsted in a world struggle, the only future for Canada would be absorption by the United States." That there was the possibility the Royal Navy, unchal-lenged in sea power since Trafalgar, might be defeated must have shaken not only Canadians, but the whole English-speaking world.

With the RCAF absent in the North through the Depression, bush air companies had sprung up to compete for airmail and government contracts, and legendary bush pilots like C.H. "Punch" Dickins had pio-neered air routes as far north as Aklavik. Typical of the breed was Grant

McConachie, who flying on gas fumes, shady credit deals, and panache, parlayed his famous charm into getting Canadian Car & Foundry to give him three Barkley Grow aircraft. The Lakehead railway car manufacturer had leaped into aviation when its Member for Parliament C.D. Howe was appointed Canada's first minister of transport. Contemporaries of the Boeing 247 and Lockheed 14, even when brand-new, the Barkley-Grows were aeronautical curiosities that Canadian Car & Foundry were soon glad to write off — but they did have radio compasses and two-way radios. For McConachie, they were enough to run a "wheels-up" airline, Yukon Southern Air Transport (YSAT). Unlike the usual float-planes in the North, YSAT's Barkley Grows freed their pilots from the tyrannies of weather and relying on visual references. In 1937, using them as leverage, McConachie was awarded an airmail contract to fly from Vancouver and Edmonton to Yellowknife and (he hoped), on to Fairbanks, Alaska.[4] The aircraft required all-weather landing facilities and radio-guidance systems, and, despite the imminent outbreak of war, the Department of Transport provided both at Grande Prairie, Dawson Creek, and Peace River, with YSAT building their own rudimentary airfields at Fort Nelson and Watson Lake. Carving the last two out of the bush almost bankrupted McConachie — he blamed the horses used in their construction for eating their weight in oats — which had to be flown in. But out of his gamble was born the Northwest Staging Route (NWSR), the line of airports through the Canadian North to Alaska. The NWSR might have remained a laudable but local achievement except for the war — and McConachie's reach, which always exceeded his grasp. Now he dreamed of YSAT flying on through Alaska to the Orient.

In this, the Canadian bush pilot got the attention of Juan Trippe, the president of Pan American Airways, who had just seen his airline's European routes cut short by the European hostilities. Before Pan American could overfly Canadian territory to Alaska, Trippe needed radio-beam stations set up along the route. No longer navigating by the stars, American pilots now only flew on radio. But as an American, Trippe couldn't get a licence to operate a radio station in Canada, so he was very pleased when McConachie offered his own basic radio cabins and airfields instead. Pan American Airways had always been the "chosen instrument" of the U.S. State Department and Trippe was so well-connected in Washington that in 1940 there would be a flurry of Exchanges of Notes between Canada and the United States, allowing Pan American Airways and the U.S. Army Air Force aircraft to routinely over-fly Canadian territory on their way to Alaska. Years later, president of Canadian Pacific Air Lines McConachie recalled:

> We had just laid down an airport at Fort Nelson in 1939 and were in the middle of putting one in at Watson Lake when the U.S. government asked the Canadian government to help them by finishing these airports so they could put land-based fighters through this good-weather route from Edmonton through Grande Prairie, Fort St. John, Fort Nelson, Watson Lake, Whitehorse, through to Fairbanks and eventually on to Nome and Russia. So these airports were the starting of the Northwest Staging Route, which later supplied Russia with aircraft. And because these airbases required sup-plies and fuel for the fighters, they had to be connected by road. This in turn became the Alaska Highway.[5]

For the airport at Teslin, all materials came in on three sternwheelers belonging to the White Pass and Yukon Company: the *Nisutlin*, the *Keno*, and the *Whitehorse*. The three vessels steamed down the Yukon River from Whitehorse, across Lake Laberge, and up the Teslin River. Each made one 240-mile trip a week, for two months, until the airport was built.

Awarded a contract by the United States military to fly the route, McConachie was given the impossible — permission by C.D. Howe, now the minister of munitions and supply (who somehow in that portfolio retained control of his prize creation — Trans-Canada Air Lines) to buy on credit brand-new Lockheed 14 airliners and (to McConachie's delight) even getting two 14s from the batch reserved for Trans-Canada Air Lines.[6]

In the only declaration of war in its history, on September 10, 1939, Canada entered into hostilities with an enemy that was part of an alliance with the potential to threaten the both the eastern and western Arctic. As it had in 1914, the United States remained neutral, considerably altering the relationship between the two countries from that day onward, especially with regard to the Atlantic approaches and the North. Initially, President Roosevelt foresaw no serious threat to the western hemisphere — unless the British and French naval fleets fell into enemy hands. But the blitzkrieg in May 1940 showed the Nazis to be seemingly invincible and the British and French were woefully demoralized. After the British defeat at Dunkirk, North Americans began to consider their own futures if Britain surrendered to the Nazis — as Joseph Kennedy, the American ambassador in London, expected them to.

The fall of Denmark on April 9, 1940, and Norway two months after, brought the war to the Arctic. The United States and Canada were very aware that the Danish protectorate of Greenland could not only become a staging point for Luftwaffe bombers and Kriegsmarine U-boats, but its cryolite mine at Ivigtut would now be available to the Germans. A mineral used in the manufacture of aluminum, cryolite was essential to the United States and Canadian aviation industries — and more so now as both countries were turning out a flood of aircraft. If the Germans took possession of or sabotaged the mine, the Aluminum Company of Canada predicted disastrous consequences to Canadian war production.[7]

When Charles Gavan "Chubby" Power became Canada's minister of defence for air in May 1940, encouraged by the British government, he and Norman McLeod Rogers, the minister of defence, planned an operation to take over the Danish cryolite mine at Ivigtut. Rogers was killed in a plane crash[8] on June 10 and James Ralston was put into the portfolio. With an invasion of Britain imminent, complete Nazi victory in Europe must have seemed very real to the new ministers. Without informing the prime minister, Power and Ralston put together "Force X," made up of RCMP and artillery officers, mining engineers, and a Canadian consul to open diplomatic relations with the Danish government in Greenland. They were to be landed at Ivigtut to reconnoiter the area for artillery emplacements and to open a Canadian consulate at Godhaven. The Royal Canadian Navy had no ships available to transport Force X to Greenland and even if there were, none were equipped for the ice conditions in the Davis Strait. With its Douglas fir and Australian gumwood outer hull and steel plate covering bow, the RCMP's tiny *St. Roch* was the Canadian government's only ice-capable vessel. But it was based in Vancouver from where it patrolled the western Arctic. Captained by Henry Larsen, the *St. Roch* left Vancouver on June 21 to attempt the Northwest Passage. There were rumours that it was to look for Nazi agents infiltrating Canada from the North[9] and sending it via the Panama Canal might have alerted Germany as to Canadian intentions — but it would never arrive in time to transport Force X.

Instead the old *Nascopie* was to be armed with a 3.7-inch naval gun and dispatched from Halifax with the force. As the first Canadian military operation into the Arctic, they would be sailing into the unknown. For one thing, all the extant charts of Greenland were in Copenhagen — now available to the enemy and secondly, no one knew if the Germans had already taken over the mine.

What Power and Ralston (and the prime minister) were unaware of was that three fast U.S. Coast Guard cutters were also making for Ivigtut on orders from the Oval Office. The first, picking its way through the storis, was the USCGC *Comanche*, which arrived on May 20, bringing the American consul, security personnel, and engineers from Alcoa, the parent of the Aluminum Company of Canada. President Roosevelt was said to be furious at what he viewed as Canadian exploitation of Denmark's unhappy state on behalf of the Aluminum Company of Canada. That there were to be military and RCMP officers aboard the *Nascopie* went against the Monroe Doctrine. Loring Christie, the Canadian minister to Washington, was called in to U.S. Secretary of State Adolph Berle's office on June 3 and bluntly told that as a neutral power, the United States was to assume full responsibility for the defence of Greenland and Iceland. (Berle, who was a professed Anglophobe, must have relished the meeting.)

Somehow for the United States, Greenland and Iceland were now included in the northern part of the western hemisphere. Washington was attempting to stabilize the situation in the Pacific and the State Department's opposition to Canadian plans to occupy Greenland stemmed from setting a precedent in the Far East. If the Netherlands were to be taken over by the Germans (as it soon would be), the Japanese would then have an excuse to seize the oil-rich Dutch East Indies.[10]

A Canadian offer for a joint defence of both Arctic islands was ignored until the following year. In March 1941, the USS *Cayuga* left Boston with the South Greenland Survey Expedition. On board with the American diplomats and naval officers was a single RCAF officer. The expedition was going to locate suitable sites for air bases, weather stations, and other military installations — all American. The new U.S. Secretary of State Cordell Hull and the Danish ambassador signed the Hull-Kauffmann Agreement on April 9, giving the United States the authority to build and operate air bases and other defensive facilities in Greenland. The construction and maintenance of airports at Narsarsuaq (better known as "Bluie West 1"), Ikateq Island ("Bluie 2"), Grondal Airport at Ivigtut ("Bluie West 7"), and at Sondre Stromfjord ("Bluie West 8") was to be completely American.[11] Although it could not have been apparent to Ottawa then, if the United States had been unable to get bases in Greenland (especially Thule in 1951), Washington would have insisted on a major defence installation in the Canadian Arctic, likely on Ellesmere Island.

As for Iceland, it took considerable persuasion on the part of Prime Minister Winston Churchill to get Icelandic premier Herman Jonassen to allow Anglo-American bases on the island. Both men were aware that President Roosevelt would brook no refusal and when the reluctant "invitation" was issued on July 1, 1941, a U.S. naval task force was already on its way from Argentia, Newfoundland, to Reykjavik. The U.S. Marines, moved from sunny California to the treeless, frozen Icelandic shore, called their new base Camp SNAFU — (Situation Normal, All F**ked Up), which says it all. Canada would not have a base on Iceland until 1944 when an RCAF squadron would be deployed to Reykjavik. By then, with the enemy no longer a threat to the Canadian mainland, Power permitted 162 Squadron Cansos to be sent to Iceland.

As for Canadian sovereignty in the High Arctic during the war, the *St. Roch* would not arrive on the east coast until October 1942 — becoming the first vessel to sail the Northwest Passage from west to east. Fulfilling the dream of Barrow, Ross, and Franklin, in 1944, the little ship would also become the first vessel to complete the Northwest Passage in one season, navigating it in both directions. Throughout the war, the government's two ice patrol ships, CGS *N.B. McLean* and *Saurel*, continued their patrol in the high Arctic, delivering supplies to defence projects in the region. Despite the technological advances that the Second World War would bring, as Franklin had known, the polar ice remained impenetrable. When the *Nascopie* failed for two years in succession to break through the ice to get to the HBC post at Fort Ross on the Bellot Strait at the southeastern end of Somerset Island, the staff was ordered by radio to abandon the post in November 1943. They were later rescued by a U.S. Army Air Force aircraft that landed nearby.[12]

The embarrassing Ivigtut episode may have prompted the Department of External Affairs to take the lead in June 1940, and broach the State Department for closer liaison between the two countries — one that was at war and the other was trying hard to remain neutral. Preliminary military discussions were held in Washington in July with the agenda focused on North American defence if or when Britain fell to the Nazis. On August 16, FDR invited Mackenzie King to meet him the next day in the border town of Ogdensburg, New York, where he would be reviewing troops. The initiative came directly from the White House with not even the State Department or External Affairs aware of the planned conference — let alone the agenda. King took with him Jay Pierrepoint Moffat, the United States Ambassador to Canada, and drove to Prescott, Ontario, where a ferry carried them to Ogdensburg. In a historic coincidence, Prescott's local militia, the Glengarry Light Infantry, had occupied Ogdensburg in 1813 to prevent invasion by the U.S. military. The prime minister's Buick was escorted by motorcycle riders to a railway yard where the president's private railway car waited. When they were on board, the train moved out of Ogdensburg to Heuvelton, a village six miles away.

Roosevelt was effusive at dinner and talked of the destroyers-for-bases negotiations with Britain and that the U.S. Navy would now have bases within the British Empire. Included in the negotiations were 99-year leases at Argentia and Stephenville in Newfoundland and the use of Gander airport that the Canadian government had recently taken under military protection. FDR thought that Canada should also contribute a base, possibly Yarmouth, Nova Scotia. King emphasized that his country did not lease sites, but would allow the United States to make use of facilities on Canadian territory.

The president then proposed the immediate creation of a joint Canadian-American board, composed of an equal number of senior military men, but led by two civilians, one from each country. This agency would study mutual defence problems for the northern half of the western hemisphere and submit recommendations to the two governments. Roosevelt explained that the new board or committee should discuss plans for defence of North America, with attention to possible attack from the northeast. Perhaps with the Ivigtut fiasco in mind, it was vital, Roosevelt said, that there should be conferences, discussions, and plans between the armed services of the two nations in case an attack were launched up the St. Lawrence or along the northeastern coast of Canada. The board would continue in existence beyond the immediate crisis. King immediately agreed to what became the Permanent Joint Board on Defence (PJBD). On Sunday morning August 18th, after attending a military service, Roosevelt and King returned to the train and drafted a joint press statement:

> Declaration by the Prime Minister of Canada and the President of the United States of America regarding the establishing of a permanent joint board on defence made on August 18, 1940 (Known as the Ogdensburg Declaration)
>
> The Prime Minister and the President have discussed the mutual problems of defence in relation to the safety of Canada and the United States.
>
> It has been agreed that a Permanent Joint Board on Defence shall be set up at once by the two countries.
>
> This Permanent Joint Board on Defence shall commence immediate studies relating to sea, land, and air problems including personnel and material.

It will consider in the broad sense the defence of the
north half of the western hemisphere.

The Permanent Joint Board on Defence will consist of four or five members from each country, most of
them from the services. It will meet shortly.

It was the summer for the signing of historic documents in railway
cars — Hitler had accepted the French surrender in one at the Compiègne
Forest on June 22. There is no historic marker at Heuvelton, New York
to commemorate the event, but what occurred in the presidential railway car had immediate and far-reaching consequences for Canadian
sovereignty.[13] Whether the Nazis occupied the mother country or not
— and with the Battle of Britain raging even while the signing took place,
it could go either way — the Dominion was now under the mantle of
American protection.

Nothing written — FDR used a pencil through the session — was
legally binding and yet the Ogdensburg Agreement, between a neutral
country and the only belligerent in the western hemisphere, had profound implications for both. The board had no executive authority and
the recommendations it made required the approval of the president and
the Canadian Cabinet War Committee. Neither leader had consulted his
advisers, their public, or representatives in this. Neither wanted to expand
it into a formal treaty or even a memorandum of understanding. Both
countries had recognized that their strategic interests were inseparable
and that a new relationship especially with regard to the Canadian North/
Arctic had been born out of necessity. From now on, neither country would
ever again act unilaterally with regard to defence of the North American
continent. The PJBD would have its greatest influence in the 16 months
between August 18, 1940, and December 7, 1941, when the United States
entered the war. Of the 33 wartime recommendations it would make —
with a single exception (the 29th) — all would be acted upon.

King certainly viewed what occurred at Heuvelton as a momentous
event — liking especially the word "permanent" that FDR had penciled
in to describe the PJBD. His greatest fear had been that the United States
would pull out after the crisis had ended and return to its isolationist

stance. This new agreement, he told Parliament, was not to be of a temporary nature: "It is part of the enduring foundation of a new world order, based on friendship and good will." The military collaboration that the agreement initiated, especially with regard to the Canadian North, had far-reaching consequences from that day onward through to the Cold War. For the Canadian public, in shock that Britain might still fall to the Nazis, the press release jointly issued by the president and prime minister signalled that the United States was emerging from its isolationist shell. A few committed imperialists (like the former Conservative prime minister, Arthur Meighen) condemned the agreement as a shift by Canada from being a British dominion to Canada as an American "protectorate." Meighen accused King of abandoning Britain, the mother country of most Canadians, in her most desperate hour, and placing the country in the control of the United States.

The membership of the board was announced on August 22. It would be led by non-government civilians with soldiers and diplomats making up the body. The colourful Fiorello H. LaGuardia, mayor of New York City, was named chairman of the United States section and O.M. Biggar, the Ottawa barrister who had once worked with Arthur Sifton in setting up the Canadian Air Force, was chairman of the Canadian section. The PJBD first met on August 26, 1940, and in its "Joint Canadian-United States Basic Defence Plan — 1940," the board specified two urgencies on the Pacific coast: the defence of British Columbia and Alaska and the protection of their sea communications, especially along the panhandle.

The board's recommendations included the expansion of the Northwest Staging Route (NWSR) and beginning the construction of the Alaska-Canadian Highway. The Alaskans naturally wanted a route that went through the panhandle (Route A), while the Canadians preferred one that cut through the Rocky Mountain Trench and followed the NWSR (Route B). There was even a lobby for a highway east of the Rockies that former premier of Alberta Charles Stewart (now the chairman of the Canadian section of the Alaska Highway Comission), considered preferable. A preliminary report issued on May 10, 1940, satisfied no one and led to further surveys. Given the events taking place in Europe — the signing of the Tripartite Pact and the battles in North

Africa and the Mediterranean Sea, a lack of interest in a road through the Northern wilderness can be excused.

The PJBD recommended that the highway follow the general line of airports, Grande Prairie–Fort St. John–Fort Nelson–Watson Lake–Whitehorse-Boundary–Big Delta. While FDR approved the PJBD's recommendations without delay, the Canadian War Cabinet Committee did not, waiting for the Treasury Board to consider the expenditures involved. The survey of sites for 3,000-foot landing strips at Grande Prairie, Fort St. John, Fort Nelson, Watson Lake, and Whitehorse had been completed by January 1940, but it took until February 1941 for Ottawa to fund their construction. For the towns on rail lines like Fort St. John (60 miles from Dawson Creek) and Grande Prairie, the shipment of men and materials was easy enough, and the White Pass and Yukon Railway could carry material from Skagway to build the airport at Whitehorse. But Watson Lake and Fort Nelson were hundreds of miles ahead of any rail line and airfield construction required horse teams and bulldozers to pioneer winter roads over the ice on frozen lakes and drivers. The spring thaw also brought all work to a halt.

On a peninsula that juts into the lake, and is surrounded by tall pines, Watson Lake is a place of rare beauty. The story of the building of this lovely, but lonely, northern airport is an example of the courage and ingenuity that characterized the building of the NWSR. In the spring of 1941, both the construction materials and the means of its transportation were assembled at Vancouver. They were a sternwheel river-steamer, three shallow-draft power boats (called tunnel-boats), and 12 barges. Then, dismantled for shipment, all were taken to Wrangell on coastal steamers. Reassembled, the boats freighted the construction material up the Stikine River to Telegraph Creek. There they and the supplies were portaged 72 miles on the old Gold Rush Trail to Dease Lake. At Lower Post, the sternwheeler hauled the barges — until it hit a rock and sank at Two Mile Rapids. The tunnel boats then continued in relays on the Dease with the freight. They took two days to go down the rushing river and six days to return. Eventually, because the Cottonwood Rapids sank so many boats, a "cat" was used to build a road around the rapids. This was joined to the final 26-mile highway to Watson Lake.

At Sandy's Point on the lake, McConachie had built a log cabin for YSAT's radio station and a second one for the crew. This last became the officers' mess in wartime, where carved into the log facing the fireplace were the names of hundreds of RCAF and USAAF pilots that flew through. Despite all difficulties, by September 1941, all five airfields were open for daylight operations only and in December the radio ranges on all sites were in operation.

This early in the war, "sovereignty" for the Canadian government had little to do with the Arctic and more with keeping control of its armed forces, reminding the British that they were not part of the War Office's own grand strategy. The mixed success that Ottawa had in this led to the first instance that Canadian troops would be used in the Arctic — the Norwegian Arctic. Through Britain in 1920, Canada had been one of the signatories of the Svalbard Treaty that recognized Norwegian sovereignty over the Arctic archipelago of Spitsbergen. When Norway was occupied by the Germans in June 1940, the British and Soviet governments wanted the island's coal mines (then being worked by Russians) and its radio and weather observation stations put out of commission. The last was especially vital to German air attacks on the Murmansk convoys.

In the summer of 1941, commanding the only troops available in strength in Britain, General A.G.L. McNaughton was asked by the chief of the Imperial General Staff for Canadian participation in such an operation. In preparation, for the first time in Canadian military history, amphibious landings, demolitions, and the construction of beach roadways were practised. On August 6, 1941, under the command of Brigadier Arthur E. Potts, "111 Force," made up of the Edmonton Regiment and a company from the Princess Patricia's Canadian Light Infantry, the 3rd Field Company, Royal Canadian Engineers, and a machine-gun company from the Saskatchewan Light Infantry departed Scotland on the Canadian Pacific *Empress of Canada* for EXERCISE HEATHER. Speculation among the troops was that they were landing in Brittany, Spain, or North Africa.

En route, Captain W.H.T. Wilson and 1 Divisional Signals were dropped off at Hvalfjord, Iceland, to send fake weather reports to the Germans that would hopefully prevent air reconnaissance of Svalbard.

Not until August 22, when they were issued with leather jerkins, sheep-skin coats, and long woollen underwear did the rank and file discover that the exercise was the cover name for OPERATION GAUNTLET, the British and Canadian raid on Spitsbergen.

Three days later, the Canadians landed at the port of Barentsburg where instead of German artillery fire they were greeted by cheering crowds of Norwegians, Russian coal miners, and a number of Free French soldiers (they were called the "Free French," as opposed to those under the Germans — the Vichy French — who had escaped through Russia). Brigadier Potts formally asked the Norwegian commissioner for permission to (as the *Life* magazine correspondent put it) "blast the island." Canadian sappers then destroyed all German radio and weather stations, 540,000 tons of coal, and 275,000 gallons of petrol. While this took place, the Russians and Free French were evacuated to Archangel on the *Empress*, which returned on September 1 to take the military and the Norwegians to Britain. Overshadowed by the Dieppe raid in August the following year, OPERATION GAUNTLET deserves to be remembered as the first time that Canadian troops were involved in the Arctic. As to Brigadier Potts, he must have been relieved that his soldiers had not required specialized winter clothing or equipment.

But the British War Department was not finished with using Canadian troops in northern climes yet. In early 1942, as a diversionary tactic to draw German units away from a proposed Allied landing in France, the British military asked Canada to consider the possibility of launching a limited attack on Norway.[14] Conceived by Lord Louis Mountbatten and code named PLOUGH, the campaign would require specialized transport, winter equipment, and training for the soldiers. The National Research Council and Joseph-Armand Bombardier were tasked with designing a suitable tracked vehicle for such terrain and several Arctic experts were asked their advice on the feasibility of military operations in extreme winter conditions. They concluded that PLOUGH would place huge demands on an already-stretched Canadian military and advised that the British be refused. Given that OPERATION JUBILEE, the raid on Dieppe was also being planned for that summer, this is understandable.[15]

But the British request led to the Canadian military considering for the first time tracked vehicles specifically designed for Arctic terrain. In response for a ministry of supply requirement for a "light reconnaissance car — armoured, tracked," the Montreal firm of Ferand and Delorme built a fully tracked two-man armoured snowmobile powered by a Cadillac V-8 engine mounted at the rear. Its ground pressure was only 20 percent of that of the ubiquitous Universal carrier, better (and incorrectly) known as the Bren Gun Carrier. Its wide tracks gave it superior mobility whether negotiating snow, mud, or swamp. Of the Ferand and Delorme vehicles built, 396 were delivered to Britain and three to Russia while Canada kept 11. Although none of them saw action during the Second World War, they were the predecessors of all military snowmobiles used in the Arctic today.

One of the most remarkable and unknown achievements in aviation during the Second World War was the ferrying of aircraft across the Atlantic. The French and British had placed orders for thousands of aircraft in the United States (in the summer of 1940 alone, British orders totalled over 26,000 aircraft to be delivered at the rate of 1,000 a month) and with the U-boats sinking ships at an alarming rate, the idea of flying them to Britain to meet the expected German invasion was a sign of the country's desperation. Also, the rows of Hudson, Liberator, and Mitchell bombers parked at the new Montreal airport at Dorval while they awaited modifications, were an embarrassment to Roosevelt and the British. The president was attacked by the isolationists who said that American generosity to Britain was being misused at the expense of the rearmament of her own armed forces.

Because of the United States isolationist lobby, neither the American, British, nor Canadian governments could get involved in the ferrying. Although transatlantic flying had barely begun, the Canadian-born press baron Lord Beaverbrook, now the British minister of aircraft production, strong-armed the Canadian Pacific Railway into organizing ATFERO (Atlantic Ferry Organization) to fly the aircraft across. Using a "foreign legion" of pilots, the first aircraft were flown from Hattie's Camp, later called Gander Airport in Newfoundland to Aldergrove, Northern Ireland, on November 10, 1940. That the seven-plane formation arrived on the other side of the Atlantic at all was through luck and the navigational skills of the navigator in the lead plane, Don Bennett (later air vice-marshal and founder of Bomber Command's Pathfinder Group). If the ferrying was to continue, a shorter, safer route, preferably over land with emergency air-fields, was required — and that involved going through the Arctic.

The passage of the Lend-Lease Act in March 1941, quadrupled the number of aircraft being flown to Britain and meant that Dorval and Gander airports were bottlenecked with the ferrying. The act did allow the British government to take over ATFERO's duties in May 1941 and set up Ferry Command. A trans-Arctic Airway between Britain and North America had been one of several dreams in the 1930s to link the continents by air and Charles Lindbergh had surveyed it in 1933 for Pan American Airways but the Arctic weather, limited aircraft endurance, and the lack of airports in Greenland and Baffin Island made it just that — a dream.

Prevented by the Americans from building airfields in Greenland and Iceland, the Canadian government looked for sites in Labrador, Fort Churchill, Southampton Island, and Frobisher Bay. In June 1941, an RCAF Stranraer flying boat took the distinguished Arctic surveyor Eric Fry, who was on loan from the Department of Mines and Resources in Dartmouth, Nova Scotia, into the Labrador area. When it landed at Northwest River, a trading post at the head of Lake Melville, Fry took a powerboat to survey the area. One evening he noticed an elevated terrace set against the sunset sky and returned to base to report it. Two days later, the whole party climbed the terrace at what was locally called Goose Bay, noticing that it was as flat as a billiards table. Later, Fry was joined by an American expedition led by Captain Elliott Roosevelt, USN, (also the president's son), and together they recommended the level plateau at Goose Bay for an airport. Away from the coast, the site enjoyed fog-free weather, but was also accessible from the ocean. On July 15, an RCAF team approved Fry's selection for the air forces of both countries to set up facilities for ferrying. A preliminary agreement was arranged with the commission of the government of Newfoundland, giving Canada permission to build the airfield at Goose Bay. A formal lease, not signed until October 10, 1944, later entitled Canada to occupy the base for 99 years. Construction began on the runways in September 1941 and proceeded rapidly.

Three thousand laborers were brought in to work, continuously bull-dozing spruce forest and building dock facilities to receive material by ship. The three temporary packed-snow runways, each more than 2,000 metres in length and able to accommodate the largest aircraft of the time, were completed in two months and the first military aircraft landed at Goose Bay on December 9, 1941.

After Pearl Harbor, the Americans built their own facilities at Goose Bay, but because U-boats posed a deadly threat in the St. Lawrence, C.D. Howe ingeniously pressed the R5727 into service, which was the "pattern" Lancaster bomber that the British had sent over to Victory Aircraft Ltd. With it, a Trans Canada Air Lines crew shuttled between Moncton, New Brunswick, and Goose Bay with supplies until May 1942. A temporary setback to the runway construction occurred when the Canada Steamship Lines *Donald Stewart*, a bulk "canaller" (so-called because it was small enough to navigate the pre–St. Lawrence Seaway lock system) was torpedoed by the German submarine *U-517* on September 3, 1942. It had been sailing for Goose Bay, laden with aviation gas and bulk cement for the expansion of runways.

In May 1942, the United States presented the PJBD with a plan for a Northeast Staging Route (NESR) through the Canadian North and Arctic to ferry single-engine fighters and complete Army Air Corps bomber squadrons to England. Called the Crimson Route, it required that the distances between the airfields be short, that the pilots be in radio contact at all times, and that the airfields should be capable of handling hundreds of aircraft passing through.

The PJBD met on June 9 to consider this — the Canadians were no doubt bemused that their American counterparts would be so ambitious given the terrain and climate of their North. Three routes were proposed: an eastern one via Fort Chimo–Baffin Island–Greenland–Iceland–Prestwick, Scotland, a central one via Kapuskasing–Richmond Gulf–Fort Chimo–Frobisher Bay–Greenland–Iceland–Prestwick, and a western one via Regina–The Pas–Fort Churchill–Southampton Island–Frobisher Bay–Greenland–Iceland–Prestwick.

The importance of the Crimson Route to the Allied war effort was relayed by the PJDB to the Canadian government in its 26th recommendation — and none too soon as the USAAF was about to ferry the entire 8th Air Force to Britain in June 1942. This time, the construction of United States bases on sovereign Canadian territory warranted no diplomatic negotiations as the Canol project had and no Exchanges of Notes that the Alaska Highway and NWSR required. Unlike the NWSR, the route was to be entirely an American responsibility. The United States built and maintained permanent airfields at Fort Churchill and Southampton Island and two "winter" emergency strips at Fort Chimo and Frobisher Bay. It also built a "feeder airstrip" called "Tweed Field" at Mingan, Quebec, which was exactly halfway between Presque Isle U.S. Army airfield, Maine, and Goose Bay. With heavy commitments at Goose Bay, the Canadian government only had the resources to build an airfield at The Pas.

With the pilot's worst enemy — the Arctic weather — some 30 meteorological stations were built by the U.S. military through the eastern Arctic. Late in September 1941, the U.S. Naval Reserve transported three small detachments to set up meteorological stations and airfields at Fort Chimo (CRYSTAL 1), Frobisher Bay (CRYSTAL 2), and Padloping Island (CRYSTAL 3). The CRYSTAL stations were manned by the U.S. military, but Canada retained the right to their use when the war ended.

When Germany invaded the USSR on June 22, 1941, concern over a Japanese attack on Alaska was heightened and the U.S. Secretary of War Henry L. Stimson (who had in 1931 had promulgated the "Stimson Doctrine" on non-recognition of territorial changes in wartime) said that a highway to Alaska had to be built immediately. But even in October 1941, King was still reluctant to invest time and money in a road, stating that he preferred to develop the NWSR.

The reports on December 8 that eight of the nine battleships of the U.S. Pacific fleet at Pearl Harbor had been sunk or were immobilized stunned King and for the first time the prime minister feared a Japanese attack on British Columbia. He also knew that all there was to protect the British Columbia coastline was the "Fisherman's Reserve" — a home guard of 17 fishing vessels and 150 officers and men drawn from the local fishing community. Possibly because Ian Alistair Mackenzie, the Member of Parliament for Vancouver Centre, had been the minister for national defence from 1935–39, the RCAF squadron based at Sea Island had managed to supplement its obsolete Blackburn torpedo bombers with modern P-40 Kittyhawk fighters.[16] But the remainder of the British Columbia coast was unprotected. Whole army divisions would now have to be diverted to the west coast and the limited war that King had hoped for was about to escalate into one that would require a national mobilization act — and conscription.

A resolution to begin construction of the Alaska Highway was once more brought to Congress on December 5, 1941, by the indefatigable Dimond. This time, the devastating attack on Pearl Harbor two days later and the subsequent Japanese expansion over the Pacific ensured that it received everyone's immediate attention. On January 16, 1942, Roosevelt called in his advisors, the secretaries of war, navy, and interior, and with General George Marshall and Admiral Ernest J. King present, asked for a decision on building the highway. Marshall was not alone in anticipating an attack on Alaska and Admiral King informed the president that with only three aircraft carriers in the Pacific, the U.S. Navy no longer had the resources to protect the Alaskan coast. Roosevelt authorized construction to begin on February 11, 1942, increasing the expenditure on March 3, doubling it from $25 million to $50 million. The American section of the PJBD then briefed their Canadian colleagues about the highway: To repay Canada for building the NWSR, the United States was willing to pay the entire cost of constructing and maintaining the highway for the duration of the war.

Even then the Canadian Chiefs of Staff Committee (like their prime minister) saw little value in the highway, as it would have no effect on the defence of the British Columbia coast. But with the United States still reeling from the shock of Pearl Harbor, King knew that Washington was in no mood to quibble and on February 12, Moffat warned him of the prevailing feeling. Bluntly put, Canada was told to swallow its sovereignty issues and acquiesce. As his own secretary of state for external affairs, King signed the Exchange of Notes with Moffat on March 18,

1942 (the same day as the first contingent of American troops arrived at Dawson Creek, British Columbia) in which the Canadian government approved the PJBD recommendation and formally accepted the offer of the United States government to undertake the building and wartime maintenance of the highway. At the insistence of the prime minister, a key clause inserted was that the United States: "Agree that at the conclusion of the war that part of the highway which lies in Canada shall become in all respects an integral part of the Canadian highway system, subject to the understanding that there shall at no time be imposed any discriminatory conditions in relation to the use of the road as between Canadian and United States civilian traffic."[17]

Now called the Alcan Highway, it would also have eight landing strips built alongside and a road from Haines, Alaska, to Champagne, Yukon, giving the U.S. Army additional facilities for distributing supplies by truck. With airfields and highways came communications. In June 1942, the Northwest Communications System began when the United States Signal Corps arranged to have line communications parallel the Alaska Highway. They ran 1,871 miles of line from Edmonton to Fairbanks using 95,000 poles and 23 repeater stations planted at 160-kilometre intervals. In mid-1945, when the Canadian Army assumed responsibility for the Canadian portion of the Alaska Highway, the RCAF did the same for the "pole" line. Within a year the RCAF turned the pole line over to the Department of Transport, which on April 1, 1947, contracted it to Canadian National Telegraph.

Choosing Route B on April 11, the U.S. Army Corps of Engineers officially started construction of the highway. The Canadian government's approach to major projects like the Trans Canada Airway was to treat them as unemployment relief schemes to get idle men doing something useful. In contrast, the U.S. military regarded the Alaska Highway as a military campaign and permafrost, swamp, mountains, rivers, and virgin forest were the enemy. Seven regiments of engineers were the shock troops to be followed by the main army of 7,500 construction workers from the United States Public Roads Commission. Cranes, bulldozers, dump trucks, and road scrapers served as the armour and artillery. Eighty-one American construction firms — to the envy of their Canadian counterparts — were the main body. Where a year before, only a few trappers and prospectors had wandered, at the height of the project a tsunami of 16,000 men and 11,000 pieces of equipment hit the North. It was a repeat of the gold rush as overnight the population of Dawson (Creek), which had numbered 3,000 residents in 1940 now overflowed to 10,000 men.

First, the U.S. Army Transportation Corps commandeered the White Pass & Yukon Railway, finding for it some narrow-gauge steam 2-8-2 locomotives from disused lines. Men and material were then transported from Skagway to the railhead of Dawson Creek from where the highway was to run through British Columbia and the Yukon. Only when it crossed the border at Snag would it be in Alaska. Its routing disappointed many Alaskans, especially those who lived on the panhandle at Juneau and Skagway and felt themselves in the greatest danger of Japanese attack. The unhappy Dimond called it, "… a mistake so great that it verges on tragedy." As commanding officer of the U.S. Army Northwest Service Command, General J.F. O'Connor had been placed in charge of all American undertakings in British Columbia, Alberta, the Yukon, and Northwest Territories. Having earlier fought his way through a bureaucratic and political jungle to build Washington, D.C.'s water-supply system, O'Connor was prepared for all critics. He defended his choice with, "The primary purpose of this road was the airfields. The secondary purpose was to have an additional route to Alaska in case of difficulties in the Pacific."

Since most U.S. Army engineer regiments had already been deployed to the Pacific or European theatres, the U.S. War Department raised construction battalions composed of black Americans to build the highway. The U.S. military was segregated at the time and the battalions were commanded by white officers who resented their assignments. Few of the black recruits had any training in engineering and most came from the southern United States and had never experienced a Canadian winter — let alone one in the Yukon. Despite all these handicaps, they managed to help push through a pioneer road in only eight months.[18]

It was a saga worthy of the country that had dug the Panama Canal 30 years before and would put a man on the moon less than 30 years later. In eight months and 12 days, at the cost of $140 million, 1,523 miles of the Alaska Highway were built through through forests, across swamps, and around mountains by U.S. Army engineers and 6,000 civilians. What pre-war should have taken five years to build was to be roughly formed in the eight months and completed in another year. Typically American, a massive publicity campaign had accompanied the truck convoys snaking their way through the wilderness and movie clips were shown through the Dominion.

On November 21, 1942, the Alaska Highway was officially opened at Soldier Summit. Mackenzie King sent a congratulatory telegram that conveyed his feelings succinctly. Canada's "… unprecedented action in granting the United States permission," he wrote, " to build the road across Dominion territory was another symbol that we are brothers in arms, waging a life-and-death struggle against a common enemy."[19] Less subtle was Ian Mackenzie, his Cabinet minister at the opening. "The soil is ours, the toil is yours," he announced. No doubt on instructions from the prime minister, he pointed out that the Alaska Highway was only part of the grand scheme. The Canadian-built NWSR was the remainder. "We have built the skyway — you the highway," Mackenzie said. The casual ingratitude of both messages must have puzzled the GI audience who were there to win the war and had no intentions of subverting Canadian sovereignty. The following year, at the request of Dimond, both countries agreed that the highway from Dawson Creek, British Columbia, to Fairbanks, Alaska, would be officially called the "Alaska Highway."

One of the most distressing difficulties facing the RCAF's detachments on the Northwest Staging Route was the problem of supply. Neither the Alaska Highway nor the Staging Route were much use without motor vehicles and aircraft, and in 1942, these were not available in the quantity required. Some degree of hardship had, of course, been anticipated, but, by December of the year just mentioned, conditions were becoming intolerable.

Taken from *Roundel* magazine, here are a few entries from the daily diaries kept by various units during this period.

> December 19th: Lockheed 7634 encountered severe
> icing conditions, and, on the south-bound trip, icing

endangered the aircraft to such an extent that only superb piloting and a great deal of good luck prevented a crash and probably fatalities. It's criminal that we should be asked to carry on northern flying without having aircraft properly equipped with de-icing and other winter equipment.... Severe temperatures being experienced in the North and still no winter clothing for personnel. Someone has bungled badly.

December 21st: Contrary to all rules and regulations, we are issuing flying-boots to all personnel, with the sincere hope that this will alleviate to some extent suffering from the cold.

December 23rd: Sqn. Ldr. Guest arrived. He reported intense cold at Whitehorse, average temperature 40 below zero. Personnel in desperate need of clothing and money. Both of these items on way, but weather delaying. Living conditions at Whitehorse deplorable. Our personnel are living in our barracks without plumbing or adequate heat, and to get their meals they must walk 1 1/2 miles to the Contractor's. Only one panel wagon available.

Sent to the Staging Route in early 1943 as the RCAF Air-Rail Transportation officer, Squadron Leader R.M. Maze and Sergeant D. Whyte would set out to drive the completed Highway. On the 17-day journey they counted 22 flat tires and had to buy or scrounge a half dozen new ones. "Almost all the bridges were of wood, hurriedly assembled and single lane," said Maze. "Just north of Watson Lake, we shot down the mountainside towards one of them. As we drove on to it, our lights probing through the night fog we suddenly spotted an Army truck speeding at us in the opposite direction. I don't know how we made it but we did. Both sides of our car were scraped, the left by the truck and the right by the bridge."

When he returned to Edmonton, Maze set to work organizing a Freight Transit Unit for the RCAF posts on the NSWR. By the autumn of 1943, a fleet of trucks was operating from the newly built refrigerated warehouse at Dawson Creek, carrying supplies to all RCAF detachments on the route. "In 1944, several people in positions of authority complained that an Air Force debased itself by moving freight on the ground," remembered Maze. "To quiet these charges, someone figured out that an airman's daily food supply, packed for shipment weighed roughly six pounds. To have flown this package from Edmonton to Whitehorse would have cost $2.40 per man per day. But by truck the cost of shipping the same package was thirty seven cents."

A convoy of RCAF trucks took seven to nine days to make the round trip from Dawson Creek to Whitehorse — except when they carried perishables. Then it was a nonstop trip of thirty-six to forty hours. This was done by flying relief drivers to Fort Nelson and Watson Lake. The total poundage carried in 1944 to the RCAF posts was five million pounds. "The winter months meant that the drivers were unable to gear down on the mountain sides lest they skid over the cliffs," the squadron leader said, "and anyway they needed as much speed as possible to get up the ice-covered hill that inevitably awaited them as soon as they had successfully reached the bottom of the previous one." In the summer, the rain made the road as slippery as ice and spring brought flash floods from the melting snow on the top of the mountains.

"It was quite possible to be driving comfortably along the Highway one moment, and the next to see deluge of icy water come rushing around a bend to wash away the road, one's car and oneself," Maze said. "But the drivers always had one thing to look forward to, however. They used to stop for a swim at the hot springs near Smith River, even when the temperature was thirty-five below and the trees and the swimmers hair thick with hoar frost."

The booming wartime economy and free-spending GIs and American civilian engineers that the Highway and Canol (short for Canadian Oil) projects brought to British Columbia, the Northwest Territories, and the Yukon meant that the locals, who had clamored in vain for decades to get Ottawa's attention, enjoyed it all. In a pattern repeated in other Northern communities, Whitehorse was transformed by the Americans from a frontier town to a modern city. Its four-man volunteer fire department was deemed insufficient for the new camps and squatters' homes that had sprung up so, without consultation with the territorial government, the U.S. Army enforced a fire code on all buildings, public and private. Seeing the town's garbage and untreated sewage being dumped in the river, the Americans built a treatment plant to prevent an outbreak of typhoid. And at the United States government's expense, a sewer system was laid through the town.

But no one had asked the Aboriginals their opinion of the highway, the airfields, or the pipeline — their sovereignty in a wartime emergency was not considered an issue. No one cared that the construction camps brought measles, venereal disease, alcoholism, and sometimes week-long forest fires to the reservations. The Natives could only watch and wonder as the trucks carrying what they called "black white men" ground by.

The construction and maintenance of the highway and NWSR airstrips required vast amounts of gasoline and oil that would in peacetime have been shipped by tanker from California. But with the shipping lanes no longer secure, the United States government looked for a secure oil supply in the Canadian North. Canol was funded by the military and built by the construction consortium, Bechtel-Price-Callahan. Its requirement and subsequent negotiations to build it were never brought before the PJBD, but were dealt with instead by the diplomats of both countries. The United States bought a complete working oil refinery in Texas, dismantled it for shipment by sea to Skagway, and then sent it by rail to Whitehorse where it was reassembled. The closest source of oil was Norman Wells on the Mackenzie River. Its ancient name was *Le Gohlini* (meaning "where the oil is") given by Natives and while exploring the region in 1789, Alexander Mackenzie had remarked on oil seepages along the river banks. In 1918, Imperial Oil established a claim at Norman Wells for the "black gold" and began drilling. The oil fields were now joined by a four-inch pipeline to the Whitehorse refinery. But to do this required 600 miles of all-weather road, telephone lines, six airstrips, and 10 pumping stations. Oil was also pumped through auxiliary lines between Whitehorse and Fairbanks, and from Carcross to Watson Lake. A line was also built between Whitehorse and Skagway to bring oil from the south when the Japanese scare had died down. In all, 200,000 tons of materials were used and over 10,000 people were employed on the Canol project. It must have come as no surprise that from an estimated cost of $30 million, the final price was over $134 million.

Considering that there were 10,000 civilian workers involved, barges moved, and docking facilities built, the Canadian government seems to have had little idea of what taking place, especially with regard to Canol. It would not be until May 5, 1943, that the Cabinet War Committee appointed Brigadier W.W. Foster the special commissioner for defence projects — but only for the Northwest. It took the British high commissioner to Canada, Malcolm J. McDonald, who toured the region to inform Ottawa of the project. Giving evidence before the Cabinet War Committee, he warned that the escalation of the Canol and highway put both beyond the scope of local government representatives and that he suspected that the United States was carrying them out with a view of the postwar situation.[20] A local Hudson Bay representative also wrote to Vincent Massey, then the Canadian high commissioner in London, about Ottawa's ignorance of what was taking place. With sovereignty worries niggling at him, King twice brought up the matter of Canol at War Cabinet Committee meetings, dictating in his diary on February 17, 1944, "I attended the Cabinet War Committee at 11. Almost two hours were spent discussing the Canol project. I held strongly with one or two others that we ought to get the Americans out of further developments there and keep complete control in our hands." But by that time, the whole Canol project was winding down.

> When a quart of milk cost $1.50 in 1944 — so you can imagine what a quart of whisky cost — a few of the RCAF and USAAF boys decided to go into business. They built three 75-gallon stills in the hills surrounding Whitehorse. They got away with it for many months, too, bringing their moonshine down to the thirsty thousands through a system of metal pipes rather like miniature Canol Pipe-lines.
>
> — *Roundel* magazine contributor

The Japanese victories early in the war — especially Pearl Harbor, the sinking of the British battleships HMS *Repulse* and *Prince of Wales* and later the surrender of the supposedly impregnable base at Singapore — all so panicked the United States that it was sure an attack on the Aleutian Islands and Alaska was imminent. The state's protection rested on the Alaskan Air Force with its six old medium bombers and a dozen obsolete fighter aircraft. But even if more aircraft had been available, there were few airfields for them. On December 10, 1941, when General John L. DeWitt the head of U.S. Western Defense Command, asked for more aircraft to defend Alaska, all that the USAAF chief H.H. Arnold could spare were assembled at Spokane, Washington — the 11th Pursuit Squadron with 25 P-40s and the 77th Bombardment Group with 13 B-25s. Installing winter maintenance equipment on them meant that the aircraft didn't leave Spokane until January 2, 1942. By the time they negotiated the rough NWSR airfields and groped their way to Alaska, six of the P-40s had crashed, six were lost, and the B-25s fared little better. To reinforce Alaska, the U.S. military also had 11 American airlines airlift troops through Canada to Fairbanks. If this wasn't enough, that spring, the United States decided to ferry aircraft to its Russian ally over the route. With such heavy traffic, the Americans wanted all airway deficiencies corrected and under their control — and immediately.

The original airway had been planned for the use of YSAT and Pan American Airways and the possibility that it might also be used to reinforce Alaska was nebulous. For Canada, ceding wartime sovereignty to the United States for the ultimate defeat of the Axis was commendable — but troubling. Allowing a foreign military (however benign) to construct and operate airfields, radio, and military installations for what had nothing to do with civil aviation was setting uncomfortable precedents. In Ottawa, politicians, bureaucrats, and the military watched the construction of the staging route airfields in the eastern and western Canadian North with growing unease. As the director of air services in Canada, J.A. Wilson was aware that airways were no longer in the mandate of the Department of Transport. On March 11, 1942, the RCAF, the Department of Transport, and the USAAF met in Ottawa to work out a compromise. The Department of Transport would install intermediate radio ranges on the airway between Fort St. John and Fort Nelson and between Watson Lake and Whitehorse and construct emergency air-fields in between each town. The USAAF would install ground-to-air radio equipment at each of the main fields along the airway and when the Canadians built the support facilities such as barracks, hangars, and mess halls, the Americans would maintain them.

Many of the USAAF aircraft ferried through the NWSR lie today on the bottom of lake beds in the North. Engine trouble, inexperienced pilots, getting lost, or running out of fuel on the route in the winter meant putting down on a frozen lake surface and so many pilots did this that the region around Watson Lake became known as "Million Dollar Valley." On one occasion, a USAAF DC-3 force-landed on a deserted bridge several miles from Watson Lake, killing the pilot and co-pilot. Two passengers survived in the fuselage for 11 days, even keeping a fire going while they heard aircraft overhead searching for them. On the eleventh day, the pair gave up hope of rescue and each with a broken leg crawled out into the bush — hoping they were heading towards Watson. For eight days they crawled through waist-deep snow dragging a small toboggan with food and water before an RCMP constable followed their tracks in the snow and found them barely alive.[21]

As to who would pay for the improvements to the Staging Route — a second compromise was reached. While the Department of Transport was waiting for a political decision on the financial arrangements, the Department of National Defence paid for the Canadian share. Aware of Japanese intentions on the Aleutians, the United States government was desperate to bring in U.S. Army engineer units immediately. But, fearing postwar repercussions that would not be in the sovereign interest of Canada, Ottawa was reluctant to agree. Colonel Biggar brought this to the Cabinet War Committee's attention and on April 22, it was decided that if the United States would pay for additional work that was beyond Canadian requirements, Canada would retain full title and control of the NWSR during and after the war.

The Department of Transport kept control of the operation of the NWSR until September 1942, when as the route was being used for military purposes, it was handed over to the Royal Canadian Air Force. Six

RCAF officers were sent to each of the airfields en route to begin the military's takeover. Their instructions convey the sensitivities of the time. They were to act as "ambassadors" of the Canadian government, which, considering they were in their own country is an interesting choice of word. But the intent was clear. At some future date, the RCAF would take over from the Department of Transport and the USAAF. While the transfer of assets with the former could be settled in Ottawa, issues with the latter were especially contentious. When the U.S. military attempted to take control of air traffic at Whitehorse, it was firmly rebuffed. With so much traffic going through, the Americans continuously attempted to expand their facilities — when the USAAF began to build an unauthorized air traffic control tower at Watson Lake as the first of many along the airway, the RCAF officers saw it as "... an effort to move towards the establishment of USAAF control organisation along the Route by a procession of limited objectives."[22] The Americans were instructed to stop unauthorized construction.

Although control of the Staging Route was to be handed over to the RCAF in September 1942, the first commanding officers of the various units arrived in July. Flying Officer S.G. French wrote of the arriving officers:

> They were chosen with two qualities in mind. The first was diplomacy: they had to be capable of ensuring friendly co-operation with the American forces (including the Engineer Corps engaged in construction of the Highway) ... Some bureaucrat in Ottawa must have run his pencil down a list of R.C.A.F. pilots until he found six former bush-pilots. Wing Commander C.M.G. (Con) Farrell went to Edmonton, and Squadron Leaders J. F. Bythell to Grande Prairie, E. S. Holmes to Fort St. John, A. C. Heaven to Fort Nelson, G. W. du Temple to Watson Lake, and J. Hone to Whitehorse. In addition, Flight Lieutenant D. M. Shields, an experienced airways traffic control officer, was sent to Edmonton to direct the establishment of a general control over the Route.[23]

Squadron Leader du Temple and his airmen scrounged some wood and built a flat-bottomed boat. Then they went to a U.S. Army maintenance camp on the Alaska Highway and talked them into "donating" a washing-machine engine to propel it. In those early days, the men at the Staging Route units were often forced to eat their emergency rations for want of supplies. The fish they caught from their boat were sometimes actually necessary for survival.

— *Roundel* magazine

In spring 1942, the RCAF's few Bolingbroke and Kittyhawk aircraft were the only effective defence of the British Columbia coast. Although a new weapon had appeared immediately after Pearl Harbor when, with Canadian permission, the U.S. War Department installed radar equipment on Vancouver Island, without aircraft to maintain continuous patrols, the province relied on the volunteer Air Detection Corps for early warning.[24] It wasn't only that there weren't any RCAF aircraft that could patrol as far north as Prince Rupert — there were no airfields on the Queen Charlotte Islands or Porcher, Pitt, and Banks islands on which to base them.

And if Canada was badly off, the Americans were in worse straits. Concerned about defence of the panhandle, the United States government had built an airfield at Annette Island, 60 miles northwest of Prince Rupert on the southern end of the panhandle although (as impossible as it is to believe today) they had no available aircraft for it. The Canadian Section of the PJBD was informed on April 27, that the U.S. War Department wanted the RCAF to ensure that it could transfer aircraft promptly from its home defence to Alaska. Local RCAF officers were given the responsibility to designate "if practicable, specific units in connection with plans for the redistribution of air strength." Obligingly, L.F. Stevenson, the RCAF air officer commanding Western Air Command, agreed to move 115 (F) Squadron's Bolingbrokes from Vancouver to Annette Island by May 5, 1942. Although they would still be under operational control from Prince Rupert, this was the first Canadian force to be based on American soil.

Even as the Alaskan reinforcement crisis abated, on May 24, the Imperial Japanese Navy sent a large task force of six aircraft carriers, seven battleships, and 57 destroyers towards Midway Island. A week later, to draw American strength away from the South Pacific (and also block U.S.-Soviet co-operation in Alaska) two small aircraft carriers, five old cruisers, and 1,600 troops left Japan for the Aleutian Islands. They were to occupy the islands of Kiska, Attu, and Adak and attack the American base at Dutch Harbor. Having broken the Japanese naval code, the U.S. Navy was aware of both approaching fleets and Admiral King sent most of his ships to meet the major one at Midway. But there were no aircraft carriers to provide air cover for the Aleutians. General DeWitt contacted the Canadian Pacific Command on May 29, and asked for two RCAF home defence squadrons (one fighter, one bomber) to be sent immediately to isolated Yakutat where they could guard the approaches to Anchorage.

Led by Power, the RCAF chiefs advised the Cabinet War Committee to refuse, saying that given the Japanese threat, the defence of British Columbia could not be weakened. DeWitt reminded Ottawa that under the terms of the Canadian-American Joint Defense Plan, the signatories had pledged to defend the North American continent — and that included Alaska and the Aleutian Islands. King always held that the defence of Alaska was an American responsibility, but he had been a politician long enough to realize that by sending even a token force to defend the state, the growing American presence in northwest Canada would be counterbalanced — and it would also serve to reassure the government of British Columbia, which was by then approaching near hysteria and considering mass evacuation of all residents of Vancouver Island.[25]

In June, Bolingbrokes and P-40 Kittyhawks from RCAF home defence squadrons as far away as Rockcliffe, Ontario, and Dartmouth, Nova Scotia, were rushed to Alaska. When No. 8 squadron's Bolingbrokes departed Sea Island, Vancouver, for Yakutat, there were no air navigation maps available past Prince Rupert and the pilots relied on old British Admiralty charts to get to Juneau. The Bolingbrokes were sent on to Anchorage, and to replace them, RCAF Beauforts took up station at Annette Island. The RCAF's foremost Battle of Britain air ace Wing

An 8 (BR) Squadron Bolingbroke and work tent at Nome, Alaska, in 1942.
This was the northern-most station used by an operational RCAF squadron
during the Second World War.

Commander Gordon R. McGregor arrived on June 4 to command 111 Squadron at Anchorage. Used to speaking his mind, McGregor voiced the opinion that if the RCAF was to meet the Japanese it had to move closer to the action.

The Japanese attacked and occupied Attu and Kiska islands on June 7 and before their carriers left, bombed the American base at Dutch Harbor. For good measure on June 20, the Japanese submarine I-26 surfaced two miles off Estevan Point on Vancouver Island and shelled its lighthouse. Not since the War of 1812 had Canada had come under enemy fire. TWO JAPANESE SUBS OFF COAST! screamed the headlines of the next day's *Victoria Daily Times*. In the aftermath of the shelling, a home guard the Pacific Coast Militia Rangers were formed to provide coastal surveillance and immediate local defence, pending the deployment of Regular Force troops. Prince Rupert suddenly received coastal defenses and (for the first time since the American Civil War) an armoured train was used on the North American continent. Pulled by a powerful 10-wheeler steam locomotive, it was manned by the army, but its movements were controlled by the Canadian National Railway (CNR). Because in peacetime this area had been a favourite haunt of Japanese fishing boats, the train patrolled the CNR line along the Skeena River between Prince Rupert and Terrace. Its movements were so secret that it killed three locals — one who was "sleeping it off" on the track and two workmen who using jackhammers did not hear (or expect) its approach.[26] After the reoccupation of Kiska, Canada's only armoured train was put into storage in October 1943 and — with no thought of history — dismantled.

On July 4, Power; Air Marshal L.S. Breadner the RCAF chief of Air Power; and Stevenson toured the defences at Anchorage to assess the situation and gave McGregor permission to move 111 Squadron to the forward Aleutian base of Umnak. The RCAF was ill-equipped to fly in Alaska — there were no maps, no radio coverage, and the P-40s didn't have the range to cover the long distances over the icy Arctic waters. Their radios were so unreliable that McGregor thought hand signals were safer. Although they had longer endurance, the RCAF's British-built Bolingbrokes and Beauforts were too far from their spare part source to be of any use at all.

Before they left, 111 Squadron's Kittyhawks were fitted with long-range fuel tanks and, at McGregor's insistence, dinghies in case their pilots had to ditch. On July 13, he and six pilots took off from Anchorage for Umnak, landing at Naknek and Cold Bay airfields to refuel. Shortly after passing Dutch Harbor on July 16, the seven fighters ran into fog and, leading the formation, McGregor ordered them to turn back. As they did so, they lost radio contact with him. Five of the pilots crashed into a cliff at Unalaska Island with one getting through. After trying vainly for half an hour to find the others, McGregor returned to Cold Bay to organize a search.

No more RCAF P-40s were flown over and the RCAF pilots at Umnak Island used USAAF P-40s instead. By September 14, the combined USAAF-RCAF force had moved to Adak to attack the Japanese on what was thought to be heavily fortified Kiska. RCAF Squadron Leader Ken Boomer would shoot down a Zero seaplane on the 25 — the only air victory in the war by a member of a home defence squadron.[27] Promoted to group captain, Wing Commander McGregor was transferred back to England in 1943 to command the fighter air cover for the planned D-Day landings. Destined to be the first (and the best) president of Air Canada, he continued to inspire loyalty from all who served with him.

In a little-known campaign, in September 1943, the U.S. military prepared to assault Attu and Kiska. The RCN ships, HMCS *Prince David* and *Prince Robert*, performed convoy escort duty for the attack force against Attu, which was regained in May. The Canadian "Flower" corvette HMCS *Dawson* escorted a troop convoy for the assault on Kiska in July. Planned by George Pearkes VC, the general officer commanding Pacific forces, the Canadian Army contribution to the assault was called GREENLIGHT FORCE and consisted of the 13th Canadian Infantry Brigade made up of the Winnipeg Grenadiers, the Rocky Mountain Rangers, the Canadian Fusiliers, the Twenty-Fourth Field Regiment (Royal Canadian Artillery), the Twenty-Fourth Field Company (Royal Canadian Engineers), and a machine-gun company from the Saint John Fusiliers. At dawn on August 15, 1943, the first to land on the beaches at Kiska was an elite American-Canadian Special Service Force. A Hollywood scriptwriter's dream — many of the men had just been released from military stockades — they would earn their nickname "Devil's Brigade" during the Italian campaign the following year.

Disappointingly, there was no one to shoot at. The whole Japanese garrison had stealthily evacuated Kiska on July 28 — by submarine. It was a Japanese victory of sorts as their 14-month occupation had successfully tied up American and Canadian resources that could have been used elsewhere. Rear-Admiral Thomas Kinkaid, the commander of North Pacific force, had known that the island was deserted, but allowed the amphibious assault to continue as a "dress rehearsal." To complement the earlier acronym SNAFU, *Time* magazine would create a special one for the Battle of Kiska — JANFU (Joint Army-Navy F**ked Up). Casualties were 28 Americans and four Canadians killed, with 50 soldiers wounded. Accidents, confusion, and "friendly fire'" were blamed. Living in tents, GREENLIGHT FORCE remained on Kiska for garrison duty for three months, returning home in November 1943.

In this war, the isolation of the Canadian North did not save it from invasion — and when the enemy did come, he landed appropriately in Labrador, the site of some of the earliest claims of European sovereignty in North America.[28] German submarines would drop off spies on Canadian soil in 1942 — *U-231* on May 14, and *U-518* on November 9, but both agents were caught almost as soon as they put ashore. Not the case with "Kurt," who remained at large until the 1980s.

Meteorologists had long known that the weather in northwestern Europe was affected by weather systems in the North Atlantic, and during the war both the Luftwaffe and Kriegsmarine set up their own weather stations in the Arctic, some manned, and others that transmitted automatically. Between 1940 and 1945, the German Navy embarked on a series of expeditions to the Arctic to obtain regular synoptic weather reports as the international exchange of which had ended with the outbreak of war in 1939. The German naval meteorological service (*Wetterdienst des Oberkommandos der Kriegsmarine*) sent out some 13 parties to Svalbard, East Greenland, and Franz Josef Land. On September 18, 1943, the German submarine *U-537* left Kiel to set up an automatic weather station on the coast of Labrador. On board was a civilian, Dr. Kurt Sommermeyer with "Wetter-Funkgerat (WFL) number 21," the sixth of 21 automatic weather stations built by Siemens, some of which were already in operation in Greenland. Three weeks later, on October 22, *U-537* arrived at Martin Bay, Cape Chidley, at the very northern tip of Labrador. Where in 1587, the British explorer John Davis had landed and named the cape after his friend John Chidley, the U-boat crew (no doubt anxiously searching the sky) took 48 hours get the canisters of equipment loaded onto dinghies to row ashore. The weather-measuring instruments along with the transmitter and 10 nickel-cadmium and dry-cell high-voltage batteries were set up 400 yards inland on a 170-foot-high hill. Every three hours, the station, named "Kurt," transmitted coded weather observations on HFB (High Frequency Band) between 3,000 and 12,000 kilohertz. It probably continued to do so long after the war ended and there was no one in the Kriegsmarine left to listen. The *U-537* arrived at the submarine base in Lorient, France, on December 8 and Dr. Sommermeyer left. The U-boat's next patrol took it to the coast of Indonesia where, in February 1944, it was sunk by the American submarine *Flounder* with all hands lost. Known only to the locals, the Nazi Labrador weather station would have been forgotten had Sommermeyer's son not found the *U-537*'s logbook in the Kriegsmarine archives in the 1980s. When the revelation of Canada's only Northern invasion during the Second World War was made public, the Canadian Coast Guard recovered what was left of "Kurt" and the canisters, mast, and batteries are on display at the Canadian War Museum in Ottawa.

The Imperial Japanese Navy was decisively defeated at Midway in June 1942, and that blunted Japanese ambitions with regard to Alaska — if it ever had any to begin with. From that month on, with coastal shipping made safe, both the Alaska Highway and the Canol project were of little use. With an annual capacity of 600,000 tons, the highway carried a moderate total of 134,000 tons and 42,000 passengers in 1943, to Alaska Defence Command. That was its brief moment of glory.

The Canol project was completed in February 1944, and the Whitehorse refinery came on line in April. Both were shut down less than a year later. Controversial from its inception, the creation of the pipeline could only be explained by the near hysteria that gripped the

Library and Archives Canada/PA- 101813.

American troops unloading pipe. Canol Project, Fort Smith, Northwest Territories.

west coast after Pearl Harbor. Unlike the airfields and highway, it had no postwar value, either — what it cost to produce a barrel of oil from Canol was more than four times higher than the world price. It was cheaper to ship oil by tanker to Anchorage or to the Alaska Highway from Skagway. Robert P. Patterson, United States under secretary of war, summed up the Canol Project saying, "I suppose that we must bow to the verdict, that the project was useless and a waste of public funds." The Canol pipeline was the only U.S.-built project that Canada made no effort to take over. Imperial Oil purchased the Whitehorse refinery at a bargain price to dismantle and transport to the recent discovery of oil at Leduc, Alberta. What was left of the pipeline was sold for scrap in 1947 and the road and airstrips fell into decay.

> Pat Ivy flew with the RCAF on the Staging Route throughout the early war years and was later killed in Europe. When Aishihik was under construction, Pat flew in one day and pancaked his Dakota after taking the undercarriage off on the top of a bulldozer. His entire load consisted of nails. "You can find nails on the runway to this day," the locals say, "— often when you least want to."
>
> — *Roundel* magazine

If the Alaska Highway and the Canol pipeline were obsolete even before they were completed, the NWSR really did fulfill its destiny. It not only opened up the Canadian North to regional aviation, but allowed the USAAF to deploy aircraft to Alaska promptly and safely. Better than that, it enabled the Soviet Union to defeat the Germans on the Eastern Front with American aircraft sent via the NWSR to Siberia. Recalling the farce in December 1941 when General DeWitt had asked for aircraft, between 1942 and 1945, with a few mishaps, 8,646 aircraft flew through the airfields successfully. But only 716 of those were destined for the defence of Alaska. Beginning September 29, 1942, the remaining 7,930 were handed over the Red Air Force. Besides C-47s and A-20s, many were single-engine fighters like P-39 Bell Airacobras and P-47 Thunderbolts that could never have reached Fairbanks without the airway. All in all, it wasn't a bad investment that had begun with bush pilot Grant McConachie's vision.

Unlike the NWSR, the Crimson Route did not live up to its purpose — at least in this war. Few aircraft were ferried to Prestwick through the most northerly bases — in all of 1944, Fort Chimo had seven landings — and all were ice patrol aircraft. The 323 air movements at Frobisher Bay were for transportation of construction personnel and supplies. The United States wanted to abandon the Crimson Route by 1944, but with Germany about to be defeated, the Canadian government thought the airfields should be maintained to re-deploy troops from Europe to the Pacific. By the time the war ended in Europe, neither country had agreed on the route's outcome.

On June 1, 1944, with headquarters in Edmonton, the RCAF Northwest Air Command was formed to take over complete operations of the route. The Yukon section of the Northwest Air Command was RCAF Station Whitehorse, with detachments at Teslin, Aishihik, and Snag. Air Vice-Marshal H.D. Lawrence told a group of officers who were to staff the new Command that they were "going to 'Canadianize' the Route." In August 1945 the Department of Transport took over the airfields at The Pas and Churchill with Southampton Island transferred in September. Mingan airfield was given over to the Department in 1949, but the United States maintained Frobisher Bay and Fort Chimo until 1950.

> Ottawa, August 21, 2009 — The Honourable Jim Prentice, Canada's Environment Minister and Minister responsible for Parks Canada confirmed that the plane discovered by Parks Canada underwater archaeologists off the coast of the village of Longue-Pointe-de-Mingan in Quebec is the wreckage of a U.S. Army Air Force plane lost in 1942. No human remains were seen during

U.S. Army Signal Corps/Library and Archives Canada/PA-130459.

Bridge across the Teslin River at Mile 837 of the Alaska Highway.

the operation this week, which was conducted principally on the exterior of the sunken aircraft.

Three dives with a remotely operated vehicle and four dives by Parks Canada's underwater archaeologists allowed them to confirm that the plane wreckage is the U.S. Army Air Force PBY 5A airplane, also known as a Catalina, which went down in November 1942 after two failed take-off attempts. The plane is in good condition and the fuselage is in one piece. The findings have been shared with U.S. officials. "Parks Canada will wait for their assessment of the information and their decision on the subsequent steps before returning to the site," Minister Prentice said.

The aircraft had been requested in early 1942 to support the establishment of a chain of airfields in Northern Canada, Greenland and Iceland, through which aircraft and supplies would flow to the United Kingdom from the eastern United States. This aircraft was used to ferry men and equipment to the airfield at Longue-Pointe-de-Mingan, Quebec, where surveying and ground clearing had recently commenced.

There were nine people on board when the aircraft foundered. Four of the crew escaped the flooding plane and were rescued by local fishermen rowing out from shore in open boats in rough seas. The five others are presumed to have perished, trapped in the aircraft by the swift flooding of the fuselage.

On August 6, Minister Paradis announced that a plane believed to be the U.S. plane had been recently discovered by Parks Canada underwater archaeologists while conducting work in an area adjacent to the Mingan Archipelago National Park Reserve of Canada, using side-scan sonar.

"The identification of the plane wreck off the coast of Mingan will now bring closure to the many people who have been so personally touched by this event that happened 67 years ago," said the Honourable Christian Paradis, Regional Minister for Quebec. "This is particularly true for the families of the deceased and the village of Longue-Pointe-de-Mingan which helped rescue the four survivors."

Parks Canada is dedicated to managing this discovery with the respect and dignity owed to the lost American soldiers. Parks Canada will be collaborating with the U.S. Government to continue the process in order to confirm the presence of remains of missing crewmembers and to explore the possibility of recovering these remains.

As to the RCN, which had begun the war with six destroyers and four minesweepers — in six years it had grown to 939 ships, including two escort aircraft carriers. But it was still a two-ocean navy — and likely to remain so. Rear Admiral Leonard Murray, the only Canadian to command an Allied theatre of operations, had his hands full with convoy escort and staying out of controversy. Unfairly blamed in 1941 for allowing the Free French Navy to take over the Vichy islands of St. Pierre and Miquelon (as he would later be made a scapegoat over the Halifax riots), Murray was not going to detach ships from the convoys for the Arctic where there was no threat. Except for the Murmansk runs, through the war, for the RCN, the Arctic Ocean did not exist.

By the last months of the war with the Allies in the suburbs of Berlin and about to land on the Japanese homeland, the Canadian North/Arctic was already being forgotten, the installations planned in the desperate days gradually abandoned. In both Ottawa and Washington, the urgency of construction from 1941 to 1942 had given way to introspection about the postwar world — and where those airfields, pipelines, and roads would fit in. The war had turned air navigation of the Atlantic into air transportation and flag carriers (state-owned airlines) were now what naval fleets had once been — i.e., extensions of a country's power overseas. The Chicago Conference of 1944 formulated civil aviation in the postwar world and made Canadian airspace and the transatlantic airfields — especially Newfoundland's Gander and Goose Bay, invaluable. Countries that had recently fought to protect each other's territorial sovereignty, now erected walls of cabotage around themselves. Mackenzie King promised the delegates at the conference that Canada was going to use her geographic position to full advantage. As in 1919, no thought was given to future wars or in this case the military possibilities of the airways — the Soviet Union was still a trusted ally.

With technological improvements in aircraft, radio, and landing facilities, the Second World War allowed the Canadian military to know the North better. The staging routes had demonstrated that existing maps of northern Canada were inaccurate and in the summer of 1944, an RCAF Canso and four Norseman floatplanes carried out an aerial survey of the Ungava Peninsula, Baffin Island, and the west coast of Hudson Bay, in order to establish ground controls for aerial mapping. Aerial surveying of the North was tasked to the RCAF and became one of its major roles in the following years, with all photographic activity centralized at Rockcliffe until it was completed in 1957.

Nor was the RCAF alone in its appreciation of the Arctic. In late 1944–45, EXERCISE ESKIMO, the first major winter exercise was held — not in the Arctic, but in Saskatchewan. Its purpose was to test existing methods of winter warfare by the USAF and the Canadian Army. Montreal Lake was selected as a target area for dropping supplies by B-17 "Flying Fortresses" and the then secret B-29. Not since the Yukon Field Force would the Canadian Army return to the North in such numbers.

The British request for Canadian assistance to invade Norway had led to introspection among those in the Canadian Army of a scientific bent who wanted to research operating in an Arctic environment. The Canadian Army Operational Research Group, predecessor to the Defence Research Board, was set up in Ottawa to assess the use of the military in the Arctic. Chief among the soldier-scientists were Major John Baird, a pre-war Arctic explorer and Colonel John Wilson. A graduate of the University of Toronto and a postgraduate of Princeton and Cambridge universities, Wilson had been awarded the Governor General's Medal, Prince of Wales Prize, the Coleman Gold Medal, and Massey Fellowship. During the war he had served as technical liaison officer with the Canadian Army overseas and subsequently as director of operational research in Ottawa. The eminent soldier and scientist was soon to be made head of the recently organized Institute of Geophysics at the University of Toronto.

The North and in particular the high Arctic had always been left to the RCMP, the Department of the Interior, and the Hudson's Bay Company. Except for the Yukon Field Force, the Canadian Army knew nothing of the northern frontier that they might soon be required to defend. The purpose of sending soldiers through the muskegs of northern Saskatchewan in -48 °F temperature was to assess their operational capability and arctic survival techniques — possibly for eventual deployment to Norway, which was still under German rule. It wasn't only the testing of winter clothing, accommodation, diet, and equipment, but for the first time in the Canadian military, the difficulties of cross-country vehicular movement over Arctic terrain were to be closely studied. Stripped of the armour and fitted with aluminum cabins, the 11 Ferand and Delorme snowmobiles were used by signals, infantry, provost (military police), and able to act as tractors to pull up to two sleds or artillery pieces.

Observers from the British and U.S. armies accompanied ESKIMO, which was followed by two other exercises — POLAR BEAR and LEMMING. The last tested six vehicles besides the Delorme snowmobiles. Also used were the American Weasel (M-29), and the U.S. Army's Halftrack (M-7). Pulling their own petrol and supplies, the LEMMING expedition left Churchill on March 22, 1945, making Padlie, Northwest Territories in 10 days, a distance of 653 miles. That they were able to accomplish this made Wilson and Baird consider more ambitious operations that would culminate in OPERATION MUSK OX after the war.

Through the 1930s and 1940s, the dominant personalities in Canada-U.S. relations were obviously President Roosevelt and Mackenzie King. Harvard alumni and co-conspirators in war and peace, and jokes at Winston Churchill's expense, both were very aware of their country's fears — and limitations. Canadians felt pride in Roosevelt writing that if the United States considered itself the Arsenal of Democracy, Canada was the Aerodrome of Democracy. One man led a nation of 11 million people and another 130 million, yet their relationship was so informal that when FDR and King met on April 20, 1941, to alleviate Canada's trade deficit after the Lend Lease Act, the Declaration was signed: "Done by Mackenzie and FDR on a lovely sunny day at Hyde Park."

On the other hand, Mackenzie King was not informed about the meeting between Roosevelt and Winston Churchill that began on August 9, 1941, and took place on Canada's front doorstep, on a pair of battleships in Argentia Harbour, Newfoundland. The Atlantic Charter meeting that would germinate into a new world order did not require him to be present. When asked why King was not invited, FDR would say, "I really couldn't take him."

For ordinary Canadians, sovereignty regarding the North, a land that outside Robert Service's poems they knew nothing of was of little importance in the worldwide struggle of liberty against tyranny. More than likely, if they thought about it at all, given the opportunities that

American soldiers unloading trucks and equipment for construction of the Alaska Highway, Dawson Creek, British Columbia, 1942.

the postwar world was about to afford them, they had no qualms with what the Americans had done in the North. Taken on junkets to see the highway, provincial politicians waxed lyrically about the peacetime benefits it would bring. The Canadian public accepted that once victory was achieved, the Alaska Highway would open up the North to settlement, farming, and mining.

The prime minister understood that Canada, as the junior partner in such an alliance, would experience difficulties with regard to its sovereignty in decision-making and control of its territory — and it is characteristic of the man that he found the money in a wartime economy to pay for all United States projects on Canadian territory. There would be no legal loopholes outstanding after the war that would allow future American governments to claim property or any privileges in the North. The Canadian government paid out the following sums for improvements in the North:[29]

The Northwest Staging Route	$31,311,196.
Airstrips along the Alaska Highway	$3,262,687.
Airstrips along the Mackenzie River	$1,264,150.

CRIMSON ROUTE along Hudson Bay	$27,460,330.
Mingan Airport, Quebec	$3,627,980.
Goose Bay Airport	$543,000.
Telephone line from Edmonton to the Alaska boundary	$9,432,208

The grand total paid by Canada to the Americans for the airstrips was $111 million. In the years to come, the United States gratuitously gave aid to many countries — especially with the Marshall Plan — but as the aviation historian J.R.K. Main would write in *Voyageurs of The Air*, for Canada, King ensured that there were no misunderstandings on this score. Sovereignty, as he understood it, came at a price.

5

Dew Line and Diefenbaker

Centuries from now, archeologists will attempt to understand their purpose. The structures rise abruptly from the icy wilderness, a remnant of buildings in an *H* layout beside metal stilts, some topped with giant white domes. As with the Great Wall of China, they look like defensive relics from another time, which is what they are.

The sum total of the greatest construction project of the 20th century, they were all but forgotten by the beginning of the next. When this electronic wall was built through the Canadian North, the continent feared the evils of Stalinism from across the North Pole, not terrorism from the Middle East. The ancestor of the present North Warning System, the three electronic "walls" (Distant Early Warning [DEW], McGill Fence, and Pine Tree), that pinpricked the North were built to safeguard American and Canadian airspace. Transformed from *terra incognita* to nuclear battlefield almost overnight, from sideshow to centre stage, the Canadian Arctic finally entered into the consciousness of those who lived below the 60th parallel — if only as a setting for the Dr. Strangelove scenario of that era.

Historians may argue that the precise date and place that the Cold War began was March 5, 1946, at Fulton, Missouri when former British Prime Minister Winston Churchill made his "Iron Curtain" speech or on March 12, 1947, in Washington, when President Harry Truman vowed to contain Soviet expansion. Whatever the date, the war that so affected the Arctic was set in motion by what occurred on Somerset Street in Ottawa, where a plaque marks the exact day and place. On a warm September night in 1945, one month after the atomic bombing of Hiroshima and Nagasaki, Igor Sergeyevich Gouzenko, a Soviet cipher clerk left his

View of typical DEW Line station with prefabricated, self-contained long buildings connected by an enclosed bridge forming the letter H.

embassy at Charlotte Street. He carried with him 109 documents detailing Soviet espionage activities in North America. Gouzenko brought them to 511 Somerset Street where he lived with his family, knowing that Soviet security personnel from the embassy would soon come after him. With the revelations in the documents, he hoped to gain asylum in Canada for himself and his family — a country whose freedoms he admired after reading in an Ottawa newspaper about a local citizen taking the city to court.

At first the clerk could not get anyone to believe him — the war had ended the month before, the Soviet Union was a trusted ally, and Canadians were preoccupied with demobilization and rationing of food and clothing.[1] Ever cautious, Prime Minister Mackenzie King hoped Gouzenko would quietly go away — referring to him in his diary as "that Russian man" before he upset diplomatic relations with the Soviet Union. But once the Department of External Affairs realized the significance of the information that he had brought, the cipher clerk's defection began the Cold War between the Soviet Union and the West, leading to the creation of the North Atlantic Treaty Organization (NATO) and the building of the Distant Early Warning (DEW) Line.

How the Canadian North, which had been protected by its isolation and bone-chilling climate, became the frontline in the defence of North America, was because of what occurred the year before. Of all the aircraft that were ferried through Canada over the Northwest Staging Route, requests for one by the Soviet Union were repeatedly ignored — the Boeing B-29 Superfortress. With a combat range of 5,230 kilometres, it was history's first truly intercontinental bomber and the media labelled it a "hemispheric defense weapon." Damaged in a raid on Japanese Manchuria on July 29, 1944, an intact USAF B-29 called "Ramp Tramp" was forced to land at the Soviet naval base in Vladivostok. As a neutral power the Soviet Union interned the aircraft, sending the crew home via Iran. Then two more B-29s landed and one crashed nearby. Using reverse engineering and adapting the design to Russian specifications, the great aircraft designer Andrei Tupolev built the Soviet Union's own B-29 (called the Tu-4), the first of hundreds flying as early as May 19, 1947.

Although it was thought that only they possessed the atomic bomb, the Tu-4 reinforced American fears of a repeat of the devastating attack on Pearl Harbor — except now the enemy would come over the Canadian Arctic — the shortest distance between Siberia and the American heartland was through Canada. More than a conduit for aid to Britain and the USSR, from the Alaskan border to Baffin Island, the Canadian North became the first line of defence for the western hemisphere. The sovereignty of northern Canada was no longer of airbases, but its airspace. Hardly had the Second World War ended when as early as September 1945, speculation appeared in the press that the United States intended to protect itself with airbases and radar stations in Canada, with Ottawa's permission — or without.

Realizing that it was controlled by the United States, Mackenzie King chided the Department of External Affairs for getting involved in the United Nations Temporary Commission for Korea. Having torn Canada away from its British connections throughout his political career, he now feared it being swallowed up by the Americans. But the prime minister was astute enough to know that to appease an increasingly jingoistic neighbour, the Canadian government would have to collaborate with the Americans in the Arctic — and at the same time maintain an active presence there. The land mass that bordered Canada's third ocean could no longer be left to civilian federal agencies like the Department of the Interior and RCMP.

Having defeated Napoleon, the Royal Navy spent its resources searching for the Northwest Passage, so too in postwar Canada (before commitments to the North Atlantic Treaty Organization [NATO] and UN peacekeeping began), the Canadian military indulged in a brief "polar passion." Although as in 1919, most of the military had demobilized with the nonprofessional soldiers reintegrating into civilian life, there was enough of the organization and wartime equipment left to do this. With the formation of NATO and the Korean War years away, there was really little else to do.

The RCAF resumed mapping the North and was now doing the same to the Canadian Arctic. In the summer of 1947, in OPERATION POLCO, an RCAF Canso from Rockcliffe would "fix" the location of the North Magnetic Pole. In May 1948, "An Aerial Reconnaissance of Arctic North America" appeared written by Flight Lieutenant Keith R. Greenaway (RCAF) and First Lieutenant Sidney E. Colthorpe, United States Air Force Reserve. The study quickly became the standard text for aerial navigation in the Arctic. Greenaway had been seconded to fly as a navigator with the U.S. Army Air Forces after the war where he was assigned to the Low Frequency LORAN Flight test program. He was one of the navigators of the first U.S. military aircraft, a B-29 to cross the North Geographic Pole on May 9, 1946. The flight originated from Fairbanks, Alaska, flew to Cape Columbia, Ellesmere Island, to the Pole, and returned to Edmonton.[2]

On subsequent flights, Greenaway discovered Ice Island T-3 in the Arctic Ocean north of Ellef Ringnes Island. He observed that Wilkins Sound was actually a channel, and that Borden Island was two islands. He would help develop polar navigation techniques, in particular the use of the directional gyroscope for maintaining heading in areas of "magnetic compass unreliability"; and interpreting the radar scope presentation of polar features, which with work at the Defence Research Board would lead to the "Twilight Computer" to assist in celestial navigational planning. In 1952, Keith Greenaway was awarded the Trans-Canada (McKee) Trophy in recognition of his contribution to the development of new methods of aerial navigation in the Arctic.[3]

Even before the war had ended, the army had conducted winter exercises with OPERATION LEMMING being the latest. Encouraged by its success, Wilson and Baird planned the next Northern foray. How would a fully mechanized force with RCAF support function in sub-Arctic and Arctic terrain? It would not only be a test of the Second World War–tracked vehicles, but of communications equipment, rations, clothing, and the physical health of the men. The pair caught the interest of Brigadier S.F. Clarke, the chief of the Canadian Army Research and the Minister for Defence Brooke Claxton. The former wanted the military to be prepared to operate effectively in the North and the latter was keen to create the Defence Research Board. Clarke must have voiced the concerns of many when he feared that the Americans might take over Canada's Arctic regions — in particular Ellesmere Island — if a Canadian presence was not inserted. Wilson reassured him that there was no issue as to whether or not Canada owned Ellesmere Island, but if the military intended to assert Canadian sovereignty in those latitudes, they might become better acquainted with it. With that, Clarke approved the proposal to develop what through planning stages in 1946 would become OPERATION MUSKOX.

Reusing the equipment from LEMMING, after cold-weather training in Shilo, Manitoba, the force was to leave from Churchill in February 1946. The whole operation was estimated to take 80 days, its route north to Eskimo Point, cross-country to Baker Lake, then to Denmark Bay and over the ice to Cambridge Bay. From there the expedition would turn southwest to Coppermine, cross Great Bear Lake to Norman Wells, then follow the Mackenzie River down to Fort Simpson and meet the ALCAN Highway at Fort Nelson. The final leg of the journey was to Grande Prairie and would culminate at Edmonton, hopefully by early May. The months chosen for the 3,000-mile trip meant that the expedition faced two problems — the Arctic in February, the coldest month, and to come south with their heavy equipment in the beginning of May through the spring "breakup."

Based at Rockcliffe, Ottawa, the RCAF would be MUSKOX's sole logistical support. With no airfields in the Arctic, its Dakotas would drop or land supplies continuously while the nimble Norsemen would pick up or drop off personnel when needed. Colonel G.W. Rowley, who spoke Inuktitut and was an experienced Arctic explorer, led an advance detachment from Churchill to Baker Lake to establish an air base and a signal and meteorological station.

OPERATION MUSKOX was divided into four main detachments: the main expedition of 48 officers and men, the base forces of 221 men, the RCAF detachment, and Colonel Rowley's advanced team. The main expedition would be transported by the 11 tracked vehicles built for the Norwegian campaign now called "Penguins." In the very last contract it would have before closing down, the Ottawa Car and Aircraft Company (streetcar builders) had made modifications to the original Ferand and Delorme designs to enclose the cabs.

At pains to demonstrate that MUSKOX had no secret agenda, Wilson invited military attachés from several Ottawa embassies to watch its staging, including Lieutenant-Colonel Peter J. Domashev from the embassy of the USSR, something that Tory party leader John Diefenbaker in the House of Commons' Opposition was quick to seize on. Wilson also invited observers from the U.S. Army to accompany them and they brought an M-29 "Weasel" snow vehicle to test. In a radio broadcast on CBC, Wilson emphasized that the focus of MUSKOX was to test military equipment and "show the flag" in the far North. But in the instructions it issued to its observers, the U.S. War Department made it clear why their men were going: "One aspect of particular interest is the feasibility of hostile attacks through the Arctic against industrial centers in the United States, either by long-range aircraft and guided missiles from bases in Asia or Northern Europe or from advanced bases established in Northern Canada or the Arctic."

The media in the United States were quick to pick up on this with *Time* magazine reporting in its November 26, 1945, issue:

Between the lines of a routine handout about an ostensibly routine military maneuver, Canadians got a
quick glimpse at the lowering future. The purpose of
"Operation Musk-Ox," said National Defense, is to study
"winter operations generally in the Arctic weather zone,"
to assess "the mobility of over-snow vehicles." But everyone knew that any foreseeable war would not be won
— or even fought — with tracked motor vehicles. What
soldiers knew was that the polar icecap was no longer
an impenetrable natural defense on Canada's topside.
So "certain technical research projects in Arctic air and
ground warfare will [also] be studied.... The expedition
is expected to obtain information of immense value."

What information bases? Sites for launching rocket bombs? Reporters
who asked such questions got only a grin and an answering question:
"What do you think?" Without once mentioning atoms, a Cabinet minister somberly said: "We all know that invasion of North America, if and
when, will come from the north, not the south.... We have to be ready.
We have to be able to live, travel and fight in the cold."

The Canadian press were little better. US AND CANADA WORK OUT
PLANS FOR JOINT DEFENCE appeared in the *Ottawa Evening Citizen* on
December 17, 1945. "Mindful of atomic age possibilities, the United
States and Canada are beginning to work out joint plans to defend
North America against any attack from Asia or Europe across the North
Polar region."

Once the symbol of the Hudson's Bay Company's sovereignty in the
Arctic, Churchill's Fort Prince of Wales served as the backdrop for the
departure of MUSKOX's main force on February 15 and Baird even had
one of the fort's 21-pounder cannons fire a ceremonial salute. In three
sections at 20 miles apart to increase flexibility, the expedition moved out,
heading north for Baker Lake. It was almost immediately enshrouded
in blizzard conditions, causing the American Weasel to be abandoned.
Once at Baker Lake, the expedition was reduced to 10 vehicles because
fuel was running low. How little was known of the terrain they were

navigating was revealed by Wilson in a later speech to the Empire Club in Toronto:

> No corrections had been made since the original survey
> by Captain Black of the Royal Navy, and two stretches
> went across for more than a hundred miles in which the
> map was a complete and total blank.[4]

The RCAF Dakotas dropped fuel supplies at Perry River, which at 1,400 miles from Churchill, was at the very edge of their range. Moving north, the convoy carried on across the smooth frozen Queen Maud Gulf to Victoria Island — crossing over the waters of the fabled Northwest Passage. They arrived at Cambridge Bay to a welcome from the local RCMP constable and Hudson's Bay Company agent and where the RCMP ship *St. Roch* was wintering. It was a historic meeting — the new guardians of Canada's Northern sovereignty with the old. The North Magnetic Pole was then only 100 miles to the east of Victoria Island and an officer from the Dominion Observatory took readings.

Turning south, the vehicles crossed the ice on Coronation Gulf, travelling for 300 miles over difficult country to Coppermine (Kugluktuk). From there they drove to Port Radium and across Great Bear Lake to Norman Wells. Like St. Bernard dogs, RCAF Dakotas and Norsemen kept watch over the expedition, dropping of necessities decades before parcel post in the civilian world.

> We had engine trouble and rather than repair on the
> spot we had radioed for another engine. We only had to
> wait 24 hours for another engine. We changed engines,
> flew the old engine out and connected up the new one.

But the worst was to come between Fort Simpson and Fort Nelson, when the expedition had to cross several rivers in the dreaded spring "break-up." The soft, mushy ground underfoot meant that the machines had to be kept in low gear most of the time, straining the engines. Nor was there stable, dry terrain anywhere for the Norsemen to land on. Tempers frayed, surplus weight was jettisoned, and transmissions had to be repeatedly repaired. The many and sudden rivers meant that the RCAF flew in advance construction parties to build bridges or rafts that the vehicles could drive or float across on. From Fort Nelson to Grande Prairie, the Alcan Highway was used. As it was still unpaved, the dust clogged all filters, overheating engines. There was a victory (or sovereignty?) parade down Grande Prairie's main street and then the vehicles were put on trains for Edmonton.

Despite attempts by the media to sensationalize it, OPERATION MUSKOX accomplished what it was meant to do. Besides introducing the army to the Arctic, much scientific data was brought back, maps were updated, experience in parachuting supplies and building airstrips was obtained, none of the men suffered frostbite, scurvy, or sun blindness — nor were any diseases introduced to the Natives. Wilson concluded his speech to the Empire Club with this warning:

> The Arctic is a good training ground. If a young officer gets lost on a training scheme at Borden or Petawawa in the summer time and his men get lost they may miss breakfast … but nothing very serious happens. But if a leader of part of an Arctic Expedition gets lost the consequences are likely to be much more severe, so it is a very excellent training ground for leaders in both peace and war.

Recommendations that came out of MUSKOX were that the snowmobiles, if extensively modified, could be used for further Arctic operations, but the Penguins could not. The winter clothing issued by the army was so inadequate that the men had exchanged their outer wear with the locals for the Native caribou skins, which were lighter, warmer, and more flexible. Besides skills learned and equipment tested, it was realized how much fuel was consumed and how vital air supply would be to any military operations in the North. In support of MUSKOX, the RCAF had moved 419 tons of cargo and flown 792,000 miles. The most important lesson was that the maintenance of a ground force in the Arctic required huge and expensive resources with constant air support.

The first of many such military exercises, if MUSKOX demonstrated anything at all, it was that the days of relying on civilian agencies for asserting sovereignty in the North had ended and that the United States was no longer the only power to contend with in the polar regions. It was time for the Canadian military to maintain a permanent presence and, through a series of military operations, to periodically test its preparedness to defend the North. Unfortunately, with defence budgets being slashed and what money was available going to equip a Special Force for NATO, the first Canadian peacetime military alliance, the North, if it was considered at all, was the poor relative of the family.

Never was this more obvious than the wartime orphan, the Alaska Highway. Even in 1945 when the Canadian Army was to take over the highway from the United States, Ottawa was still unsure as to its relevance to the Canadian North. The NWSR airfields were of more use than the still unpaved highway, which had after all been built for the defence of Alaska. Just before the handover scheduled for April 1, 1946, The Department of National Defence (DND) sent advance parties to grasp the nettle, estimating that the takeover would cost $5.7 million. Based at Whitehorse, the Northwest Highway System (NWHS) military unit was formed to maintain the highway and with the exception of RCAF support, became almost an independent brigade of the Canadian Army. "Civilianizing" what was a military road provided good practice for the Royal Canadian Engineers and when families of the NWHS troops were allowed to move into nearby military camps, the DND found itself providing schools, hospitals, skating rinks, and sports facilities. But the government drew the line at paving all 1,965.6 kilometres of the highway that lay in Canada. Minister of Defence Brooke Claxton said on June 21, 1954, that as the road was a "civilian operation" it would be "… more practical and economical if it were taken over by the Department of Public Works." Later, his Conservative colleague George Pearkes, Diefenbaker's minister of defence, offered to give the highway to any department (federal or provincial) in the government that wanted it, but there were no takers and the NWHS continued its stewardship. The United States offered financial assistance to pave the highway, but as in 1941, the sovereignty issue raised its head. When President Eisenhower and Prime Minister John Diefenbaker discussed a plan in July 1958 to share the costs, the Canadian government pointedly did not pursue it. Not until 1977 would Canada allow the United States to pay for a reconstruction of certain portions of the Alaska Highway. But the Exchange of Notes had this proviso:

> This Agreement shall not be construed so as to vest in the United States any proprietary interest in the highways, and upon completion of the project, or any part thereof, the highways shall remain, in all respects, an integral part of the Canadian Highway System.

Held in January/February 1950, EXERCISE SWEET BRIAR took place along the Alaska Highway, in which the Canadian Army fought an aggressor force that had captured Koidern near the Alaskan border. Although there were umpires on both sides, it was to be as realistic as possible with the aggressors (American troops) speaking only Spanish for interrogation purposes. In this the first jet warfare exercise, the aggressor air force would fly in F-82 jet fighters from Alaska's Ladd Field and the RCAF would meet them with 410 squadron's Vampires from Rivers, Alberta. The Vampires flew 127 sorties through the exercise, which highlighted their many shortcomings — the tiny British-built aircraft was wholly unsuited to Arctic conditions. But the most serious hardship for the troops was the Whitehorse Winter Carnival.

> It took place in a small wooden hall well filled with noise, smoke, smells, troops and civilians. There was little in the way of entertainment other than two crown and anchor boards, a dice game and a rather tired troupe of dancing girls dressed in costumes alleged to have been the vogue for entertainers in the gold rush days....
>
> — *Roundel* magazine

The next exercise, SUNDOG TWO, was held in February 1951, 85 miles from the army's Experimental and Training Station at Churchill. The locale was chosen because the Directorate of Military Training in Ottawa noted it was "... representative of the true, barren Arctic Canada where the next conflict would be." The "enemy" was the 1st Battalion, Royal 22nd Regiment, which were moved by tractor train into their position. Long-range RCAF reconnaissance determined where they were and paratroops of the 1 Royal Canadian Regiment were flown from Rivers, Alberta, and dropped by parachute and glider. Although the "enemy" was skillfully concealed, the paratroops flushed them and the position was cleared. The directorate handout said that the exercise provided "much factual data on Arctic airborne operations, in addition to testing new equipment." Those who were on it especially remember erecting the new five-man Arctic tent in a strong wind.

Under pressure from its allies, on December 29, 1950, the Liberal government took the decision to triple the defence budget from $403 million to $1.45 billion. But it was to send RCAF squadrons, naval forces, and a division of troops to bolster NATO. That was where Soviet expansion was expected — not the Arctic. And although Korea was seen as a Communist diversion, in February 1951, Parliament was told that a brigade group was to be sent to the peninsula. The Canadian North — if it needed defending — was to be left to those who lived in it.

The three OPERATION BULLDOG exercises held from 1951 to 1954 were designed to assess how those locals could defend their hometown from enemy invasion. BULLDOG II was also held on the shores of Hudson Bay near Churchill — the scenario of the eight-day exercise was that invaders had landed in the sub-Arctic and captured a weather station. A company of the 1st Battalion, Royal 22nd Regiment, once again played the role of the enemy. Buildings were erected at the site to simulate a northern weather station. To create the realism and difficulties of northern operations, all personnel, weapons, equipment, and supplies of the attacking force were parachuted into battle. Using Edmonton as the main base for operations and Churchill as an advanced base, the army and RCAF were required to launch an airborne assault to reduce this "lodgement." No. 1 Tactical Air Command RCAF, based at Churchill, controlled transport and medical evacuation with two of the new C-119 "Packets."

Perfectly suited for this sort of exercise were the Canadian Rangers. Once the British Columbia coast watchers, the Canadian Rangers were formally established as a corps of the Reserve Militia by an order-in-council in 1947. Their role as stated at that time was, "… to provide a military presence in those sparsely settled northern, coastal and isolated areas of Canada which cannot conveniently or economically be covered by other elements of the Canadian Forces."

The Rangers were to conduct surveillance of the local terrain in sparsely settled areas of the country. Instead of regular force troops being stationed at great expense in northern and isolated coastal areas, the Rangers, who would not for a variety of reasons join the regular forces, were seen as a cost-effective solution to enforcing Canadian sovereignty during and long after the Cold War. "The guerrilla must move amongst the people as a fish swims in the sea," wrote Mao Tse-tung and the DND visualized the Rangers as a "people's army," giving the vast expanse of the North to be watched over by those who lived there — loggers, hunters, bush pilots, and fishermen, Aboriginal and white, who in their daily lives were the military's "eyes and ears." Not only did the Rangers use local human resources who were protecting their own backyards, but, dear to every politician's heart, the patrols required minimum funding and guidance from Ottawa. With little training, obsolescent .303 Lee-Enfield rifles and complete knowledge and love of their own communities, the Rangers, could now act as scouts, guides, and guerrillas in both war and peace.

Unlike the prima donnas of the Cold War — the ruinously expensive Avro Arrow, the non nuclear–tipped BOMARC missiles, and the SAGE computer system, the Rangers received little money, no public attention or recognition — and perhaps that is what ensured their survival through successive governments, almost untouched to the present day. But nowhere was their ingenuity and value to local sovereignty more clearly demonstrated than in the "Battle of Yellowknife Airport."

Yellowknife's proximity to the USSR and also having one of the few airports in the North that could sustain heavy aircraft made it a strategic Cold War asset. In 1955, National Defense planned OPERATION

BULLDOG III to test the ability of the local Rangers to harry an invading army until conventional reinforcements could be deployed to the area. Once more, a battalion of the Royal 22e Régiment was the enemy and tasked with staging a mock invasion of Yellowknife Airport. The defending forces of the No.7 Company Canadian Rangers were 65 part-time soldiers who were local hunters, bush pilots, and prospectors. Their commanding officer (and the local justice of the peace, acting magistrate, town surveyor, and geologist) was John Anderson-Thomson. The Scottish immigrant had served as a commissioned officer in both the First and Second World Wars and was eminently suited to defending the North. His Rangers were ordered to secure the airport from February 23 to March 8 when the Princess Patricia's paratroops could land and take over from them — if they survived that long.[5]

On the morning of the invasion, several members of the Rangers who owned airplanes were cruising around in the sky. Just as the Van Doos had finished unloading and deplaning, they swooped in and began their bombing run, dropping small bags filled with lamp black (which was used for making ink), their "bombs." The fine carbon powder got into everything the Van Doos had, their tents, sleeping bags, and even their rations. The "bombing" was so successful, that if real bombs were used, the whole invading force would have been wiped out. The umpires supervising the operation declared that the Rangers had won their first battle.

When the exercise resumed shortly after that, the Rangers decimated the soot-covered Van Doos — who stuck out like sore thumbs against the white snow — from their hidden machine-gun nests. The umpires announced the Rangers the victors of the second battle.

The Rangers were so successful that the umpires ordered them to retreat beyond the airport road, so that the Van Doos could finish unloading, and setting up camp. After the dismayed Van Doos were ready, the exercise started up again, and the Van Doos started to slowly make their way to the airport road with an easy victory in mind when the Royal Yellowknife Air Force (RYAF) struck again. A pilot in a Stinson bush plane was in the process of pulling down the Van Doos radio antenna with his wheels, when he saw three of the Van Doos in a huddle and dropped a bag of lamp black on them. One of the people in the huddle was the Van Doos commanding officer, so they were now without a leader and without communications equipment. This was to be the Rangers third win in as many hours.

Pole Star Blues
Sung by the Royal Canadian Regiment to the tune of
"Trail of Aching Hearts"

We ain't had a beer for many a day,
And dames are a thing of the past,
The only thing we hear out here,
Is the North wind's horrible blast.
For some go down to the sea in ships,
Others fly high in the sky,
But we'll walk the trail of the five man tent,
Till the day we die,
For VRI.

The umpires decided to even out the odds by grounding the RYAF, declaring John Anderson-Thomson a casualty, and making the Rangers retreat even farther away from the airport, telling them to prepare for a night attack. Before long, the Rangers had gotten a fourth victory declared for them. For the next and final exercise, the Rangers were told that they would have to secure an enemy-free zone on Back Bay in which Princess Patricia's paratroopers could land. Once they landed, they followed five kilometres of trail that was built by the Rangers, back to the airport without the Van Doos even knowing they were there. Their short, but successful assault on the Yellowknife Airport brought an end to OPERATION BULLDOG III for the Rangers who were elated that they had won all five exercises against the best troops in Canada.

U.S. Air Force aircraft had begun making weather observation flights to the North Pole in early 1946. The route, known as "Ptarmigan," was from Ladd Field, Alaska, directly to the North Pole by way of Point Barrow and back. As the Germans had done in the Second World War, it was a means of obtaining observations of temperature, humidity, pressure, amount and type of cloud formation, turbulence, precipitation, and visibility. The round-trip of 3,600 statute miles had to be flown "within the weather" at no higher than 10,000 feet and to do so, the B-29 carried 8,000 gallons of fuel for a long 17 hours. It was a near-suicidal, gruelling mission, but essential to weather stations around the world.

Fortunately for the Americans, the Danish government granted the United States permission to build a Danish/U.S. weather observation station at Thule, Greenland, on June 28, 1946, ensuring that it was civilian in intent and had no connection with the 1941 agreement that had allowed the building of the "Bluie" military bases in the south. While an airstrip was being constructed at Thule, OPERATION NANOOK, a U.S. Navy task force of six ships led by icebreakers left Boston to make its way to Lancaster Sound.

Once the airstrip at Thule had been completed, a U.S. naval PBM aircraft reconnoitered Ellesmere's northern coast, and Cape Columbia was selected as the future site for a joint Canadian/U.S. weather station. With the American task force already on location and winter approaching in the high Arctic, it was thought expedient to have this station built at the same time and in May, discussions had already begun in Ottawa to do so. But the Canadian government was not going to be rushed into anything and asked for time to examine the proposal. On August 14, 1946, Washington formally requested permission from Ottawa to establish several joint meteorological stations across the Canadian Arctic. After examining the proposal through the summer and fall, the Interdepartmental Meteorological Committee recommended to the Cabinet Defence Committee on November 23 that the stations be built. They were not to be airbases, radar stations, or even LORAN air navigation sites, but that did not prevent press speculation that the USAF was about to station interceptor aircraft in Canada's North as a defence against the imminently expected hordes of Soviet Tu-4s.

As if to quell such rumours, Mackenzie King's Cabinet gave its approval on January 28, 1947, for a Joint Arctic Programme with the U.S. Meteorological Division of the U.S. Weather Bureau (USWB). A statement from both governments followed in February about "mutual availability of military facilities in the North." At the United Nations in New York, secretary of state for external affairs and heir apparent Louis St. Laurent went to great pains to emphasize that the United States government had not asked for bases in the North. When asked about OPERATION MUSKOX, the prime minister said "… because our troops must of course have experience of conditions in these regions…." Weather reporting, accurate mapping, and aviation facilities were what Ottawa had in mind for the Arctic — not defence against Russian bombers by the Americans.

The following spring, on March 4, 1947, C.D. Howe announced that the Canadian government planned to establish five Arctic weather stations within the next three years at Winter Harbour on Cornwallis Island, Mould Bay on Prince Patrick Island, Isachsen on Ellef Ringnes Island, Eureka Sound, and at Cape Columbia on the very tip of Ellesmere Island. These Joint Arctic Weather Stations (JAWS) were to be erected with the assistance of the USWB. The U.S. Coast Guard and Navy would supply the transportation necessary for their establishment and half of the staff, rations, and technical equipment.

Colonel C.J. Hubbard (USWB) and D.C. Archibald of the meteorological branch of the Department of Transport of Canada were given the responsibility for the planning and operation of the stations. Beginning in April 1947, men and equipment were flown from the U.S. airbase at Thule, Greenland, to Slidre Fjord, in southwestern Ellesmere Island, for the construction of the Eureka weather station. Because of sovereignty issues, Canadian officials were always part of the air, shipping, and icebreaker support that the U.S. Navy and Coast Guard provided. That summer, U.S. Naval Task Force 68 attempted to reach Winter Harbour, Melville Island — named by William Parry when he was forced to winter there in 1819–20, so that a station could be built there. But heavy ice and damage to one of the escorting icebreakers prevented this and a more accessible site at Resolute Bay was chosen. From the airfield completed here in the spring of 1948, reconnaissance flights were made to select sites for the two weather stations at Mould Bay and Isachsen.

Located on coasts, stations like Resolute were open during the summer, so that the bulk of their supplies as well as those for the satellite stations could be brought by sea. The satellite stations were also on coasts, but in more remote areas with hazardous shipping conditions and only icebreakers (with little cargo space) could be expected to reach them. As Canada had no icebreakers, the original plan called for the satellite stations to be maintained by RCAF airlift in the spring and parachute drop during the rest of the year.

With the stations at Mould Bay and Isachsen operating, in the summer of 1948, an attempt was made to send icebreakers to set up the final satellite weather station at Cape Columbia. For an airlift of the many tons of supplies, equipment, and materials needed, a cache was first to be put ashore to build a runway on the sea ice. To do so, two icebreakers, the USN *Edisto* and USCG *Eastwind*, left Thule on July 30. Sister ships in the "Wind" class, they had been originally designed to carry a Grumman Duck seaplane. Now modernized, the *Edisto* had a helicopter on its aft deck. The *Eastwind* lost its forward propeller and fell behind, but on August 2, the *Edisto* anchored off Cape Sheridan due to heavy ice conditions preventing it from proceeding farther along the coast toward Cape Columbia. The area around Cape Sheridan was then reconnoitered by the ship's helicopter to find a substitute site. Soon, a few kilometres to the northwest between Dumbbell Bay and the Dumbbell Lakes, a likely site was found. Colonel Hubbard and W.I. Griffith of the Canadian Meteorological Division examined the area and selected the future site for the station at 82° 30" 6' N latitude, and 62° 19" 47' W longitude. They chose it because it was accessible by sea (only by icebreakers), the Dumbbell lakes had fresh water and could be used as a winter airstrip and finally, part of Cape Belknap was level enough for the construction of a land airstrip.

Unloading began immediately, but by the time the *Eastwind* arrived, a change in the wind pushed the ice pack on shore and before it could be trapped, the icebreakers retreated to open sea. There were still several

National Defence Imagery Library.

Early Alert with Jamesway hut and antenna. Originally a weather station, it became a listening post for Soviet activities and assertion of Canadian sovereignty in the Arctic.

men on shore and while a few were brought back by helicopter, others had to be left behind without shelter because of a sudden fog, and were taken off by helicopter 36 hours later. When the ice eased on August 5, the remainder of the provisions was landed at Dumbbell Bay, including a T-9 bulldozer for clearing the snow off the bay ice to make a runway, an aircraft engine heater, 12 drums of fuel, cargo sleds, a Jamesway hut for shelter, and other supplies.

A name for Canada's most northernmost station was yet to be chosen. All equipment destined for it had been labelled "Cape Columbia," but since the cape was almost 100 kilometres to the west, this was obviously no longer an appropriate name. On November 17, 1948, the chief of the USWB, E.W. Reichelderfer, wrote to Andrew Thompson, controller of the Department of Transport's Meteorological Division to name the station. He suggested two names, "Alert," the name of Nares's ship in the British Arctic Expedition or "Belknap," the name of the naturalist surgeon on the *Alert*. Both names were submitted to the Board of Geographical Names in Ottawa for a decision. On January 6th, 1949, "Alert" was adopted.[6]

With a Canadian/U.S. crew, Alert would have the largest staff of all stations: four rawinsonde (for measuring and transmitting wind speed and direction) observers, two radio operators (one of whom would also be qualified as a radio technician), a cook, and a mechanic. In addition there would be four temporary employees, a carpenter, and a three-man airstrip construction and maintenance crew. A Department of Transport employee, Leo Lafranchise, who had previous experience in setting up weather stations elsewhere in Arctic Canada, was to be in charge. In alphabetical order, the first 12 at Alert were: Charles J. Clifton, executive officer/rawinsonde observer (U.S.); Selwyn M. Dow, radio operator (Canada); Woodrow W. George, cook (U.S.); Sam Griggs, mechanic (U.S.); Peter J. Johnson Jr., airstrip mechanic (U.S.); Leo J. Lafranchise, in-charge/rawinsonde observer (Canada); Elwood J. McCormick, airstrip mechanic (U.S.); Willis G. Morgan, senior airstrip mechanic (U.S.); James Scovil, carpenter (Canada); Griffith A Toole, rawinsonde observer (Canada); Stanley Whiteman, radio technician/operator (U.S.); and George Zahary, rawinsonde observer (Canada). Personnel assigned to Alert from elsewhere in the Canadian Arctic went to Thule from Resolute Bay; the others flew north via Goose Bay and Frobisher Bay and by April 3, all arrived at Thule.

> Food was taken more or less continuously because there were not enough eating utensils for everybody. There was a large supply of frozen meat, "C" and "5 in 1" rations and during the first couple of weeks many meals consisted of steak, canned fruit, juice and coffee, each man making his own. A welcome treat was a chocolate cake sent up by a military cook in Thule when one of the crew had a birthday.

Setting up what was to be the most northern permanently inhabited settlement in the world (Alert is 450 nautical miles from the geographic North Pole) proved as was to be expected, an ordeal. On Easter Sunday, April 9, an advance party was sent to prepare a runway on the ice of Dumbbell Bay. Under Lafranchise's direction, Clifton, Morgan, and Whiteman left Thule aboard a USAF ski-wheel C-47 aircraft while a C-54 transport flew "cover" and made parachute and free drops of fuel and equipment. The snow-covered surface of Dumbbell Bay had been packed by the wind into ridges which made the C-47's landing very rough. The cache already ashore was buried in drifting snow in and had to be dug out. All supplies including an engine preheater (in case the one at the cache proved unserviceable), tent, rations, radio, batteries for radio and tractor, emergency supplies, and an aircraft altimeter had to be man-hauled by a sled, which collapsed under the weight of its load. A weather balloon was filled with helium and sent up, with a wire attached to serve as an aircraft beacon antenna.

With the temperature at minus 46 °C, the Jamesway hut (4.9 metres squared in size) was set up on top of a knoll, a short distance from where it had lain in the cache. Bunks were put up inside the Jamesway and an oil space heater was installed and started. While this was going on, Morgan dug out the T-9 and after preheating it, got it working. With the T-9, a runway was laid out in the middle of the bay and except for Whiteman, who kept a continuous radio watch from a tent heated by a small coal stove, the others began to clear snow from its surface. By April 14, the runway was 1,000 metres long and only one barrel of fuel for the tractor remained. It would be another four days, however, before aircraft could bring more fuel from Thule, because of delays in the airlift to Eureka. On June 10, a USAF C-54, bringing with it the first mail, aborted a landing at Alert because of poor weather — much to the relief of the station crew as the surface of the airstrip was beginning to melt and one of them had a very vivid dream the night before of an aircraft crashing.

> During the airlifts, the pilots were always "kind" enough to shut down the port engines but kept at least one starboard engine running. At -40 °C, that prop wash, even from the opposite side of the aircraft, was a tad chilly. Cargo was unloaded on plank ramps and slid (manhandled) to the ground. If a fuel drum got away, we'd just let it roll and collect it when there was more time. The aircrew didn't dilly-dally at Alert!

In those early days, the aircraft that serviced the stations were USAF C-54s and RCAF North Stars and on the average, 20–30 tons were delivered daily. At Alert, it was mainly USAF C-54s from Thule that brought in the supplies — which was good, because the American crews were part of the worldwide MATS (Military Air Transport Service) and prone to drop off cans of the latest Hollywood movies for the station's Bell & Howell projector. The most suitable of all aircraft were the USAF C-119 "Packets," with their rear clamshell loading doors, the model later also bought by the RCAF for servicing the DEW Line and nicknamed "Flying Boxcars." Two RCAF Lancasters from 405 Squadron, Greenwood, Nova Scotia, were also used for long-range ice reconnaissance and supply to the joint Canadian/United States northern weather stations. The first airlift to Alert ended May 2, 1950, after 308 tons had been delivered and a third Jamesway had been built. Weather Station "Alert" was operating and Canadian sovereignty at the top of the world had been executed.

C-119 Packet taking off from DEW Line base. While many commercial airlines were used in this the greatest airlift in history, the backbone was made up of the giant U.S. Air Force "Globemasters" and the RCAF C-119 "Flying Boxcars."

The RCAF North Stars were loaded at Resolute and fitted with special unloading ramps to be used at Isachsen and Mould Bay.

Unlike its sister services, the Royal Canadian Navy (RCN) was ill-equipped to offer much to Arctic operations. As it had never shown any interest in the Arctic, it had no icebreakers. During the war, protecting the Atlantic convoys, the RCN had specialized in anti-submarine warfare. But Canada had ended the war with the world's third-largest navy — among its 400 ships, it had two aircraft carriers, two cruisers, eighteen frigates, and nine minesweepers. The war had been the heyday for the RCN when, having won its independence from the Royal Navy, it had attained the status (however temporarily) of a "big ship" navy. Having come of age, the RCN now looked to consolidating those gains in peacetime. But the dropping of the atomic bombs and the use of strategic bombers (to say nothing of the rumours of rocket warfare) meant that the RCN, like other navies, was unsure of its role in the postwar world. The insecurity came at a time when Ottawa was keen to downsize the armed forces — and the cruisers, aircraft carriers, and the naval air arm were especially vulnerable.

On the other hand, Arctic involvement for the U.S. Navy dated as far back as 1830 and now with the largest fleet in the world, this continued after the war. In March 1946, the U.S. Navy launched OPERATION FROSTBITE, with the aircraft carrier USS *Midway*, three destroyers and a tanker conducting exercises in Davis Strait. A hint of things to come was the presence in Baffin Bay of the submarine USS *Atule*. The RCN had been asked to participate with the U.S. Navy in OPERATION NANOOK that same year as the joint USN/Marine exercise was held in Canadian territorial waters off Viscount Melville and Lancaster Sounds with the Marines landing near Dundas Harbour on North Devon Island. The Canadian government declined the offer, but sent an observer.

RCN staff officers watched with envy at the U.S. naval activity in the Canadian Arctic while they without ice-strengthened vessels, could not even supply Canadian weather stations. Captain H.N. Lay, director of naval plans and intelligence from December 1945 to April 1948, wrote in October 1946 "that the idea of a purely Canadian Arctic Expedition is an excellent one. We know that U.S.S.R. is [*sic*] taking a considerable amount of interest in the Arctic regions, and we have some reason to suspect that a Russian submarine has been operating in the Davis Strait."[7]

In 1947, the RCN planned its own OPERATION ICEWORM, but got bogged down in the types of ships to send and their fuelling capabilities. But as the British had discovered in the Victorian era, nothing said sovereignty better than a naval vessel. Lay proposed an RCN cruise (it was not an operation) into Hudson Strait and Bay for "familiarization" with the waters, radio testing, "within the auroral belt," bathythermograph readings, hydrographic soundings, and magnetic observations. The cruise was to be conducted when the strait and bay were ice-free, i.e., between mid-August and mid-September, since the hulls of the destroyers could not withstand the ice. To dispel any ideas that this was a military operation, it was given no name. Mackenzie King saw no value in sending aircraft carriers on a sovereignty cruise to the North. Neither carrier, HMCS *Warrior* nor *Magnificent,* was winterized. *Warrior* was barely equipped for the Atlantic. The prime minister did agree to allow the *Magnificent* to take part on the assurance of its previous owners, the Royal Navy, that its heating system and upper-deck machinery was "arcticized." Mackenzie King also thought sending the *Magnificent* "too grandiose" for such a venture — aircraft carriers were unsuited to Arctic waters — but it had just been commissioned on April 7, and both the RCN and the prime minister understood that the taxpayer would have wanted to see it in action.

These were to be the first Canadian warships to enter Canada's Arctic waters and chosen were the new (to the RCN) aircraft carrier HMCS *Magnificent,* under the command of Commodore G.R. Miles, with 19 Carrier Air Group aboard; the tribal destroyer HMCS *Haida,* commanded by Lieutenant-Commander A.F. Pickard; and HMCS *Nootka,* under the command of Commander A.H.G. Storrs.

The duration of the voyage was from September 2 to 28, 1948, with no thought of remaining on station later. The ships sailed from Halifax, first anchoring off Wakeham Bay where 20 years before, Squadron Leader Lawrence had based his Fokker Universals. With Ottawa parsimonious about paying for fuel, *Magnificent* only went as far as Wakeham Bay, where it topped off the destroyers with fuel. The *Haida* and *Nootka* continued on, entering Hudson Bay and going to Churchill.

Also involved in joint tactical exercises were two RCAF search-and-rescue aircraft, a Canso and a Lancaster from 103 SAR (Search and Rescue)

Flight, Greenwood, Nova Scotia. The Lancaster was able to practise radar and homing exercises and patrols with the destroyers. The destroyers visited Churchill for four days where the governor general flew in and they were open to the public for tours. After calling at Coral Harbour on Southampton Island, they refuelled at Port Burwell from the tanker *Dundalk*, which had been sent from Halifax, and returned home.

It was purely a "show the flag" cruise and newspapers and newsreels featured publicity shots of RCN ships navigating past towering icebergs with the *Magnificent* living up to its name. Observers from other navies and civilians were also on board, including the British High Commissioner to Canada Captain Sir Robert Stirling-Hamilton; the U.S. Naval Attaché to Canada Captain Benjamin Scott Custer; the geophysicist A.A. Onhausser from the Dominion Observatory; and members of the Canadian Army and the RCAF.

Stirling-Hamilton and Custer left the ships at Churchill and what happened to them next would demonstrate how much the RCAF's presence in the North had increased in the postwar period. On September 12, a U.S. Navy Beechcraft flown by Custer with Stirling-Hamilton and three other passengers took off from Churchill for The Pas. When it did not arrive, the RCAF's (SAR) HQ in Winnipeg launched OPERATION ATTACHÉ to look for them. The largest SAR operation ever held in the North, at one time it had 35 aircraft in action. Custer had brought the aircraft down on muskeg and would later say the cause of the crash had been Stirling-Hamilton's compass, which was too close to the aircraft's compass, causing him to lose his way. The five men remained with the aircraft for a week, living off the rations on board and then began walking in the direction they hoped was south. Four days later, they were spotted by an RCAF Lancaster and rescued. In a magazine interview, Custer later blamed untrustworthy RCAF ground crews in Ottawa for "looting" the Beechcraft's emergency supply of guns, machetes, and an axe that would have allowed them to live off the land. More erratically, he went on to say that just before they were rescued, he had been thinking of the Donner Party (who were forced to resort to cannibalism).

The primary lesson the RCN had got from the cruise was that without an icebreaker, a naval presence in the North was not sustainable.

The formation of NATO in 1949 and the government's White Paper that year committed the navy to protecting coastal waters (which included the Arctic Ocean) and allied Atlantic shipping lanes. Funds for a naval icebreaker had been approved, but only just — as NATO commitments precluded any further Arctic presence after that. The government's determination to use a naval warship to underline Canadian sovereignty in the Arctic — after years of relying on the innocuous *St. Roch* and *Nascopie* — was entirely out of character and subject to change.

Laid down at Marine industries shipward in Sorel, Quebec, in November 1949, the RCN's first diesel-electric ship, HMCS *Labrador* was modelled after the "Wind" class and had a helicopter deck for a Piasecki helicopter. Her hull was specially designed for icebreaking, plated from waterline to keel in rolled high-tensile steel 1 5/8 inches thick, with no scuttles below the upper deck. She also had heeling tanks fitted with reversible-propeller pumps that shifted tons of water from side to side at 40,000 gallons per minute, fast enough to make the ship rock herself free when she got caught in pack ice. Crewed by 24 officers, 208 sailors, and 10 civilians from the Defence Research Board (according to the RCN, her primary function was research), *Labrador* was designed to be at sea for months in a very thinly settled region with a severe climate; consequently, she was the first RCN ship with a central heating, ventilation, and air-conditioning system that even filtered and humidified the air below decks. She was also the first RCN ship with bunks instead of hammocks and a modern cafeteria that doubled as a movie theatre.

HMCS *Labrador* set sail from Halifax on her maiden voyage on July 23, 1954, her destination, appropriately, for the Labrador Sea. On August 25, she rendezvoused with her sister ships USCGS *Northwind* and *Burton Island* and went through the Northwest Passage to survey the Beaufort Sea. The voyage was kept secret for fear that she would break down and require American assistance. Her arrival in Esquimalt on September 27, 1954, made HMCS *Labrador* the first warship to transit the Northwest Passage — a feat that neither the Royal nor U.S. Navies had accomplished. This was not lost on the government, which finally had an RCN ship capable of patrolling the Arctic Archipelago. Until the *Labrador*'s voyage, the U.S. Navy had considered the Arctic to be their

Mare Nostrum. The building of the DEW Line began the following year and on June 15, 1955, the *Labrador* was put to use doing hydrographic surveys and preparing the beaches at the chosen sites. It also provided icebreaking support for the 60-ship convoy that arrived in early August for the line's construction.

Captain Bill Landymore had served on HMS *Belfast* with distinction on the Arctic convoys to Murmansk. Now the director of naval plans and operations in Ottawa, he saw little use for the *Labrador* in the RCN when it could better serve in Arctic research for other government departments. He did not grasp the symbolic implications of a naval ship rather than a research one to project Canadian sovereignty. Landymore's navy was focused on supporting NATO operations in the Atlantic, not icebreaking to supply DEW Line and JAW stations. The chief of naval staff, Vice-Admiral H.G. De Wolf was aware of the symbolic implications of *Labrador*'s cruises in the Arctic and would write: "There is a very real value in showing the white ensign in the Canadian North where the stars and stripes are so much in evidence."[8] But, told to reduce expenditures by Pearkes, he transferred the *Labrador* to the Department of Transport in 1958. When asked about further Arctic sovereignty cruises, George Hees the Transport Minister said the *Labrador* was needed for icebreaking duties on the St. Lawrence in the winter.

Travelling under the ice pack was almost as old as the invention of submarines. In 1901, Hermann Franz Anchütz-Kaempfe, a German scientist and explorer, proposed reaching the North Pole by submarine. The British explorer Sir Hubert Wilkins actually attempted such a voyage in 1931, but had to turn back when the submarine was damaged by the edge of the ice pack. During the Second World War, German U-boats had sheltered under the ice, and after the war, the U.S. Navy sent submarines up to the very edge of the sheet. But these were conventional submarines that needed to surface to recharge their batteries. Opening an entirely new frontier (i.e., navigation beneath the Arctic ice) the USS *Nautilus*, the world's first nuclear-powered submarine, transited the Beaufort Sea completely underwater to the North Pole in the summer of 1958. That the Soviet Union was soon having its own nuclear submarines roaming under the Arctic ice came as no surprise to anyone.

In lieu of winter patrols in the Arctic, the RCN protected Canadian sovereignty with listening posts as part of the National Signals Intelligence (SIGINT) organization. For example, the former Crimson Route base Frobisher Bay, Labrador, found a new lease on life in 1950 as the RCN and the U.S. Navy coordinated their Atlantic HF/DF (High Frequency Direction Finding) Network to provide mutual support for maritime warfare. The single RCN ship deployment was in August 1961, when the River class frigate HMCS *Cap de la Madeleine* was sent to Frobisher Bay to build a crew barracks at the station. On the other side of the continent in the Northwest Territories, Naval Radio Station (NRS) Inuvik CFV was established in 1961.Commissioned on September 10, 1963, it became HMCS *Inuvik*. In 1966, with the Armed Forces unification, the station was renamed CFS *Inuvik*.

By July 1950, the summer resupply of Alert was proceeding apace with supplies dropped off at Thule where Hubbard and J. Glenn Dyer (his assistant) were directing their air drop with the RCAF's ice-reconnaissance Lancaster. Bringing in needed spare parts for the bulldozer, shortly after noon on July 31, the Lancaster arrived over Alert. It flew directly over the airstrip, so that its passengers could look at the progress made and then to make the drop, it turned to approach the station from the east. Immediately over the station, the parachute appeared, but it fouled the aircraft's elevator. The aircraft dived into the ground, exploding in a cloud. Everyone began running toward the column of smoke from which flames, flares, and other minor explosions were now coming. Johnson took the Weasel from the garage, picked up Griggs, and went on ahead of them.

There were no survivors. The main fire burned for an hour while the RCMP at Resolute Bay was contacted. The bodies were covered and snow fences were set up around the remains to keep the foxes away. Pending a decision by the authorities about an investigation, a constant guard was set on the crash site, where a large packing case and a small coal stove were set up on a cargo sled for shelter. All those on board had been killed immediately: the crewmembers Wing Commander D.T.

French D.F.C.; Flight Officer (F/O) T.D. Martin; F/O J.R. Dubé; F/O J.E. McCutcheon; Flight Lieutenant (F/L) L.M. Maclean; F/L J.F. Swinton; Leading Aircraftman R.L. Sprange; and passengers Dr. D.W. Kirk, from the Department of Mines and Technical Surveys; and Colonel C.J. Hubbard, from the United States Weather Bureau. All were especially saddened to learn that Hubbard had been one of those aboard.

The next day, despite deteriorating weather, the second Lancaster made a number of sweeps across the station to examine the crash. It reported that the ice was navigable for a ship to within 450 kilometres of Alert, but from there on navigation was impossible. But one of the Dumbbell lakes was sufficiently open for a flying boat to land and an RCAF Canso from 103 Rescue Unit, Greenwood, Nova Scotia, was to arrive the next day to pick up the remains of the victims of the crash. Hubbard's family had requested that, according to his wishes, he be interred at Alert. The difficulties encountered by the Canso in getting the bodies out forced a decision to also bury the Canadians at Alert. Accordingly on August 7, the ground beside the grave dug for Hubbard was opened and a joint military funeral was held at the most northerly cemetery in the world. On another August day in 1952, in the light of both the midnight sun and a full moon, a cairn was unveiled dedicated to the memory of the seven RCAF servicemen and two civilian observers who perished when the Lancaster crashed. Those who stood listening while the "Last Post" echoed out along the shores of the Lincoln Sea included representatives of the RCAF, the U.S. Navy, the Department of Mines and Resources, and the U.S. Weather Bureau.

Its proximity to the Soviet Union meant that it was only a matter of time before the JAWS at Alert would also be used for intercepting radio signals. In 1956, the RCAF then involved with the construction of the Distant Early Warning Line throughout the high Arctic, established a building uphill from the DOT's JAWS station to house "High Arctic Long Range Communications Research," or signals intelligence operations.

National Defence Imagery Library.

Graves at Alert for those who died in the crash of the RCAF Lancaster on July 31, 1950.

National Defence Imagery Library.

The family of Colonel C.J. Hubbard of the U.S. Weather Bureau requested that he be interred at Alert, in accordance with his final wishes.

—*—

Maurice Drew, who was there in 1960, never forgot some difficulties in breathing the air at Alert.

> When it got super cold, it was hard to breathe. How cold did it get? Well, any moisture in the atmosphere would freeze into large crystals that would scatter light from headlights and severely degrade normal vision. The air was so dry that when we were indoors our skin cracked and often bled. But that was only in winter. Summers were a bit more tolerable. When the wind blew in summer, the talcum-like dust got into every nook and cranny. We ate it, breathed it and washed our clothes in it. There was no escape.

The next year, the Alert Wireless Station was conceived as an intercept facility to be jointly staffed by personnel from the RCN and the RCAF. The first listening posts in the high Arctic, both Alert and Resolute, were in operation until September 1958, when Resolute was closed down and Alert became an official listening post with control transferred from the RCAF to the Royal Canadian Corps of Signals (RCCS). It was staffed with personnel from the three services until such time as RCCS could man it on their own. When they moved in, additional buildings were constructed — a mess, three barracks/accommodations buildings, a power house, and vehicle-maintenance building. The operations building housed the radio intercept and cryptographic equipment. Initially, 27 RCCS men were posted to Alert at any one time. They were the Chief Radio and Telegraph operator, 18 radio and telegraph operators, one radio equipment technician, and one teletype and cipher technician.

In 1957, Darryl Catton was a young man of 18 when he was told he was being sent far into the Canadian Arctic to build a military installation at a place called Alert. As a Royal Canadian Air Force construction

National Defence Imagery Library.

Igloo Gardens Musk Ox Steak. Good cooks who kept the men happy with their three "squares" a day were prized.

hand with two Construction and Maintenance Units in Calgary, he had never deployed anywhere, never mind the high Arctic. "I was one of the original members of a party of 28 who put up Alert in between 1956 and 1957," says Mr. Catton, who retired from the RCAF after eight years of service. "We were flown up to Thule, Greenland, from Edmonton to begin putting up buildings and improving the runway at Alert."

The job was arduous and the conditions rough — no radio, no TV, no alcohol, or entertainment. Just a really good cook. It took five weeks of continuous flying to get the men their construction materials flown in from Thule. Once they arrived, the men worked for months on end putting up prefab buildings and turning a makeshift runway into a permanent one.

National Defence Imagery Library.

Before political correctness: The yearnings of the "Frozen Chosen" at Alert.

"One of the most difficult tasks our team had was moving the bodies from the site of the Lancaster bomber crash," recalls Mr. Catton. "I wasn't personally involved but we were such a small group the men would sit around at night and talk about their various projects. That was a difficult one, exhuming the bodies and moving them to a more permanent location." Although the men thought they were there to expand the weather station that had been there since 1950, what they were actually doing was building a listening post to keep an eye on the Russians — after all it was the Cold War. "We had Russian aircraft flying over all the time," recalls Mr. Catton. "At the time there was an island called T-3 a few kilometres away occupied by the Russians — they were keeping tabs on us. We were told Alert was a weather station but we found out later it was actually a listening post. We wondered why one of the buildings was out of bounds. We started putting radios in there and sometimes we snuck in there and started twiddling the knobs to hear people from all over the world."

Although he was only in Alert for six months, the experience has stayed with him for most of his life. "What stands out for me is the peace and quietness of Alert. Once you walked away from the base, away from the sound and the noise of the diesel engines it was really serene — almost a religious experience — to think that maybe only a handful of people in 1957 had walked that land — I didn't really appreciate that until I got older. It was quite an experience and it's followed me through my whole life."[9]

The first Soviet atomic bomb was dropped on October 18, 1951, from a Tu-4 at an altitude of 10 kilometres, and detonated 400 metres above the ground. With the Berlin Airlift, the formation of NATO, and the Korean War at its height, the lines between Communism and the Free World were now clearly drawn. In 1952, the Massachusetts Institute of Technology's Lincoln Summer Study Group of scientists met in the Lincoln Laboratory where many of the principles of radar had been for-mulated. One of the group was J. Robert Oppenheimer, who had created the Manhattan Project and, typical of the Second World War scientists, they were used to dreaming on a large scale. To buy time in a surprise attack by Soviet bombers, they recommended the immediate building of radar sites across Alaska and the Canadian North, plus air and sea exten-sions of radar "pickets" over the Pacific and Atlantic oceans.

Of limited use in detecting Soviet "bogeys" ("Bear" bombers) and obso-lete once missile-carrying submarines, ICBMs, and cruise missiles were deployed, as Hadrian's Wall had once been for the Romans, the psycho-logical reassurance that the DEW Line gave to a generation of North Americans was worth the effort and expense. The stimulation to invest millions of dollars in the Canadian Arctic came from the stalemate of the Korean War and Secretary of State John Foster Dulles's "New Look" strategy of massive retaliation. Canadians were wary about incautious American actions (particularly in Korea), but as early as February 12, 1947, Mackenzie King and President Harry S. Truman had agreed to joint defence co-operation. With the exception of John Diefenbaker, postwar Canadian prime ministers understood that total sovereignty of Canada's North was (like politics) the art of the possible. Sandwiched between two nuclear powers, they accepted that Canada could not afford its own defensive strategy, but at the same time did not want to surrender complete sovereignty to Washington. For the Canadian military and particularly for RCAF Air Marshal Roy Slemon, chief of air staff in 1953, a joint Canada–United States air defence was inevitable.

"The United States of America, without prejudice to the sovereignty of Canada, shall have quiet enjoyment of the Leased Areas." In language that was more Wordsworth than legal, the Exchange of Notes in December 1952 gave the USAF a 20-year lease "free from the payment of all rent and charges" of RCAF facilities at Goose Bay, Labrador. Once the vital ferry link for Allied aircraft during the Second World War, Goose Bay continued to be of importance throughout the Cold War with the USAF stationing interceptor aircraft and helicopters to support DEW Line stations. Given its location and isolation, there was never any quibbling about Canadian sovereignty here. Strategic Air Command's bombers and tankers were deployed to the "leased RCAF areas" from other SAC bases and more than 12,000 USAF personnel and their families were living on site. On November 10, 1950, when a SAC bomber flying between Goose Bay and Davis-Monthan air base, Arizona, jettisoned three unarmed nuclear bombs over the St. Lawrence near Saint-André de Kamouraska, Quebec, the plutonium cores were fortunately in storage at Goose Bay.[10] The Doppler Melville radar station built nearby was operational in October 1954. In the late 1950s, the Royal Air Force also returned to Goose Bay, using it as a tactical flight training area for their Vulcan bombers.

In January 1953, the United States was given permission to construct two trial DEW Line sites on Herschel Island in PROJECT CORRODE. The following month, Minister of Defence Brooke Claxton discussed with the newly elected President Eisenhower the building of the DEW Line, but no decision was made. But the North had become a priority to

Aerial view of Ellesmere Island — as forbidding today as always.

Now almost forgotten, the Distant Early Warning (DEW) Line was one of the greatest engineering feats of the 20th century. The 58 radar sites built between 1955 and 1957 from Alaska to Greenland would change the Canadian North forever.

Refuelling aircraft at a DEW Line base. During the airlifts, the pilots shut down the port engines, but kept the starboard ones running. At -40 °C, the prop wash, even from the opposite side of the aircraft, was a tad chilly.

The farthest extension of Canada, CFS Alert is named after the vessel commanded by Captain George Nares of the British Arctic Expedition of 1875–76, the first ship to reach this shore.

Unloading C-119 at Resolute Bay: With the rear clamshell loading doors open, the aircrews did not hang around longer than they had to.

Canadian Coast Guard Ship Henry Larsen *in Strathcona Sound near Nanisivik, Nunavut Territory, during* OPERATION NANOOK.

Right: *Canadian Forces winter gear.*

Below: *Canadian Forces Alert. OPERATION NUNALIVUT 10 Sergeant First Class Jens Bonde, chief of training for the Danish military's Sirius Dog Sledge Patrol, and Captain Nathan Trescher, from 440 Squadron Yellowknife, unload a dog from a Canadian Forces Twin Otter.*

National Defence Imagery Library.

Photo by Corporal Shilo Adamson, Canadian Forces Combat Camera.

Iqaluit, Nunavut. Canadian Rangers take part in a military parade, August 25, 2008, in Pangnirtung, Nunavut, to mark the close of OPERATION NANOOK.

Iqaluit, Nunavut. Gunner Brittany Heatherington, a member of the Arctic Response Company Group deployed to OPERATION NANOOK 09 *in southeastern Baffin Island.*

A CC-138 Twin Otter from 440 Transport Squadron flies low over a Canadian Ranger patrol after dropping fuel and food at a forward cache location during OPERATION NUNALIVUT 2009.

Photo by Captain Cheryl Major, public affairs officer, RCSU Northern.

Her Majesty's Canadian Ship (HMCS) Montreal *(centre), Her Danish Majesty's Ship (HDMS)* Vaedderen *(foreground), and United States Navy ship (USS)* Porter *(background) in the Labrador Sea to participate in* OPERATION NANOOK.

Canadian Rangers from the 1st Canadian Ranger Patrol Group (1 CRPG) meet up with a 440 Squadron CC138 Twin Otter aircraft near Eureka, Ellesmere Island, Nunavut.

Iqaluit, Nunavut. After his arrival at the forward supply point for the Arctic Response Company Group, Prime Minister Harper greets the members of the Canadian Rangers, dedicated to the Canadian Arctic Sovereignty Operation, OPERATION NANOOK '09.

Washington, and speaking to the House of Commons on November 13, 1953, President Eisenhower emphasized the need for a common continental defence. By coincidence (although it had been planned for some time), three days later, the bill to create the Department of Northern Affairs and Natural Resources was introduced in the House. The government was at last accepting the existence of 40 percent of the country's land mass and its inhabitants.

On March 21, 1954, Claxton announced what was possibly the worst-kept secret in North America. A transcontinental chain of air defence radar stations was to be built north of the Arctic Circle. But, he reassured Canadians, the expense of building the Line was not Canada's problem, as the United States government had undertaken to pay for construction and maintenance, while employing Canadians to build and staff the stations on Canadian soil. In fact, work had already begun; the contracts had already been awarded when President Eisenhower had signed the enabling legislation on February 15. To tie in with an integrated continental air defence system based at Cheyenne Mountain, Colorado, the DEW Line had to be operational by July 1957.

This did nothing to satisfy the Progressive Conservative Opposition leader John Diefenbaker, who, in inimitable style, raised the questions in the House on March 25. "This is not the place for me to question what means of defence we have. I do not know. The House of Commons does not know. We do know that we are spending great sums of money on defence, but we do not know what these defences are.... I do not know whether we have an effective radar screen. I do not know whether we have effective interceptor aircraft."[11]

As in the Second World War, how much the Canadian government knew about the United States plans for the North is debatable. On April 12, Claxton explained that he could not give a list and did not note the locations of radar sites because "... it would enable a potential enemy to check the efficiency and effectiveness of its own sources of intelligence."[12] But he professed not to be comfortable "... with President Eisenhower's open determination to get the DEW Line built immediately if not sooner, but the Cabinet finally decided that the U.S. plan should be allowed to go ahead, as long as Canadians are guaranteed employment on the project."

What emerged was that the DEW Line was to have 12 sectors, from the Aleutian Islands, with its main station at Cold Bay, Alaska, then straddling the Davis Strait and on Baffin Island and its main station at Cape Dyer. Each sector had four types of sites: a main radar station with storage facilities, basic recreational amenities, and a mixed crew of civilians and Air Force personnel (the USAF in Alaska and Greenland and RCAF in Canada); one or two intermediate stations, each staffed by a chief, a technician, and a cook, two to five unmanned auxiliary sites, checked periodically by airlifted maintenance crews, and a "rearward" communications site to maintain contact with the south. In all, 58 DEW Line stations were to be built, including 30 in Canada from Cape Dyer in the east to Komakuk Beach, Yukon, in the west.

For such a mammoth undertaking, the two countries set up a military study group to work with industry. In 1953, the Bell System had tested Second World War–era radar technology in Alaska and when it concluded that this was feasible across the Arctic, the PJDB recommended to Ottawa and Washington that the DEW line be constructed. In December 1954, the Western Electric Corporation was given the contract for the American part of the DEW Line with the Foundation Company of Canada in Montreal and the Northern Construction Company in Vancouver subcontracted for the eastern and western Canadian sections. The rotating radar antennas needed special housing of their own to withstand a range of temperatures from minus 18 °C to plus 18 °C and wind velocities of up to 240 kilometres per hour. The architect Buckminster Fuller (who would use the same principles in the American pavilion at Expo 67), would design an unusual structure called the geodesic dome. Called a radome, its replaceable panels were made of fibreglass-reinforced plastic. The operational target date was two years from the signing of the contracts and scheduled for July 1957 to coincide with the joint signing of the NORAD (North American Air Defence) Agreement.

If the main DEW Line construction was completely paid for by the United States, the "backup" fence, the Mid Canada Line or McGill Line, was not. Begun on June 23, 1954, this was Claxton's face-saving compromise on sovereignty — the concept, construction, and funding of the Mid Canada Line was to be all-Canadian. The idea came from

Dr. W.B. Lewis of the AECL Chalk River Laboratories, Ontario, and Professor G.A. Woonton from McGill University. The latter had met with United States officials in Washington as early as 1951 to discuss the Doppler Effect to detect aircraft. In October 1953, the Defence Research Board supported the idea that a Doppler detection "radio fence" system along the 55th parallel would work and notified the RCAF. Because of the association with McGill University in its development, it became widely known as the "McGill Fence." The Mid Canada Line was to be a chain of eight manned and 90 unmanned radar sites along the 55th parallel from Hopedale, Labrador, to Dawson Creek, British Columbia. A 24-kilometre-wide strip along the 55th parallel was approved with the RCAF providing aerial photos and the army contour maps. The Cabinet gave its support in the summer of 1954 and siting engineers checked out the locations the following year so that material could be procured and marshalled for the construction.

To be effective, the manned and unmanned McGill Fence radar stations had to be sited at exact coordinates — whether in dense bush country, with its hundreds of lakes, or on the permafrost tundra or on the treacherous muskeg. As there were no airfields, roads, or railheads to get the construction equipment and supplies to the site, this is where a relatively new invention — the helicopter — came into its own. Industry had few such machines then, so to locate the radar sites and then service them, on June 1, 1954, the RCAF formed its first all-helicopter squadron — 108 Communications Flight at Bagotville, Quebec. Then it ordered Piasecki/Vertol H-21s, Sikorsky H-19/S-55s, and H-34/S-58s. Squadron Leader R.T. (Bob) Heaslip, the RCAF's most experienced helicopter pilot, was appointed 108 Squadron's commanding officer and his first job was to ferry the helicopters from their factories in Morton, Pennsylvania, and Bridgeport, Connecticut, to Bagotville. Later, H-12s from Search and Rescue units across Canada were also transferred to 108 Communications Flight. With few helicopter pilots, the RCAF opened its own school in Rivers, Manitoba, where it had a few well-used S-51 Dragonflies. As Okanagan Helicopters, British Columbia, had been using the more advanced S-55s on the Alcan construction project; the RCAF helicopter pilots received advanced training on H-19/S-55s from them. Here they also learned to how to operate in the mountains, haul nets, sling drums, and hook up cargo.

By June 1955, the helicopter units were operational and moved out of Bagotville to Knob Lake, Quebec, and later Baie-Comeau, Quebec, Cochrane, Ontario, and Grande Prairie, Alberta, transporting men to survey the sites. Many times, because of the terrain, the surveyors had to be lowered by the hoist from a hovering helicopter, as the muskeg wouldn't support the weight of the machine for a conventional landing. Vertol Aircraft (Canada) converted eight RCAF H-21s for use on the line. Nicknamed the "Flying Banana" because its shape-supported tandem rotors, the H-21 would later service DEW Line sites, but with a range of only 230 nautical miles, they required extensive refuelling and fuel caches had to be put in place by tractor trailers. By 1956, 108 Communications Flight had moved to Rockcliffe, Ontario, to begin hauling the towers and electronic equipment to the McGill Fence sites. Thanks to the use of helicopters and the ingenuity of their RCAF crew, the Mid Canada Line was operational by January 1958. For his contribution in using helicopters to build it, Squadron Leader R.T. Heaslip was awarded the McKee Trophy.

Earlier than both the DEW and the Mid Canada Line was the Pine Tree Line. In 1946, the PJBD had recommended that both Canada and the United States consider a warning system on approximately the 49th parallel that would shelter the American Midwest, the east coast, Ontario, and Quebec, and cost $450 million. Congress gave approval for funds and in January 1951, the PJBD presented "Recommendation 51/1 for the Extension of the Continental Radar Defence System." Canada was to pay one-third of the cost and personnel for the Pine Tree Line would be split between the USAF and the RCAF. Neither in the Canadian North nor high Arctic, the Pine Tree Line would be situated on the 53rd parallel in the west and along the 50th parallel in the east (to cover Toronto, Montreal, and Quebec) and connect to the DEW Line through Hopedale, Labrador. Pulse-based and easy to jam, it would have problems throughout its existence with civilian aircraft and was always of questionable value.

To build the DEW Line, an army of personnel had to be hired, trained, and transported to the North. For the huge quantities of equipment and supplies, more than 113,000 purchase orders were issued to

4,650 supplier companies in Canada and the United States. Purchase orders ranged from 9,000 tons of aluminum for 57 garages and 16 hangars, 2,000 tons of reinforced steel, and 28,500 tons of cement for foundations. Thirty quarter-million gallon tanks, 200 smaller tanks accounted for 2,900 tons of steel. Steel required for the building and erecting of 160 antenna towers ranging from 25 feet to 400 feet in height. For the construction and first year of operation 50 million gallons of gasoline and lubricating oils were needed — this did not include the aviation and automotive fuel that had also to be furnished. Completion on schedule depended how soon the materials could get there by sea and airlift. The former was planned for the shipping season in the summer of 1955 and the latter was to begin immediately.[13]

It was the largest commercial airlift operation in history, with 45,000 commercial flights in 32 months, delivering 120,300 tons over an average distance of 720 miles per flight. Involved were some 50 Canadian and 31 U.S. commercial airlines. The DEW Line construction was a heaven-sent boon for struggling freight airlines in Canada, which had been shut out from lucrative cross-Canada routes by the Trans-Canada Airlines monopoly. By transporting materials and personnel where there were few existing airstrips, radio, or navigational aids, the airlines remained solvent for another decade. For DEW Line sites in the east, Maritime Central Airways won the contract with Associated Airways in the country's centre and rather fittingly, Grant McConachie's Canadian Pacific Airlines did so in the west.

The airlift and sealift were supplemented by barge transport down the Mackenzie River as with the Canol pipeline 12 years before. Sometimes ice strips had to be located as much as 40 kilometres away from the sites, and completing the final delivery was by tractor train or "cat trains." The sites on Baffin Bay for example were 610 metres above sea level and roads had to be built up the steep, precipitous cliffs to them.

EXCHANGE OF NOTES (May 5, 1955) BETWEEN CANADA AND THE UNITED STATES OF AMERICA GOVERNING THE ESTABLISHMENT OF A DISTANT EARLY WARNING SYSTEM IN CANADIAN TERRITORY

The Canadian Ambassador to the United States of America to the Secretary of State of the United States of America.
CANADIAN EMBASSY
Washington, D.C., May 5, 1955.
No. 306

Sir,

I have the honour to refer to my Note No. 791 of November 16, 1954, regarding the joint establishment by Canada and the United States of America of a comprehensive warning and control system against air attack. My Note read in part as follows:

"The Canadian Government has now considered a proposal put forward through the Permanent Joint Board on Defence that the construction of the Distant Early Warning element of the over-all joint Canada-United States warning system should be the responsibility of the United States Government. The Canadian Government concurs in this proposal subject to the conclusion at an early date of an agreement as to the terms which shall govern the work. At the same time, however, the Canadian Government wishes to state its intention to participate in the project, the nature and extent of such participation to be determined in the near future."

I am instructed by my Government to inform you that its participation during the construction phase of the project will consist of giving assistance to the United States authorities in organizing and using Canadian resources, and to helping by making available the facilities of the armed forces and other agencies of the Canadian Government when appropriate. I am also instructed to state that the Canadian Government intends to participate effectively in the operation and maintenance phase of the project, the character of such participation to be determined on the basis of studies to be carried out during the construction phase.

My Government now proposes that the annexed conditions should govern the establishment by the United States of a distant early warning system in Canadian territory. If these conditions are acceptable to your Government, I suggest that this Note and your reply should constitute an agreement effective from the date of your reply.

Accept, Sir, the renewed assurances of my highest consideration.

[FROM:] A.D.P. HEENEY,
Ambassador
[TO:] The Honourable John Foster Dulles,
Secretary of State of the United States,
Washington, D.C.

Not wishing to repeat the carte blanche given to the United States in the Second World War, Ottawa took pains in the annex of the Exchange of Notes to ensure that Canadian sovereignty was protected. And it wasn't only that game laws would be obeyed, communications with the Natives regulated, or that all scientific data obtained in the construction was to be given over to Canada.

The key points in the annex were:

- Canada will acquire and retain title to all lands required for the system.
- Canada grants and assures the United States, without charge, such rights as access, use, and occupancy

as may be required for the construction, equipment and operation of the system.

- Airstrips at installations in the DEW System shall be used by the United States solely for the support of the System. If it should be desired at any time by the United States to use an airstrip for other purposes, requests should be forwarded through appropriate channels.

- There shall be no local disposal in the north of supplies or materials of any kind except with the concurrence of the Department of Northern Affairs and National Resources, or the Royal Canadian Mounted Police acting on its behalf.

Less known was the building of the Tactical Air Navigation (TACAN) sites across Canada by the United States. Because of their use in commercial aviation, on June 23, 1955, Ottawa permitted the United States to undertake surveys for TACAN facilities at St. Anthony, Cutthroat Island, and Saglek in Newfoundland; at Seven Islands in Quebec; at Cape Christian in the Northwest Territories; and at Port Hardy, Fort Nelson, and Sandspit in British Columbia. Operational by 1959, the TACAN sites revolutionized aviation in Canada, replacing the wartime single-beacon navigation systems and allowing for true "aerial highways" across the country.

When there were concerns as to the allocation of DEW Line contracts, on April 11, 1956, Prime Minister Louis St. Laurent placated Members in the House that Canadian laws would be applicable and enforced at all sites. When an explosive article in the May issue of *Maclean's* magazine called Canada "the world's most northerly banana republic" and that Canadians had sold their sovereignty in the North to the Americans for contracts, the Opposition seized on the issue. What was especially galling to media was the flying of the Stars and Stripes beside the Red Ensign at all sites and that the Americans demanded security clearances from visiting Canadian journalists. Opposition defence critic George Pearkes, VC, who had been associated with the embarrassing OPERATION GREENLIGHT in the Aleutians during the Second World War, questioned the wisdom of allowing the Americans to contract and man the line, ending his speech in the House with "… having some pride in our own sovereignty we would have preferred Canadians doing that work."[14] On June 22, Party leader John Diefenbaker weighed in by asking what the government was doing to "assure Canadian sovereignty" on the line. Somehow Diefenbaker saw air defence of the North American continent not so much as a bilateral issue, but tied into NATO's overall command structure.

Another threat to Canadian sovereignty in the North was FULLHOUSE. This was the code name for Strategic Air Command's "strike from the homeland" concept. As with all early jet aircraft, the B-47 and B-52 bombers had limited range and to get to targets deep in the Soviet Union, they required pre- and post-strike refuelling. To ensure this, USAF tanker aircraft were based in Lakenheath, United Kingdom; Thule, Greenland; and Argentia, Newfoundland (the facilities obtained through an arrangement with the British before 1949). In time of war, these bases would be unable to handle the traffic, but also become prime targets themselves. Slow-moving and heavy with fuel, the KC-97 tankers needed to be on station well in advance to rendezvous with the faster B-47 jet bombers. To do this, the USAF wanted 12 more bases — 11 in Canada and one at Sondrestrom, Greenland. At a top secret meeting of the Cabinet Defence Committee on June 13, 1956, those present feared that if refuelling facilities in Canada were granted, it would not be long before demands were made for bomber bases themselves. At the meeting, Prime Minister Louis St. Laurent, Secretary of State for External Affairs Lester Pearson, Chief of Staff General Charles Foulkes, and Chief of Air Staff Air Marshal Roy Slemon took comfort in the fact that no nuclear bombs could be removed from the United States without presidential approval, hence demands for the storing of nuclear weapons in Canada were unlikely. But all were also aware that refusing the request for tanker facilities would lead to considerable difficulties with the United States. Although SAC had not been assigned to NATO, its deterrent effect was the most important single element in the defences of that organization and one of Canada's roles in NATO was to support the strategic bombing effort of the United States.

The RCAF was well aware of FULLHOUSE and Air Vice-Marshal C.R. Dunlap, vice-chief of air staff, recommended that the Americans handle this with caution. Although the bases would require a minimum USAF maintenance crew to be stationed in Canada, Dunlap was aware that Ottawa would more than likely refuse the demand. He was partially correct — before even considering it, the Canadian government stalled by asking for complete details. After a survey conducted by the USAF, the number of sites were reduced to nine, to which the RCAF agreed was feasible and the matter was handed over to the Department of External Affairs to negotiate. Then the USAF reconsidered again — the faster Boeing KC-135 Stratotankers were becoming available and the number of bases was reduced to four: Churchill, Frobisher, and two in northern Alberta. Six KC-135 tankers were to be permanently deployed at each with an additional 20 to fly in an emergency. A relieved Canadian government agreed to this and the air refuelling facilities were inserted into the NORAD agreement of June 20, 1958. Sovereignty was not impinged upon, and in any case, the advent of the submarine-launched missiles soon made SAC's manned bombers less essential. In 1963, the USAF moved out of their air refuelling bases in the Canadian North. The exception was Goose Bay, where the USAF would not leave until 1976.

With so many Americans in the Arctic, the Canadian government worried that its sovereignty might be in question, especially in uninhabited regions. Prime Minister Louis St. Laurent delivered a major speech in the House in December 1953 that the government had administered the North "… in an almost continuing state of absence of mind." Dependant on family allowances and government relief (as the fox-fur market was disappearing) had made the Inuit lose their self-reliance and cluster in certain regions especially in northern Quebec, while others were uninhabited.

At a time when Canadians were outnumbered by American military personnel in the North and the Privy Council was being made aware of an increasing number of incidents that infringed on Canadian sovereignty, in 1952, the USAF prevented the CGS *C.D. Howe* from anchoring at Padloping Island and the USAF base at Thule instructed an RCAF Lancaster to cease aerial photography of the coast of Baffin Island — sovereignty was again an issue. Lester Pearson, the secretary of state for external affairs, urged the Cabinet to employ some means to preserve Canadian sovereignty over the vast wastelands of the Arctic. As the 1933 International Court of Justice case said, human activity was essential to sovereignty and relocating the Inuit from cramped conditions in northern Quebec to the high Arctic was a solution to the "Eskimo problem."

On July 25, 1953, seven Inuit families from Port Harrison, on the Ungava peninsula, embarked on the *C.D. Howe*. On August 28, the ship picked up families from Pont Inlet, Baffin Island, and the following day arrived at Craig Harbour, Ellesmere Island. Some families disembarked and others transferred to the CGS *d'Iberville* to go to Resolute Bay. The Inuit had no idea where they were or that they were going to be separated — or that relief benefits were to be abolished since they were expected to become self-reliant in the strange area. Not providing housing was consistent with the project's rehabilitation ideology. There was no way they could return home or even notify their relatives where they were until the 1970s, when commercial aviation arrived in the area.[15]

Conquering the Arctic to erect radar equipment for the DEW Line was accomplished by degrees. Not only was the terrain desolate, rugged and treacherous, as the first British sailors had discovered in 1830, it was also either in darkness from October to May (with pitch-blackness from December to February) or blinding sunlight in June and July. With the railheads hundreds of miles to the South and roads nonexistent, nothing could be sent overland, and like the construction of the Alaska Highway and staging routes, building the DEW Line took on the aspects and urgency of a military campaign much like D-Day. As with that operation, first, small parties probed and established "beachheads" before the major force landed. They were the mapping teams that travelled hundreds of kilometres and reviewed more than 80,000 aerial photos. Then, surveyors and site engineers were set down by ski planes, carrying only their shovels. They cleared enough snow so that C-47s could land with small bulldozers and fuel drums. With these, airstrips could be built for the four-engined DC-4s and North Stars. Periodically, strong winds negated the labour of many days when huge quantities of snow were blown over the cleared ice strip. The equipment brought in enabled the giant C-124 Globemasters and C-119s to arrive with the remainder of the material, which included the living quarters. Now the sealift could begin.

Here was a drama in two acts with a finale — each set a year apart to take advantage of the short shipping season. Two convoys of ships leaving from either side of the continent — from Seattle and Halifax — had to get in to the sites quickly or as near to them as possible, unload and get out fast to avoid being trapped for the long winter. Each convoy had a complement of 60 ships: tankers, tugs, Second World War Victory ships, repair vessels, and LSTs (Landing Ship Tanks). Icebreakers preceded both convoys to smash their way through ice into open water. Once the ships were on location, often U.S. Navy demolition experts had to plunge into the icy waters to place explosive charges on hidden reefs before the cargoes could be landed by LST or barge. Three ships were towed home when two lost rudders and propellers and one was "stoved in" by ice and its engine room flooded.

If the sites themselves were unimaginatively named like WAT-X, PIN-DA, BIR-X, or BAR-4, many of their locations were relevant to the history of the North. For example, Liverpool Bay had been so named in 1826 by two of Franklin's homesick midshipmen. The location of Gjoa Haven had always been known to the locals as the "Land of Fat" because of the plentiful blubbery game around but it was where Roald Amundsen wintered with his ship *Gjøa*. Martin Frobisher had landed at Resolution Island on July 28, 1576, while attempting to discover the Northwest Passage. Ten years later, Cape Mercy would be named by his friend John Davis before he returned home to fight the Spanish Armada. And Hall Beach was named by the unfortunate Charles Francis Hall before he went off to his death.[16]

When it was officially operation on July 31, 1957, there were 1,500 civilians employed on the line, most in Canada. While there were libraries, hobbies, and movies for the men, the topic of conversation (along with politics, religion, and women) was what would happen if the Russians really did send their bombers across. Those who manned the radar sites remember that all were aware that they were on the front line of the Cold War — and that they were also in the safest place to be — why would the enemy waste a bomb on a trailer with 15 men? The ultimate fear for them was that if the unthinkable happened, what sort of world would there be left to live in?

The incentive to work the line was exactly as it had been for Franklin's men: money. Civilians earned on the average $9,000 to $10,000 annually — close to what they would be making in urban Canada — except that full room and board, transportation, medical, and clothing allowances were taken care of — and there was nothing to spend it on. At that time, they were required to sign for an 18-month tour while Canadian military personnel were posted for a 12-month period, broken at the fourth and eighth month for a visit to the base at St. Hubert, Quebec and a one-week leave at home.

To build the DEW Line cost the United States (in 1957 dollars) about $400 million. Twelve aircraft crashed and at some sites, the wreckage remains there. Worse, when some of the DEW stations were deactivated, they would scar the North with rusted buildings, thousands of oil drums and soil contaminated with Polychlorinated biphenyls (PCB), hydrocarbons, and heavy metals. With environmental site inspections begun in 1989, the Canadian Forces Dew Line Clean-up (DLCU) Project is presently involved in the clean-up of chemically contaminated soils, the stabilization of existing landfill sites, and the demolition of surplus infrastructure. The human cost of building the DEW Line would be high, as well, with 30 men killed and many more injured.

But rivalling the completion of the Panama Canal in 1914 and putting a man on the moon by 1969, the building of all three radar chains was the greatest engineering and logistical feat of the 20th century. As with the Alaska Highway and Canol pipeline, which were also gestated at a time of crisis, when the United States moved to satellites to detect Soviet missiles, the line would be relegated to the collective memory with those other Cold War fixtures — air raid drills and bomb shelters. With the advent of cruise missiles, its 1950s technology became wholly ineffective. As U.S. Secretary of Defense James R. Schlesinger said: "Since we cannot defend our cities from strategic missiles, there is nothing to be gained from trying to defend them against a relatively small force of Soviet bombers."

Material Transported
By Aircraft: 140,400 tons
By Naval Convoy: 281,600 tons
By Cat Train: 17,600 tons
By Barge: 20,300 tons
TOTAL: 459,900 tons

Construction

Gravel produced was more than 9,600,000 cubic yards, enough to build two replicas of the Great Pyramid or a road 18 feet wide and one foot thick from Jacksonville, Florida to San Diego, California.

Airstrips in the Arctic covered 26,700,000 square feet, or 625 acres. 46,000 tons of steel were used — more than enough for the U.S. Navy aircraft carrier USS *Forrestal*. 1800 piles were sunk an average depth of 12 feet into permafrost. Generating capacity of power generation equipment installed is 155,000 kilowatts per day — enough to supply a city the size of Spokane, Washington.

Personnel

Over 1,600,000 people worked on products for the DEW Line. Three construction companies employed more than 20,000 people in two and one half years on direct work. Peak numbers actually inside the Arctic at any one time was about 7,500 men.

Miscellaneous

Shipped in 32 months was 22,000 tons of food in 1,000,000 containers; 12 acres of bed sheets; 6 acres of

rugs; 3 miles of window shades; 100,000 copies of 600
different manuals prepared to cover operation and
maintenance of the line.

The DEW Line became operational at almost the same time that
John Diefenbaker came to power and the new prime minister and his
minister of defence, George Pearkes, found themselves in the uncomfortable position of having to accept the NORAD agreement on May 12,
1958, thus allowing the American commander at its Colorado Springs
headquarters to order Canada into war. Handing over the country's
sovereignty so easily was something that Diefenbaker regretted in later
years. But with early Liberal opposition ineffective, the prime minister
called an election and campaigned on opening up the North.

The audience in the Winnipeg Civic Auditorium on February 12,
1958, were in for a treat — this was prime Diefenbaker:

> Sir John A. Macdonald gave his life to this party. He
> opened the West. He saw Canada from East to West. I
> see a new Canada — a Canada of the North. As far as
> the Arctic is concerned, how many of you here knew the
> pioneers in Western Canada. I saw the early days here.
> Here in Winnipeg in 1909, when the vast movement was
> taking place into the Western plains, they had imagina-
> tion. There is a new imagination now. The Arctic. We
> intend to carry out the legislative program of Arctic
> research, to develop Arctic routes, to develop those vast
> hidden resources the last few years have revealed.

Having spent part of his youth in the North, he promised "Roads to
Resources," a $75-million road-building program that was to open up
the North for mineral exploration.

The populist platform suited the times and he returned to Ottawa
on March 31, with (until then) the largest majority in Canadian history.
The former small-town Saskatchewan lawyer adulated President Dwight

Eisenhower, seeing him as another prairie boy made good. Without consulting Cabinet or Parliament, on the advice of Pearkes and the chairman of the chiefs of staff, General Charles Foulkes, the prime minister was quick to commit Canada to NORAD, which he somehow saw as part of a multilateral defence system like NATO rather than bilateral and controlled by the United States.

On October 8, 1958, Pearkes raised the "Canadianization of the DEW Line" in Cabinet. Aware of the prime minister's feelings, the ministers took the decision to replace USAF operators at the four main DEW Line stations with RCAF personnel.[17] The minister of national defence authorized the RCAF member on the PJBD to inform the board at its October meeting of the Canadian government's intentions. The prime minister announced in January 1959, that the RCAF would take over all operational (but not administrative) control of the DEW Line and the airfields. But for to defending the North — one of his campaign platforms — Diefenbaker discovered that he had no troops to spare. Pearson's Nobel Prize for peacekeeping ensured that whenever there was a crisis somewhere in the world, the Canadian public wanted their military patrolling it — whether it was the Suez Canal Zone, Lebanon, or the Congo. For if there was some glamour (and much boredom) in those war-torn regions, there was certainly none in the North.

The perceived insults that the prime minister felt from the charismatic, telegenic, young President John F. Kennedy did nothing to help. Nor did the intrigue by the Canadian military chiefs to undermine his refusal to accept nuclear weaponry — with Pearkes (on General Foulkes's recommendation) cancelling the iconic Avro Arrow and then being forced to accept second-hand American Voodoo interceptor aircraft in its place. Canada would pay for 66 Voodoos taken from National Guard stocks by completely taking over the Pine Tree Line in 1955. Now, Liberal rising star Lester Pearson could bring up the DEW Line issues of flying of the Stars and Stripes and security clearances in the House. The cordial relations between president and prime minister that characterized the Roosevelt and Eisenhower years were long gone and the media were quick to discern that Diefenbaker was equating sovereignty with anti-American (and anti-John F. Kennedy), especially when he famously accused Kennedy of stealing his "New Frontier" slogan. Unable to forgive the Americans for not buying the Canadair CL-44 and then the Avro Arrow (thus losing Tory support in Montreal and Malton) the prime minister's ego and self-destructive streak overwhelmed him at a critical period in the Cold War. If Canada complied with the United States in accepting nuclear armament to be based on Canadian soil, he warned that, "We will be their vassals forever." The sovereignty issue dogged Diefenbaker throughout his increasingly erratic prime ministership.

On August 1, 1960, the U.S. Navy sent a nuclear-powered submarine, the USS *Seadragon*, on its first voyage to the Arctic. Ordered to proceed through the Northwest Passage, she entered via the Lancaster Channel, going past Resolute, through the Viscount Melville Sound, and under the ice at McClure Strait to the Beaufort Sea. This occurred without the furor that the voyage of the SS *Manhattan* would cause nine years later, the voyage of the USS *Seadragon* attracted no criticism in the media or government. In fact, RCN Commodore Owen Connor Struan Robertson, the former commander of HMCS *Labrador*, would serve as the ice pilot for the submarine's voyage.[18] For an RCN officer to be onboard a U.S. Navy nuclear submarine was a unique honour, but Robertson's reputation as an ice pilot in both navies was legendary. He was then serving as the senior RCN officer in Washington and given the sovereignty sensitiveness, it made good sense to have him on the *Seadragon*.

What did follow from the naval activity in the North was the 1961 Brock Report, which mentioned for the first time a three-ocean Navy and submarine patrol of the Arctic. Under the aegis of Rear Admiral Jeffry Brock, it promised that the RCN was going to reassert Canadian Arctic sovereignty, on a "research and operational evaluation" basis.

Unknown to the public, the DEW Line was put on high alert on October 5, 1960, when radar returns from the new Ballistic Missile Early Warning System (BMEWS) indicated a massive Soviet missile launch. Air Marshal Slemon was deputy commander of NORAD that day, and with the U.S. Air Force commander away on an inspection tour, it would have been his decision to contact President Eisenhower and advise whether a retaliatory attack be launched. Unflappable as always, Slemon asked, "Where is Khrushchev?" When told that the Soviet premier was at the

United Nations in New York, the RCAF officer wisely held off contacting the political leaders. After the DEW site at Thule indicated nothing, it was later discovered that the Soviet missile "blips" were BMEWS signals bouncing off the moon. NORAD was stood down, and through Slemon, avoided what might have been a nuclear holocaust.

Alvin Hamilton, Diefenbaker's minister for northern affairs, ensured that the prime minister did not forget his campaign promise of implementing the "Roads to Resources" program — especially from Dawson City to Inuvik. Although much of the country it was to pass through was still unexplored and Public Works in Ottawa had little idea what the costs were, what would one day be the all-weather Dempster Highway to the Arctic Circle was begun as soon as the Conservatives returned to power. The Liberal Opposition criticized the need for such a project and the cost overruns, calling it the "Roads to Remorses" (the isolated construction workers had a better name — "Roads to Divorces") with Pearson saying it was needlessly being built "from igloo to igloo." When the Liberals returned to power, funding vanished and environmental issues were discovered that caused the road to peter out — it became the "Road to Nowhere." It would not be until August 18, 1979, that the Dempster Highway was completed with Erik Neilsen, the local Member of Parliament and Prime Minister Joe Clark's minister for public works, opening it. Diefenbaker was to have officiated at the opening, but had died shortly before. An empty chair marked his place on the dais.

In 1961, Diefenbaker was also the first Canadian prime minister to actually visit the North. Arriving by the RCAF *Northstar*, he would dedicate the town of Inuvik, Northwest Territories, officially inaugurating the birth of the community. Speaking at the same location on August 28, 2008, Prime Minister Stephen Harper announced that Canada's new northern flagship Polar class icebreaker would be named after Diefenbaker. "He was a man who saw Canada and Canadians not as they were," said Harper, "but as they could be — a country and a people destined to become one of the greatest nations on earth. But only, he realized, if we accepted the challenges and seized the opportunities presented by the North."

If there was ever justification for the effectiveness of the DEW Line, it was that the Soviets decided to put missiles in Cuba because the

American underbelly was unprotected. The Cuban Missile Crisis proved to be the acid test for Diefenbaker, the DEW Line — and Canadian sovereignty. Pushing crop insurance and debt reduction onto farmers in the west, Douglas Harkness was an unpopular minister of agriculture and with Pearkes's resignation, Diefenbaker moved him to the defence portfolio. In politics, as in comedy, timing is everything, and to be the minister of defence on the brink of a nuclear showdown was the wrong time for Harkness. With the missile-carrying Soviet ships approaching Cuba in this test of nuclear "chicken," Diefenbaker feared Canada was being "stampeded" by Kennedy, and he rashly proclaimed that the "Cuban business was no affair of Canada's." Along with Howard Green, his vociferous minister for external affairs, Diefenbaker managed to alienate Harkness, most of the Cabinet, the Department of External Affairs, the chiefs of staff, and the media. When he also offended the Americans by casting doubt on the fuzzy U-2 spy plane aerial photographs showing missile launchers in Cuba (he wanted a UN inspection tour of the sites), Diefenbaker's defence minister quietly complied with President Kennedy to order all Canadian Forces to DEFCON 3, the defense readiness position of high alert.

General McNaughton once said, "The acid test of sovereignty is control of the armed forces," and his political boss Mackenzie King had also once feared a revolt of his generals. Perhaps alone among Canadians then, Diefenbaker refused to accept the unpleasant and inevitable — that with the DEW Line and NORAD, Canada had been forced to compromise on its Northern sovereignty. In doing so, he forfeited the support of his own party, Bay Street, the press, the NATO allies, the immensely popular President Kennedy — and all Canadians. But as Mackenzie King could have told "The Chief," sovereignty comes at a price.

Whether manned or unmanned in whatever the latest upgrade, the DEW Line remains a permanent feature of the Canadian Arctic. But, as historian Desmond Morton would write, Canada's reward for participating in the DEW Line was belated American acceptance of its Arctic claims.[19] Rather than take away from it, the United States was forced to acknowledge Canadian sovereignty. Whatever its environmental and strategic shortcomings (and there are many), constructing and maintaining it all these years not only opened up the Arctic to transport and communications, but made Canadians accept their responsibilities to 40 percent of their country's land mass and two-thirds of its coastline. For Ottawa to have invested in the North as well as UN commitments and a NATO garrison and RCAF Air Division in France and Germany was an unprecedented deviation from its Euro-focused defence strategy, and perhaps the beginning of the "Canada First" Arctic sovereignty.

6
On Guard for Thee

After the Liberal election in April 1963, the military became less preoccupied with the North. About to be reorganized, unified, and "civilianized," that was understandable. If Prime Minister Diefenbaker's defence ministers had been divisive, they paled in comparison with Paul Hellyer, Lester Pearson's first defence minister. Basic training in the military is humiliating enough once, but in the closing days of the Second World War, when he switched from one service to another, poor Hellyer had endured it twice. Perhaps that was where the idea for the integration of the three branches of the armed forces came to him.

Claxton had begun the process, but Hellyer (who hoped by this to become Pearson's heir apparent) is remembered for ramming the legislation through with an aggressive "Damn the Torpedoes" attitude.[1] Influenced by the Glassco Commission on efficiency in the federal government, the minister established one integrated Canadian defence policy, one overall defence program, one Canadian Forces Headquarters (CFHQ), and one chief of the defence staff (CDS) with authority over the three service chiefs. While ending the last vestiges of Britishness, unification caused senior staff resignations — the most prominent of whom were Rear Admiral Bill Landymore (who had written off HMCS *Labrador*) and Rear Admiral Jeffry Brock, then the vice-chief of naval staff. Unification coincided with the peace movement of the 1960s, causing a diminishing of respect by the public for the institution itself. Then, having caused more casualties than a Panzer division, Hellyer would leave in 1967 to be minister of transport.

But worse was to come. Now called the Canadian Forces, proud regiments that had turned back the enemy at Vimy and the Gothic Line were demoralized and decimated by slashed budgets, bilingualism, gender equality, parliamentary meddling, and self-serving deputy ministers — all culminating in April 1968, with the election of Pierre Trudeau, a prime minister who had little appreciation for the military at all.

The government's indecision about the Forces' strategic role, especially during the Pearson years, led to what few assets it had in the North becoming "civilianized." When the Strategic Air Command (SAC) staging facility at Churchill closed in 1963, the Canadian Army and RCAF moved out a year later. The base was transferred to the Department of Transport with Associate Minister for Defence Lucien Cardin explaining that Churchill would always have an administrative garrison so that it could be used as an advanced staging base for Arctic operations. The year also saw the transfer of the Alaska Highway (still unpaved) to the Department of Public Works, which was already overwhelmed with the Dempster Highway — and the RCAF and the army leaving Whitehorse. The RCAF and SAC also left Frobisher Bay in 1964, turning it over to the Department of Transport.

The sole RCN icebreaker, HMCS *Labrador*, had been decommissioned and transferred in 1962 to the newly created Canadian Coast Guard (CCG). Historically part of the Department of Marine and Fisheries since 1867, the "orphan agency" would be moved to the Department of Transport when it was formed in 1936, remaining with them until 1995 when it became part of the Department of Fisheries and Oceans. But unlike its counterpart in the United States, the Canadian Coast Guard was an unarmed, civilian organization that would not have a legislated mandate for enforcement of maritime security. The enforcement of Canada's maritime sovereignty remained the responsibility of the Canadian Navy (now called the Canadian Forces Maritime Command), with the RCMP responsible for the enforcement of laws in Canada's territorial sea. Despite that, from 1962 onward, the symbols of Arctic sovereignty would be the Canadian Coast Guard's distinctive red-and-white ships and helicopters. In September 1964, Captain N.V. Clarke took the (now) CCGS *Labrador* up Kennedy Channel, between Ellesmere Island and Greenland passing Hans Island, to reach the most northerly position ever attained by any Canadian ship until then. But except for the periodic visits in the summer, the RCN would abandon the North to the RCAF. Besides Air Force personnel at Alert and on the DEW Line sites, little remained of the Canadian military except for the radio stations at Churchill, Whitehorse, Frobisher, and Inuvik. Then, in 1967, Churchill, Whitehorse, and Frobisher were shut down.

The Defence White Paper of 1964 ignored the North all together, diverging from continental defence for a flexible response to Third World scenarios. Nobel Prize–winner Lester Pearson repackaged the Canadian Forces into international policemen, committing scarce troops to Yemen, the India-Pakistan border, and Cyprus, where they remained for thirty years.[2]

Remembered as the "pinko prime minister," Pierre Trudeau was quick to use the military when he invoked the War Measures Act on October 16, 1970, during the FLQ Crisis. He also questioned Canada's role in NATO, never accepting that the historic obligation to the Alliance meant stationing 10,000 soldiers and nuclear-armed CF-104s to protect Europe. His defence minister, Donald Macdonald made the army in Canada responsible for internal security, assistance in natural disasters, and environmental protection — roles it was unaccustomed to at that time. In a realignment of priorities, Canada's last aircraft carrier, HMCS *Bonaventure*, was decommissioned, even as a permanent military command called Canadian Forces Northern Area (CFNA) was established in Yellowknife in 1970, with a view to treating the North as a single theatre of operations.

The air force temporarily returned to the North in large numbers in 1971, when, with aircraft from No.433 and No.434 Squadrons, it tested the new CF-5 fighter's winter-weather capabilities by conducting operations in Frobisher Bay and Whitehorse. But the exercise was less for defending Canadian sovereignty and more because the CF-5s were to reinforce NATO's Norwegian flank in the Canadian Air/Sea Transportable (CAST) battle group.

But contrary to Trudeau's "flower power" image, defence spending was a high 2 percent of the Gross Domestic Product (GDP) during his tenure — in contrast with fellow Liberal prime ministers Jean Chrétien and Paul Martin when by 2005, little more than 1 percent of GDP was spent. While persuaded by German Chancellor Helmut Schmidt to buy

National Defence Imagery Library.

Testing the CF-5 fighter's winter-weather capabilities.

Leopard tanks for Canadian Forces in Europe, Trudeau realized that to rely on meagre military resources to pursue Arctic sovereignty, especially with the United States and Soviet Union, was to court disaster. Instead, his government opted to use legal means and world opinion to do so.

The discovery of major oil deposits in 1968 at Prudhoe Bay, Alaska, made oil companies contemplate transporting oil in supertankers with icebreaking capabilities rather than a pipeline to Valdez. The largest American merchant vessel then, the tanker SS *Manhattan* (said to be equivalent in size to the Empire State Building lying on its side), owned by the Atlantic Richfield oil company, was refitted with an icebreaker bow. From the beginning, the oil company and the U.S. Coast Guard consulted with the Canadian government and in return for its cooperation, Ottawa was to receive valuable scientific data from the "project." Trudeau told the House of Commons on May 15, 1969, that his government welcomed the *Manhattan* "project" and that the legal status of Canada's Arctic waters "was not an issue." On August 15 — by happenstance the date that President Teddy Roosevelt opened the Panama Canal in 1914 — the tanker left Chester, Pennsylvania, to navigate through the

Baffin Sea and Viscount Melville Sound to Prudhoe Bay, where it was to take on crude oil and return. Flying the Canadian flag as protocol demanded, and with a Department of Transport representative on board, the SS *Manhattan* was continuously (and symbolically) escorted by the icebreaker CCGS *John A. Macdonald*, which helped to get it through the ice. The Coast Guard's only heavy icebreaker, the CCGS *Louis St. Laurent* had just been commissioned and was too late to enter the fray.

When blocked by ice at McClure Strait (where in 1853, Robert McClure himself had been forced to abandon HMS *Investigator* for the same reason), the *Manhattan*'s captain turned onto a southerly route, going through the narrow Prince of Wales Strait and sailing south of Banks Island.[3] A token barrel of crude oil was loaded at Prudhoe Bay and

National Defence Imagery Library.

Tanker SS Manhattan.

then the ship returned, arriving in New York Harbour on November 14. It had been a successful venture and plans were made by the Humble Oil Company to repeat the voyage in 1970.

The voyage of the SS *Manhattan* made Canadians conscious of their North — but more of its fragility than sovereignty — like nothing else had done before or has since. The wreck of the supertanker SS *Torrey Canyon* off the Cornwall coast in Britain two years before had been the first such environmental disaster and Canadians feared that if tankers were allowed to navigate the Northwest Passage, a massive oil spill in the fragile ecosystem of the Arctic was a certainty.

Prime Minister Trudeau knew the Arctic better than his predecessors — in 1968 he had camped on Ellesemere Island, fished for Arctic char, and attended church in Fort Chimo. Wearing fur regalia that guaranteed front-page publicity, he would also open the Arctic Winter Games on March 9, 1970.

The Nixon administration held that Canada had no legal basis for an assertion of sovereignty over the Arctic Archipelago waters. On Trudeau's instructions, the Canadian ambassador to Washington, Marcel Cadieux; Alan Beesley, legal adviser to the minister of external affairs; and Ivan Head of the prime minister's staff, called on the State Department on March 12 to discuss Canada's position relating to the Canadian Arctic Archipelago. The ambassador stated that no Canadian government could take a position inconsistent with Canadian sovereignty over the waters of the Canadian Archipelago.

"During the discussion," Executive Secretary Theodore L. Eliot, Jr. would write to Henry Kissinger, the president's assistant for national security affairs, "it became clear that the Canadians were not interested in having our comments, suggestions, modifications, or alternatives."[4] In 1965, the Pearson government had extended the traditional three-mile territorial sea with a nine-mile exclusive fishing zone — but this was mainly for the east and west coasts. Cadieux now informed Eliot that his government was considering drawing straight baselines around the outer perimeter of the Arctic islands that would assert Canadian sovereignty over large areas of the high seas and would (at least in the Canadian view) constitute the whole area as internal waters.

The Americans were also told that the prime minister talked about an international regime of the Arctic (a concept which the United States endorsed in principle, but feared in practice), saying that unless this regime were to come into being "immediately" and meet all of the Canadian requirements, Canada would have to act unilaterally since it was faced with "imminent irreparable damage." Legislation on a 100-mile pollution zone, Cadieux said, was to be introduced in Parliament within the next two weeks.

Eliot's appraisal of the meeting to Kissinger was that the consequences of the intended Canadian action were serious — and not only for private American interests. "They are critical for national security interests and seriously degrade the entire United States law of the sea posture on which military mobility depends." From the standpoint of the United States, which had focused on keeping the world's straits and channels open for its navy since the Cold War, Canada's claim threatened to create an unwanted legal precedent elsewhere in the world, for example in the Straits of Malacca or Hormuz. If the Northwest Passage was considered an international strait, submarines would not have to surface and alert Canada as to their presence, and military aircraft would have the right to use the airspace above.

On June 17, Parliament approved the Arctic Waters Pollution Prevention Act, declaring a 100-mile control zone around the islands north of 60 and banning the discharge of waste. For the first time in history, the special nature of the Arctic region was legally recognized, as was its need of protection, especially in relation to recent developments to the exploitation of its natural resources. Canada was to impose civil liability against ship owners for the illegal deposit of waste from ships in Arctic waters. In response, a United States Foreign Relations document stated, "We cannot accept the assertion of a Canadian claim that the Arctic waters are internal waters of Canada … Such acceptance would jeopardize the freedom of navigation essential for United States naval activities worldwide."

Almost 40 years later, the federal government would introduce new legislation to enlarge its sovereignty. On December 4, 2008, a bill amended the 1970s Arctic Waters Pollution Prevention Act, changing the definition of "Arctic waters" from 100 nautical miles to 200 nautical miles. Under the UN Law of the Sea, a country's "exclusive economic zone" extends 200 nautical miles offshore. This would bring the new enforcement zone in line with the United Nations treaty under which Arctic nations like Canada could negotiate their territorial boundaries.

And it wasn't only the Arctic waters that were in danger of pollution. Nothing revealed the region's environmental fragility more than when a Soviet attempt to launch a COSMOS 954 satellite into orbit failed. On January 24, 1978, debris from the nuclear-powered surveillance satellite scattered a large amount of radioactivity over a 124,000-square-kilometre area in Canada's North, stretching southward from Great Slave Lake into northern Alberta and Saskatchewan. Dubbed OPERATION MORNING LIGHT, the clean-up operation was a coordinated event between the United States and Canada. Using special radiation sensors, Canadian and American teams flew over the contaminated area, trying to detect parts of the satellite's power source, which had 110 pounds of enriched uranium, on the ground's surface. By October, when the search was called off, it was estimated that about 0.1 percent had been recovered. If anything positive could be said about the crash, it (and the Three Mile Island accident a year later) led to the development of the Federal Nuclear Emergency Plan.

"Trudeau made the North part of Canada's idea of itself," Jeremy Kinsman, the Canadian high commissioner to London (and former speechwriter for the prime minister), would write in a paper he presented at a colloquium on Pierre Elliott Trudeau at Southampton Institute in December 2001. "His initiative to assert Canadian sovereignty in the Arctic for the purposes of environmental protection was a precursor to the drafting of a new Law of the Sea convention…. If the Trudeau administration did nothing else that was new in foreign policy, this concrete and very real contribution to international law and to Canadian sovereignty would stand as a fine monument."

In the eulogy to his father, Justin Trudeau recalled:

I was about six years old when I went on my first official trip. I was going with my father and my grandpa Sinclair up to the North Pole. It was a very glamorous destination. But the best thing about it is that I was going to be spending lots of time with my dad because in Ottawa he just worked so hard.

One day, we were in Alert, Canada's northernmost point, a scientific military installation that seemed to consist entirely of low shed-like buildings and warehouses. Let's be honest. I was six. There were no brothers around to play with and I was getting a little bored because Dad still somehow had a lot of work to do. I remember a frozen, windswept Arctic afternoon when I was bundled up into a Jeep and hustled out on a special top-secret mission. I figured I was finally going to be let in on the reason of this high-security Arctic base.

I was exactly right. We drove slowly through and past the buildings, all of them very grey and windy. We rounded a corner and came upon a red one. We stopped. I got out of the Jeep and started to crunch across towards the front door. I was told, no, to the window. So I clambered over the snowbank, was boosted up to the window, rubbed my sleeve against the frosty glass to see inside and as my eyes adjusted to the gloom, I saw a figure, hunched over one of many worktables that seemed very cluttered. He was wearing a red suit with that furry white trim. And that's when I understood just how powerful and wonderful my father was.

With Soviet submarines lurking under the polar ice to escape U.S. satellite detection, the United States viewed passage through the Arctic waters from a security point of view while Canada saw it from a national sovereignty perspective. In northern deployments (NORPLOYS), the Canadian Navy had been sending a few surface vessels annually to the eastern Arctic since 1971 (e.g., HMCS *Preserver* visiting Chesterfield

Inlet in 1974, HMCS *Ottawa* going to Coral Harbour in 1977), and in NORPLOY 1986, two ships went to the Barrow Strait. But as usual with ice preventing further patrols, they remained on station for barely two months. Nothing had changed in the 40 years since HMCS *Magnificent* had entered Hudson Bay. As far as its third ocean was concerned, Canada still had a summertime navy. Franklin and Larsen understood the problem, that despite the technological advancements in marine transport, ice reigned supreme in the Arctic, on the surface at least.

In 1985, the USCGS *Polar Sea* left Thule to navigate the Northwest Passage to the Beaufort Sea. Washington had asked that Canadian officials accompany the icebreaker and promised it would abide by the Arctic Waters Pollution Prevention Act. But it rejected Ottawa's demand of formal permission to go through the Northwest Passage (a request for permission would have been interpreted as American recognition that the passage represents Canadian internal waters). Although it wasn't asked, Prime Minister Brian Mulroney granted that "permission" for the voyage, saying that denial of Canada's Arctic sovereignty was "an unfriendly act." His government promised to increase Canada's military presence in the Arctic and acquire an icebreaker for year-round use for Canadian naval vessels.

In the Commons, Secretary of State for External Affairs Joe Clark confirmed the obvious: "When we looked for ways to defend that sovereignty, we found that the Canadian cupboard was bare." To which the Liberal member Jean Chrétien succinctly replied: "Now that the horses are gone, they come and try to close the gate."

In a finely crafted speech on the subject, Clark would state:

> Canada is an Arctic nation. The international community has long since recognized that the Arctic mainland and islands are part of Canada like any other, but the Arctic is not only part of Canada, it is part of Canadian greatness ... Canada's sovereignty in the Arctic is indivisible. It embraces land, sea and air. It extends without interruption to the seaward facing coasts of the Arctic islands. These islands are joined, and not divided, by the waters between them .... The policy of the Government

is to maintain the natural unity of the Canadian Arctic archipelago and to preserve Canada's sovereignty over land, sea, and ice undiminished and undivided.[5]

When Prime Minister Brian Mulroney made Erik Nielsen defence minister in February 1985, the Canadian Forces must have hoped for better days, especially in the North. A wartime bomber pilot, when a Member of Parliament for the Yukon in 1963, Neilsen had protested the army giving up its base in Whitehorse and leaving the Alaska Highway. In the brief span that he was defence minister, at the "Shamrock Summit" at Quebec City on March 18, he would sign the Memorandum of Understanding on the Modernization of the North American Air Defense System. At a total cost of $7 billion, the North Warning System (NWS) of 13 Long Range Radar (LRR) and 39 Short Range Radar (SRR) stations (with 36 in Canada) as "gap fillers" was to be deployed across northern Alaska, northern Canada, and down the Labrador coast. Canada was to pay 40 percent of the total $1.3 billion and manage the system. Funded entirely by the United States was the $2.3 billion Over-the-Horizon radar to extend air and sea coverage over the Atlantic and Pacific approaches. Airborne radar coverage across North America would be provided by USAF Airborne Warning and Control System (AWACS) aircraft, which would have partial Canadian crews. Now there were to be permanent Forward Operating Locations (FOLs) for CF-18 fighter aircraft and Dispersed Operating Bases (DOBs) for the AWACS aircraft constructed at existing airfields in the Arctic.

Nothing demonstrated defending Canada's Arctic sovereignty better than an "intercept" of a Soviet "Bear" bomber. In 1985, Chris Hadfield was a 25-year-old CF-18 pilot flying out of CFB Bagotville, Quebec, in defence of Canada's North under NORAD. He would perform the first intercept of Soviet "Bear" bombers off the coast of Labrador — a feat that the future astronaut repeated seven more times. Remembering the "intercepts," Hadfield would later say: "I think it was important — not that they were going to launch their missiles and not that we were going to do anything hostile, but to demonstrate the ability to defend ourselves, to demonstrate that we know what is going on within our borders."

Henry Perrin Beatty had begun his political career in 1975 as the Conservative critic for sovereignty. On October 17, 1986, the young defence minister warned his Toronto audience that Canadian sovereignty in the Arctic "... cannot be complete if we remain dependent on allies for knowledge of possible hostile activities in our waters, under our ice." In particular, he said, "...we need to consider how to ... maintain surveillance under the Arctic ice. The three conventionally-powered submarines we have today cannot do the job. The Soviets and the Americans have nuclear-powered submarines which can cope with Arctic conditions, but we do not and must consider how best to deal with this problem." The first White Paper on Defence in 16 years: "Challenge and Commitment: A Defence Policy for Canada" appeared in 1987. Estimating that the military's equipment was going to "rust out" very soon, it promised a 2 percent defence spending increase over the next 15 years and the beginnings of a "Canada First" commitment. The Norway CAST reinforcement was cancelled and to make it a three-ocean navy, the Maritime Forces were to get six anti-submarine frigates and 10–12 nuclear-powered submarines, this last to cost an estimated $5–8 billion in total.

In 1965, the Pearson government had considered buying a few American Skipjack class nuclear submarines for patrolling under the Arctic ice cap. Beatty's nuclear submarines would traverse the Northwest Passage in a fortnight, allowing for rapid reinforcement between the oceans — and also deterring the Soviet submarines that were regularly within Canadian Arctic waters. But designing a conventional submarine from the keel up was beyond Canadian capability, let alone one with nuclear propulsion. The British and French were eager for Canada to build their own nuclear submarine forces under licence but the French Rubis-class submarines were outdated. And as much as the British would have liked Canada to licence-build their Trafalgar-class submarines, because their nuclear reactors were based on a Westinghouse design, the transfer of technology would involve a renegotiation of the 1959 bilateral treaty between the United States and Canada on the Cooperation for Mutual Defense Purposes.

The simplest solution would have been to lease or buy "off the shelf" U.S. Navy nuclear submarines. But having continually challenged

Canada's claim to the territorial waters of the Arctic Archipelago, the U.S. Navy was not about to co-operate. Besides, both superpowers were loath to transfer nuclear submarine technology, even to their most trusted allies. While the fear of nuclear accidents was bad enough, when the Soviets gave India a Charlie-class submarine, the Chinese immediately threatened to do the same for Pakistan. Considering that Canada had cut back its NATO commitments, the Americans were concerned that Beatty and the DND did not fully appreciate what the financial burden of running a nuclear submarine fleet would be. Besides, coping with Soviet submarines under the ice was dangerous enough for the U.S. Navy without neophyte Canadians getting involved.

On the diplomatic front, Washington's new ambassador to Canada, Tom Niles, publicly promised that there would be no more *Polar Sea* incidents. Through negotiations led by Derek Burney, Mulroney's chief of staff on January 11, 1988, Canada and the United States came together to sign the "Arctic Cooperation Agreement" in which: "The Government of the United States pledges that all navigation by U.S. icebreakers within waters claimed by Canada to be internal will be undertaken with the consent of the Government of Canada." While the Canadian ambassador to Washington, Allan Gotlieb, said it "significantly enhanced" Canadian sovereignty, the agreement did not alter either country's legal position vis-à-vis the Arctic waters.

But the U.S. Navy's intransigence reckoned without President Reagan's close friendship with Prime Ministers Mulroney and Margaret Thatcher.[6] It took a visit to the White House for Mulroney — when the president said, "What this continent needs is another Irishman" — and a personal letter from 10 Downing Street to ensure that in April 1988, over the objections of his naval advisors, Reagan agreed to the transfer of highly classified nuclear technology to Canada.

Then followed long months of negotiations between the United States and Canada as the former attempted to "educate" the latter on the industrial infrastructure that it would have to acquire to maintain its own nuclear submarine fleet before such technology could be given. Besides the costs being prohibitive, there were many Canadians who questioned the use of submarines in demonstrating Arctic sovereignty

— they couldn't "show the flag" underwater. Although Mulroney reduced the number to five or six submarines, by February 1989, 71 percent of Canadians polled opposed the underwater option. On April 27, the Canadian government, chastened and not a little relieved, dropped the idea of nuclear submarines protecting the Arctic.

The history of the Versatile Pacific Shipyards in Vancouver can be traced to the old Burrard Dry Dock where the *St. Roch* had been built in 1928. In March 1987, over the Quebec shipyards that had competed, the British Columbia yard was awarded the contract to build the world's largest icebreaker for the Canadian Coast Guard, receiving a Letter of Intent to do so from Transport Minister John Crosbie. At $320 million, the *Polar 8* was to be a 100,000-horsepower behemoth (and was originally was to have been nuclear-powered) that demonstrated to the world that the Canadian cupboard was no longer bare. Able to smash through 12-metre-thick ice, the Canadian icebreaker would outclass the USCGS *Polar Sea* and anything the Soviet Union had. It would perform surface and underwater surveillance, transport troops, monitor Soviet communications, support scientific survey, and with its unlimited ocean-going capabilities, could even be deployed to Antarctica.

Unfortunately, like the Avro Arrow, the *Polar 8* was an easy target for its detractors. Costs rose with the expectations — from $320 million to $700 million and the Liberals took to calling the icebreaker "the billion dollar flag."[7] Although his government faced a massive budget deficit and Mulroney was fighting an election, even up to May 1989, the prime minister bravely offered his personal assurance that the super icebreaker would be built, calling it "a very important instrument for the assertion of sovereignty in northern Canada." More far-sightedly, during a visit to Leningrad in November, he would become interested in Soviet President Mikhail Gorbachev's "perestroika proposal" for the Arctic states to end militarism and set aside their differences. Taking his cue, Mulroney would propose that a council of Arctic countries come into existence to coordinate and promote co-operation among them.

The first sign that the *Polar 8* was going down and taking its captain with it came in January 1990, when Beatty was moved to the Department of Health. In February, Finance Minister Michael Wilson took the axe to the icebreaker, which had never left the blueprint stage. He also closed seven military bases and reduced operations in others.

The Gulf War that August, the end of the Soviet Union soon after, the Bosnian conflict, and the confusion of Somalia after that — all of these events pushed the Arctic off the television screen and Commons agenda for the government, the Canadian Forces, and the public. The lack of focus on northern activities for the Canadian Forces from 1991 to 2001 was a result of events happening elsewhere in the world and their resources being drawn in other directions. Then there were environmental issues. In 1991, HMCS *Preserver*, following her deployment to the Persian Gulf, was tasked to undertake a NORPLOY. However, because she had a single hull, such a voyage would contravene Canadian environmental legislation such as the Arctic Waters Pollution Prevention Act and the Arctic Shipping Pollution Prevention Regulations.

When the Canadian Forces in the Arctic did make the news, it was under tragic circumstances. On October 30, 1991, an AIRCOM CC-130 Hercules transport aircraft flying from Edmonton, via Thule, was on final approach to the Alert airstrip. The pilot apparently was flying by Visual Flight Rules instead of Instrument Flight Rules. The aircraft crashed two miles short of the runway, killing five of the 18 passengers and crew. Rescue efforts by personnel from CFS Alert, USAF personnel from Thule, and CF personnel from bases in southern Canada, were hampered by a blizzard and local terrain. The crash investigation recommended all CC-130s be retrofitted with ground-proximity detectors.

Prime Minister Mulroney's legacy to the North would be the signing of the Nunavut Land Claims Agreement Act (NLCA) in Iqaluit on May 25, 1993. Marking the end of 30 years of negotiation by the Inuit to settle land claims, it addressed their rights to sovereignty over 2 million square kilometres of land and adjacent marine areas, about 20 percent Canada's land mass. This was especially important to Canadian sovereignty, a fact reflected in Article 15 of the Land Claims Agreement, which states that: "Canada's sovereignty over the waters of the Arctic archipelago is supported by Inuit use and occupancy."

The bills to ratify the NLCA and to create Nunavut received royal assent on June 10, 1993, by which time Brian Mulroney had handed over leadership to Kim Campbell. Parliament passed the NLCA and the Nunavut Act on July 9, granting the Inuit of the eastern Arctic their own territory and self government. Nunavut officially came into being on April 1, 1999, carving out a new jurisdiction from part of the Northwest Territories. These two major initiatives transformed the future of northern Canada. At last the Inuit had made the "outside world" understand that before the Europeans, they had Aboriginal title and sovereignty "… of the lands, waters and land-fast ice therein in accordance with their own customs and usages."[8] It was in effect a bilateral treaty between two nations, one of whom, despite decades of mistreatment by the other, was allowing them use of their ancestral lands.

Although incoming Prime Minister Jean Chrétien had been minister of Indian and northern affairs from 1968 to 1974, besides ridiculing the Conservatives' *Polar 8*, Beatty's submarines, and cancelling new Search and Rescue helicopters, some of which would have been used in the Arctic, his northern visions were modest. There would be little concern for Arctic security during the 1990s, the Liberals opting to protect it through cheaper, multilateral institutions, the most important of which was the Arctic Council. Formally established on September 19, 1996, by the "Ottawa Declaration," the Arctic Council, made up of Canada, Denmark/Greenland/Faroe Islands, Finland, Iceland, Norway, Sweden, the Russian Federation, and the United States was a forum for providing co-operation, coordination, and interaction among the Arctic states. But the council was prohibited from addressing security-related issues — the clause inserted at the insistence of the Americans, who did not want an international organization limiting their freedom of action in the region. Nor were any of the other states convinced that that the Northwest Passage was a sovereign Canadian waterway.

Chrétien's Foreign Affairs Minister Lloyd Axworthy met with Nunavut Premier Paul Okalik, Yukon Deputy House Leader Scott Kent, and Inuit, Gwich'in, Métis, and Yukon First Nation leaders on June 9, 2000, to unveil the Liberal's "Northern Dimension" of Canada's foreign policy. It outlined his government's foreign policy objectives, focusing on promoting Aboriginal peoples' participation in the Arctic Council, helping to establish a University of the Arctic and a Canadian and circumpolar policy research network, developing opportunities to assist Russia in addressing its northern challenges, and promoting the means for circumpolar countries to develop trade across the Arctic circumpolar region.

The Arctic Security Interdepartmental Working Group became one of the most important instruments available to Ottawa to coordinate domestic Arctic security policy. A biannual forum at which federal and territorial government officials could discuss and coordinate activities, the first meeting was held at Yellowknife in May 1999, and attended by the Canadian Forces, the RCMP, Coast Guard, Revenue Canada, Citizenship and Immigration, the Canadian Security Intelligence Service (CSIS), Foreign Affairs, and International Trade. In his opening comments, Colonel Pierre Leblanc, then the commander of the Canadian Forces Northern Area (CFNA), explained his rationale for hosting this symposium: "The North is a vast and beautiful part of our country. It contains enormous natural resources, but it is also a very fragile ecosystem. It behooves all of us to look after it properly. Ultimately that is the aim of this symposium: to provide a better coverage of northern Canada from a security point of view."

Responsibility for Canadian Forces' routine operations in Canada and its approaches was traditionally delegated to the three services: the navy, army, and air force. Given its practical regional structures, the army was granted the lead for most contingency operations within Canada and was the main regional point of contact for civil authorities. A small operations cell within National Defence Headquarters provided overall coordination and some longer-term planning. But the events of September 11, 2001, changed that. The threat of the nuclear holocaust posed by the former Soviet Union and the Warsaw Pact had been replaced by terrorism, drug smuggling, and pollution.

—*—

Instead of invasion by a foreign power as in the Cold War, the NARWHAL series begun in July/August 2002, which were Arctic exercises by the Canadian Forces aimed at supporting other government departments in their area of responsibility. The simulated threats were sabotage to oil production or a commercial airliner disaster in the far North. In August 2002, HMCS *Goose Bay* and HMCS *Summerside* conducted a NORPLOY visiting Killiniq and Iqaluit, supporting rangers from the First Canadian Ranger Patrol Group (1 CRPG) with a patrol to Resolution Island at the southern approach to Frobisher Bay. But Canada's contribution to the war on terrorism had depleted its availability for sovereignty patrols in the North. OPERATION APOLLO, the subsequent naval deployments to the Middle East, caused the deployment of 14 of 17 Canadian warships and 96 percent of naval personnel in seagoing billets. There were few ships to send North without taking away from other operations.

In August 2004, held in the Cumberland Peninsula area of Baffin Island, Nunavut, EXERCISE NARWHAL 04 involved locating a downed simulated foreign satellite that had crashed on Canadian territory. More than 600 sailors, soldiers, and airmen, and air women from the following military organizations took part: Canadian Forces Northern Area (CFNA) Headquarters, 427 Tactical Helicopter Squadron, 440 Transport Squadron, G Company, 2nd Battalion, the Canadian Ranger Patrol Group, the Royal Canadian Regiment, Canadian Forces Experimentation Centre (CFEC), the Directorate of Space Development, and the CCGS *Henry Larsen*. The Maritime Coastal Defence Vessel (MCDV) HMCS *Goose Bay* was one of the class especially designed for coastal surveillance, sovereignty patrol, and working with other government departments. It rendezvoused with the frigate HMCS *Montreal* and together they crossed the Arctic Circle. It was the first time that an MCDV had crossed the Arctic Circle, and the first time in 15 years that a major warship had crossed the line in Canadian waters.

"I don't know how you can say you're a Canadian unless you have a deep love for the North," Prime Minister Paul Martin told the media on December 14, 2004. Meeting with First Ministers Joseph Handley (Northwest Territories), Dennis Fentie (Yukon), and Paul Okalik (Nunavut), his government was to release a framework for the first-ever jointly developed Northern strategy to put $120 million into the infrastructure of the region. As prime ministers are wont to do in the summer, Martin posed in the familiar prime ministerial photo op: by the snow-peaked Baffin Island Mountains with a giant iceberg in the bay. On that trip, he told the locals assembled in the Pond Inlet school gymnasium: "One of the responsibilities of government is to protect the sovereignty of the land." This must have amused the Inuit audience who had been protecting their land (and sea ice) for generations.

The outspoken General Rick Hillier was appointed as chief of defence staff in February 2005. After the Chrétien deficit-cutting years, Hillier breathed new life into the Forces, updating its command structure more amiably than Hellyer had 40 years before. With the minister's endorsement, the general announced the creation of Canada Command (CANCOM), Canada Expeditionary Command (CEFCOM), and Canada Special Operations Forces Command (CANSOFCOM). Unlike Hellyer, he did not require amendments to the National Defence Act to do so — or approval of Parliament. The 2005 Defence Policy Statement (DPS) directed that: "The Canadian Forces will continue to perform three broad roles: protecting Canadians, defending North America in cooperation with the United States, and contributing to international peace and security."

In May 2005, Vice-Admiral Bruce MacLean and his staff released "Securing Canada's Ocean Frontiers: Charting the Course from Leadmark." It outlined the naval vision until 2025, calling for integration with other government departments through the Marine Security Operations Centres (MSOC), increased surveillance capabilities and presence in Canadian waters, including the Arctic, and the development of littoral capabilities, including support for joint operations ashore.

Conducting that surveillance and Northern presence was one of the primary objectives of OPERATION HUDSON SENTINEL held that August. A joint sovereignty operation in Hudson Bay, it involved the deployment of navy, army, and air force personnel and members of "V" Division RCMP and the CCGS *Radisson*. Two MCDVs, HMCS *Glace Bay* and HMCS *Shawinigan*, circumnavigated Hudson Bay and the frigate HMCS *Fredericton* was engaged in a northern fishery patrol off the east coast of Baffin Island.

"Use it or lose it." Prime Minister Stephen Harper first uttered the expression that would become synonymous with his approach to the Arctic on December 22, 2005. As Conservative candidate for prime minister, he stood before a giant map of Canada in a Winnipeg hotel and announced that if elected he would strengthen the country's military presence in the Arctic, including buying three armed icebreakers. "You don't defend national sovereignty with flags, cheap election rhetoric and advertising campaigns," Harper said. "You need forces on the ground, ships in the sea and proper surveillance." Arctic sovereignty is a tried (and tired?) old election issue — for who could argue against it? It was also in Winnipeg that John Diefenbaker had spoken of his Northern Vision in 1958 — which had come to little. As previous prime ministers discovered, promises made during an election campaign are rarely carried out — especially if they involve the Arctic. In Prime Minister Harper's case, the war in Afghanistan, a rising deficit at home, and deployments to earthquake-ravaged Haiti would prevent (or delay) some promises from being implemented.

When elected in January 2006, the Conservative government's "Canada First Northern Strategy" was intended to establish sovereignty in the Arctic and increase Canada's military presence in the North, by:

- Stationing three new armed naval heavy icebreakers in the area of Iqaluit that will include 500 regular force personnel for crews and support;
- building a new military/civilian deep-water docking facility in the Iqaluit area;
- establishing a new Arctic National Sensor System for northern waters that will include underwater surveillance technologies;
- building a new Arctic army training centre in the area of Cambridge Bay on the Northwest Passage, staffed by an estimated 100 regular force personnel;

- stationing new fixed-wing search-and-rescue aircraft in Yellowknife;
- providing eastern and western Arctic air surveillance through stationing new long-range uninhabited aerial vehicle (UAV) squadrons at CFB Goose Bay and CFB Comox;
- revitalizing the Canadian Rangers by recruiting up to 500 additional Rangers, increasing their level of training, activity, and equipment; and
- providing an army emergency response capability through the new airborne battalion and airlift capacity stationed at CFB Trenton to provide a rapid emergency response capability throughout the entire Arctic region.

Canada Command was stood up on February 1, 2006, and given military responsibility for the defence of North Canada and North America. Headquartered in Ottawa, the command oversaw six sub-commands, known as regional joint task forces. Additionally, Canada Command was made responsible for the overall effective operation of the federal coordinated maritime and aeronautical search and rescue system and the provision of air resources in response to aeronautical and maritime Search and Rescue (SAR) incidents. For this purpose, the country was divided into three search-and-rescue regions, Halifax (eastern Canada), Trenton (central Canada), and Victoria (western Canada). The Trenton Search and Rescue Region, with its higher headquarters in Winnipeg, Manitoba, provides search-and-rescue-coverage for most of the North. Canada Command was also responsible for responding to major air disasters in the North, and would support responses to other disasters or humanitarian crises as requested. The Canada Command crest became official on January 15, 2007. The dragon on the left denoted a defender of treasure. The wyvern on the right represented valour and protection and the command motto, which is inscribed in Latin on the crest, is "*Protegimus et Defendimus*", which means "Protect and Defend."

By the time EXERCISE NARWHAL 06 was held, CFNA had been reorganized and renamed as Joint Task Force North (JTFN). As its first major exercise, new command and control procedures put in place could be practised. This time, along with the Canadian Forces, were participants from National Energy Board, Enbridge Pipelines, Imperial Oil Resources, the Town of Norman Wells, Public Safety Canada (Arctic Region), Public Health Agency of Canada, the Government of Northwest Territories: Emergency Measures Organization, and the Territorial Emergency Response Committee.

JOINT TASK FORCE (NORTH)

Headquartered in Yellowknife, Joint Task Force North, (JTFN), is responsible for CF operations in the North, which is Canada Command's single largest region. JTFN's area of responsibility encompasses approximately 4 million square kilometres, or 40 percent, of Canada's land mass and 75 percent of its coastal regions. The commander of JTFN reports to the commander of Canada Command. JTFN's role is to exercise Canadian sovereignty north of the 60th parallel, to coordinate and support CF activities in the North, and to provide liaison with the territorial governments and peoples of the three northern territories: Northwest Territories, Yukon, and Nunavut. In addition to its headquarters in Yellowknife, Northwest Territories, JTFN maintains detachments in Whitehorse; Yukon; and Iqaluit, Nunavut.

The government also announced the establishment of a multipurpose facility for Arctic military training and operations in August 2007. The Canadian Forces Arctic Training Centre (CFATC) in Resolute Bay will be used year-round for both winter warfare and Arctic training, and routine operations. The facility can also be used as a command post for emergency operations and disaster response. The CFATC will also provide a location to pre-position equipment and vehicles, thereby generating an increased capability to support regional military or civilian emergency operations in this rugged and remote region of the country.

CANADIAN NAVY

The Canadian Navy plays a key role in asserting sovereignty along Canada's three coasts and routinely sails in the nation's northern waters. With the government's intention to acquire new ships and establish a berthing and refuelling facility that will support the navy in the Arctic, there will be a marked increase in the navy's presence in Canada's Arctic waters.

The planned acquisition of six to eight ice-capable Arctic/Offshore patrol vessels will enable the navy to conduct seaborne surveillance operations in the Arctic during the navigable season, and on the east and west coasts throughout the year. These new patrol ships will enhance Canada's ability to enforce its right, under international law, to be notified when foreign ships enter Canadian waters, and will further enhance the CF ability to support other government departments in responding to emerging security challenges such as organized crime and illegal immigration, and in carrying out drug interdiction operations and environmental protection. The first ship is expected in 2014.

The Department of National Defence Berthing and Refuelling Facility at Nanisivik, Nunavut, will help Canada exert a sustained naval presence in Arctic waters during the navigable season. Strategically positioned inside the eastern entrance of Parry Channel, and more than 1,100 nautical miles by sea north of Iqaluit, this facility will serve as a refuelling location for naval vessels on station in the high Arctic, and as a place to embark equipment and supplies, transfer personnel, and work closely with the CCG, who will also have access to the facility. The Nanisivik facility is expected to be fully operational by 2015.

Two Marine Security Operations Centres (MSOCs), located in Halifax, Nova Scotia, and Esquimalt, British Columbia, maintain vigilance over Arctic waters. The navy currently hosts these MSOCs, but they represent a "whole of government" approach and an equal partnership between departments and agencies involved in marine security. MSOC facilities are staffed by personnel from the five core partners that have a vested interest in marine security: Canada Border Services Agency, National Defence, Department of Fisheries and Oceans Canada (including the Canadian Coast Guard), the RCMP, and Transport Canada.

The current capability of the MSOCs allows them to collect and synthesize marine information within existing legal frameworks in order to enhance the government's capability to respond to marine security threats and thereby protect Canadians. Responsibility for monitoring marine activity in the Arctic is shared between the east and west coasts.

CANADIAN AIR FORCE

The air force, in conjunction with NORAD, maintains four Forward Operating Locations (FOLs) where it can pre-deploy fighter aircraft in response to, or anticipation of, unwelcome activity. The FOLs are located in Inuvik and Yellowknife, Northwest Territories, and in Iqaluit and Rankin Inlet, Nunavut. They provide all the necessary infrastructure and supplies to support the air force's CF-18 fighter aircraft in these remote and isolated regions.

These days, regular Northern Patrols are conducted by CP-140 Aurora maritime patrol aircraft. With an endurance of 17 hours and a range of almost 10,000 kilometres, these strategic surveillance aircraft safeguard Canada's waters from emerging security challenges such as illegal fishing, immigration, drug trafficking, and pollution violations. There are plans to augment these patrols with satellite-based systems and uninhabited aerial vehicles (UAVs).

When interviewed, subject matter experts within Canada Command said:

> We are in a period of transition, from a construct where northern surveillance is being conducted solely by aircraft to a new construct where we will have persistent, wide area surveillance sensors which include space based RADARSAT 2, space based AIS (Automated Identification System) and the CCG run, ground based LRIT (Long Range Identification and Tracking). In June of 2010, Canada Command assumed responsibility for

the Polar Epsilon Project Arctic Surveillance (Land) when it achieved Full Operational Capability. Canada Command now has access to RADARSAT2 imagery of the north. We are still working to refine the RADARSAT capability for maritime surveillance in the north. In the future, with the persistent, wide area surveillance assets in place, the mobile resources such as Aurora's, and possibly UAVs, will be able to provide reactive, cued reconnaissance to investigate contacts identified for follow up by the persistent surveillance assets.

The UAV project is still in the requirements definition phase, with many technological hurdles such as the command and control over the long distances involved, as well as the usual range, sensor fitment and airspace control issues to be solved before going to contract and entering operational use.

As a final point, tremendous advances have been made since the roll out of the MSOCs (Maritime Security Operations Centers) which bring a "whole of government" approach to surveillance of the maritime approaches to Canada, including the north. As well as sharing data collected by other government departments during their surveillance activities to get a better overall picture for everyone, DND also contracts for unused capacity of OGD surveillance assets. In the North, Transport Canada deploys a Dash 7 aircraft to support Environment Canada Ice Reconnaissance as well as the TC pollution patrol mandate. As this very capable surveillance asset is based in Iqaluit from late June to October conducting surveillance anyway, additional surveillance flights are a good leveraging of existing government surveillance assets to improve everyone's Maritime Domain Awareness(MDA) in the north.

That in a nutshell is what we foresee as the way ahead. There are many technical and fiscal issues to be worked through to reach this end state, as well as evolving technology which may be considered, but achieving MDA for the 3 Oceans that border Canada is a significant challenge, given the vast areas to monitor.

The only formed Canadian air force unit based full-time in the North is 440 (Transport) Squadron. Operating four Canadian-designed and produced CC-138 Twin Otters, this Yellowknife-based squadron conducts airlift, utility, and liaison flights in the Yukon, Northwest Territories, and Nunavut, as well as any assigned search-and-rescue missions. The squadron operates the rugged Twin Otters in some of the harshest weather conditions on the planet and has the capability to conduct "off-airport" operations on skis in the winter and on tundra tires in the summer. "The Twin Otter has supported a wide number of roles while supporting Canada, the Canadian Forces, and Canadians," explains Lieutenant-Colonel Dwayne Lovegrove, commanding officer, 440 (T) Squadron. He would later write:

> Looking back on my limited time flying this aircraft, a few impressions and stories linger. OPERATION NUNALIVUT 2010, held during most of April last year, provided many of us with a fantastic opportunity to employ the Twin Otter to the extremes of its abilities. 440 Sqn deployed two aircraft in support of this operation to CFS Alert, arriving early in the month. It was an incredible experience, including just getting there. Our ski-equipped Twin Otters almost seemed to enjoy being flown every day despite the bone-chilling temperatures found at that latitude and time of year, leaving us with only a few minor maintenance snags to fuss over. We quickly became pretty good at getting the wing "skins" (protective covers) and engine blankets on and off the aircraft, with the bite of the extreme temps providing tangible motivation. The weather was largely VMC

(visual meteorological conditions) for the most part, allowing for breathtaking views of the starkly rugged, mountainous landscape.

It is difficult to describe the scenery to anyone who hasn't been there … a sea of jagged peaks and deep valleys, many sporting massive glaciers that reminded me of a dog's extended tongue! You really had to watch the weather, for despite the cold, tidal forces created many open leads of water whose "arctic sea smoke" could quickly envelope a large area in ice fog with little warning. As several of us were relatively new to operating the aircraft on skis, we set out in the first few days to find nearby fjords to "work up" in, practicing the procedures that would allow us to tackle the more formidable sea ice later on. What powdered snow exists up there tends to accumulate in the fjords, making for landings that were far smoother than what we would soon experience. Our confidence bolstered, we soon got into the real work of flying JTFN personnel and Rangers out to Ward Hunt Island, and onto the sea ice.

Getting in and out of Ward Hunt was a challenge. A short, narrow landing strip had been marked out with black garbage bags by someone before us, but getting onto it meant paralleling the ridge and its accompanying "saddle back" which always featured a solid crosswind on landing. If you didn't nail the touchdown point right off, you quickly were faced with overshooting in order to avoid rocketing onto the uneven sea ice and surrounding ice shelf. Similarly, failure to maintain directional control in the post-landing phase would find you hurtling either towards stacked oil drums or the rock face of the adjoining "mountain." Riding on the skis, you don't have any brakes for landing, so salvation lies in the judicious use of rudder and the skilled application of reverse propeller thrust. Once stopped and shut down, aircrew immediately became ground crew, faced with the prospect of loading/unloading fuel barrels, burdensome snowmobiles, and in a couple instances, dogs from the Danish "Sirius" patrol. Unused to sensations associated with flying in a small aircraft and bouncing around on skis, almost every husky heavily soiled its cage. With the internal airflow in the aircraft coming up through the cockpit and out the pilot's vented windows, the expeditious offload of the animals quickly became an immediate priority!

After a few days of working out onto Ward Hunt Island, we entered the next phase which involved inserting a Ranger patrol out onto the sea ice some 80+ nautical miles from shore. Finding a suitable landing site was the first challenge. Only the newest of sea ice is smooth; ice thick enough to reliably support the landing of fixed wing aircraft typically features several patterns of drift snow, and is far more rugged in nature than what meets the eye. What appears to be soft ripples of snow actually is more consistent with construction-grade Styrofoam, or worse. Landing on such surfaces feels akin to belly-flopping onto cement, with the snow ridges creating miniature ski-jumps that cause the aircraft to thump hard, often setting off the ELT (Emergency Locator Transmitter). Takeoffs are even worse, as these same ski-jumps repeatedly launch the aircraft prematurely into the air in a series of mini-stalls before it is ready to "slip the surly bonds" of gravity. After my first sea-ice landing, I fully expected to find the airframe rippled with a trail of broken parts behind, but the ruggedness of the Twin Otter won out. It is during such operations that one truly gains a deep respect for this uniquely Canadian aircraft — it really is built like the proverbial outhouse of old.

A number of other images are ingrained in my mind, including many gained while flying the aircraft over the same Ellesmere Island but during the summer. I haven't even mentioned my fond memories of Tanquery Fjord and the nearby glacier unofficially called "The Hand of God," so named as it appears to reach down from on high, but that is yet another story again.

NORAD

NORAD also maintains the North Warning System. Tied in with other NORAD radars, the system forms a radar buffer zone 4,800 kilometres long and 320 kilometres wide that stretches from Alaska, across Canada to Greenland, allowing NORAD to detect all approaching airborne activity.

TECHNOLOGY

The Polar Epsilon Project is a $60-million space-based initiative using imagery and information from Canada's radar satellite, RADARSAT-2, to provide enhanced land and sea surveillance capabilities for the CF at home and abroad. RADARSAT-2 is ideally suited for Arctic land surveillance due to its polar orbit and radar characteristics of all-weather, day-or-night sensor capability. The satellite's near real-time processing of images will allow a more efficient and timely CF response to help maintain Canada's Arctic situational awareness and to address potential situations such as environmental and humanitarian crises, including search-and-rescue operations, natural disasters, and large oil spills.

The Polar Epsilon Project includes satellite ground stations that will process data from RADARSAT-2 to produce imagery products in near real-time that can then be used to support CF operations and the activities of other federal departments or agencies as well as to monitor activity or changes in the Arctic.

The Northern Watch Technology Demonstration Project, led by Defence Research and Development Canada (DRDC), explores various technologies that may be utilized to provide enhanced Arctic security and surveillance. The key project areas focus on combinations of assorted surface, underwater, and space-based sensors and systems that may ultimately provide the CF and the government of Canada with additional resources to monitor and protect the Canadian Arctic.

OPERATIONS

The Canadian Forces currently conduct three major sovereignty operations each year, in the high, western, and eastern Arctic respectively. While the precise objectives of each operation differ, they all share the same overarching purpose: to exercise Canada's sovereignty in the region, to advance the CF capabilities for Arctic operations, and to improve interdepartmental coordination in response to Northern security issues. These operations are conducted under the command of JTFN, but with the participation of partner departments and agencies.

RECURRING OPERATIONS

The OPERATION NUNALIVUT series are enhanced Ranger sovereignty patrols. The operation employs the unique capabilities of the Canadian Rangers to support JTFN operations in the extreme environment of the high Arctic, as Ranger snowmobile patrols provide a presence and demonstrate a response capability in the most remote areas of the North.

The NUNAKPUT series are conducted in the western Arctic and are integrated JTFN operations that take place each summer in co-operation with the Canadian Coast Guard and the RCMP. The aim of the operation is to exercise sovereignty and practise interoperability, focusing on the Beaufort Sea region, including Herschel Island.

The NANOOK series are joint, interagency sovereignty operations conducted in the eastern Arctic. Planned and directed by JTFN, it highlights interoperability, command and control, and co-operation with interdepartmental and intergovernmental partners in the North.

Major Steven Burgess is a senior logistician in the Canadian Forces and in 2011 was posted to CANOSCOM (the CF lead for operational level support) as a J5 Domestic Planner (Northern Desk Officer). Responsible for developing operational level support plans for current Northern operations, he would write this:

> As a general concept, the Canadian Forces (CF) endeavours to develop and/or maintain the ability to rapidly and effectively project joint forces in order to respond to safety and security challenges in the North. In cooperation with our Northern Mission partners, we conduct annual sovereignty ops including land, air and sea elements in order to support the Canadian Government's Arctic Policy and Northern Strategy.
>
> As interest in the North continues to grow, there has been an explosion of activity within our northern territories and waterways from both non-military and military sources. The Government of Canada (GoC) has outlined four fundamental "pillars" that make up its Northern Strategy. To that end, we must be able to demonstrate an enhanced capacity to operate in the North including a demonstrative ability to save lives in austere locations in times of crisis. Within this framework, the CF continues to develop capabilities and shape its activities accordingly.
>
> The GoC's four "pillars" comprising its Northern Strategy are:
>
> * Ability to exercise Arctic Sovereignty;
> * Protecting Environmental Stewardship;
> * Promoting Social and Economic Development; and
> * Improving and devolving Northern Governance.

In step with the government's approach to the North, the CF has developed its own strategic objectives. First, we must be capable of conducting surveillance of Canadian territory including the air and maritime approaches in the North. Coupled with this is the ability to exercise Canada's sovereignty in the North while demonstrating a visible Canadian presence throughout the region. Secondly, there is a need to identify and develop supporting relationships with OGD (Other Government Departments) and OGA (Other Government Agencies) operating in the North including DFO, CG, PS, RCMP, INAC, Transport Canada and NRC, to fulfill their mandates. Thirdly, the CF must continue to improve its 24/7 Search and Response capabilities that are able to reach those in distress anywhere in Canada, notably the North. Fourthly, we must continue our present commitments to continental defense, including through NORAD, and endeavor to create new and build upon existing defense relationships in the region thus strengthening operational links.

Over the years, there has been a great deal of discussion as to how to exercise our sovereignty. We continue to refine our definition in order to meet the government's expectations of the CF in the North. Is it as simple as having Canadian Rangers from Joint Task Force North (JTF(N)) execute patrols throughout the region or do we need to be able to project larger military forces from the south into the North that are capable of conducting large-scale operations? And, more importantly, what do we want these forces to be able to do there and for how long?

As activity in the North increases, the potential threats to our environment increase as well. There is a great deal of eco-tourism, mineral exploration, scientific research, etc. that has been steadily increasing over the past few decades as access to the far North improves. With this increase in northern traffic, the CF must be

Photo by Master Corporal Blake Rodgers, Formation Imaging Services Halifax, Nova Scotia.

Her Majesty's Canadian Ship (HMCS) Corner Brook *sails past an iceberg while on Arctic patrol during* OPERATION NANOOK.

able to respond more effectively and efficiently to natural disasters and other emergencies, i.e., a Major Air Disaster (MAJAID) and maritime incidents. Whether we have the lead or not, the CF must be able and prepared to either execute the operation or assist Other Government Departments (OGD) in doing so. Our responses must be in step with a Whole of Government (WoG) approach.

OPERATION NANOOK

OP NANOOK is an annual operation conducted primarily in the Eastern Arctic (Baffin Island/Lancaster Sound region) during the August timeframe. It is a JTF(N) planned and directed (under the authority of Canada Command), joint and integrated sovereignty operation. It highlights interoperability, command and control, and

cooperation with interdepartmental and intergovernmental partners in the North.

Canadian Operational Support Command
(CANOSCOM) support to OPERATION NANOOK

Established in 2006, CANOSCOM has been working with Canada Command and JTF(N) since 2008 in
order to develop the support concept for the NANOOK
series of operations. Throughout the deliberate planning process, it is our responsibility to identify operational support requirements, satisfy operational level
taskings, and assist Canada Command in identifying
remaining gaps in the overall support plan. Given the
limited assets available to JTF(N), we generally deploy a
Joint Task Force Support Component (JTFSC) in order
to provide the appropriate level of support required.
The JTFSC provides operational level support consistent with CANOSCOM's current mission support role
for CF operations, including: theatre activation support,
Strategic Line of Communication (SLOC) operations
during all phases of a mission, other specialist capabilities during sustainment and mission closure support.
These activities involve CANOSCOM planning, coor-
dinating, and force generating support specialty capabilities in co-operation with Canada Command, JTF(N),
and the lead force generators in the areas of supply, land
transportation, vehicle maintenance, movements, food
services, general engineering support (temporary camp
construction, etc.), communications and information
systems, military policing, health services, operational
personnel management, and operational support capability contracting.

Unique Challenges

To say that supporting military operations in the North is challenging is a gross understatement of the present reality. There are many unique problems associated with not only mounting and deploying forces from their home bases in the south, but even more when trying to devise innovative solutions for the follow-on sustainment they will require. The Arctic is one of the harshest living environments in the world. It is difficult to gain a full appreciation for this when you live and work in the temperate climates of Canada's southern regions.

One of the most significant challenges we face when deploying forces for NANOOK is the weather. Even during the summer period, the temperatures are often below freezing, high winds are common, there is a potential for snow and an abundance of fog and ice in the harbours and at the local airports. This makes the movement of people, equipment, and material very problematic. The vast majority of the CF's movements is via strategic airlift, i.e., the C-17 Globemaster and CC-130 Hercules. There are no land lines of communication (highways) to leverage and movement by sea is limited to very small windows of opportunity (generally twice yearly, totalling approximately eight weeks) due to the ice floes and inhospitable sea conditions. Even though there are now extended periods of time where "open water" exists in the high, eastern Arctic, our Naval ships are not ice-capable at this time. There is still a great deal of one-year ice in the shipping lanes making even routine movement difficult and potentially dangerous. As we continue to increase our presence north of Iqaluit, this has become one of the limiting factors to CF projection of maritime forces into the Arctic Bay/Nanisivik and Lancaster Sound region, making coordination with

Photo by Corporal Rick Ayer, Formation Imaging Services, Halifax, Nova Scotia.

HMCS Montreal *passes an iceberg in Strathcona Sound near Nanisivik, Nunavut Territory, during* OPERATION NANOOK..

intergovernmental agencies such as the Coast Guard extremely important in achieving the government of Canada's mandate for the North.

Local infrastructure like airfields, roads, hotels, water/sewage stations, etc., where it is available, is limited in capability and is most often not capable of accommodating the demands of a significant deployment of CF assets. Essentially, what you have is what you bring. This places great importance upon detailed planning at every level (from the operational to the tactical) prior to deploying. A close balance needs to be developed for every operation in the North between CF self-reliance and utilization of local resources without negatively impacting community support systems. OP NANOOK can provide significant financial stimulus to the communities involved, however the capabilities and capacities of the communities are limited and often finite, based on their limited replenishment windows by air or sea. We carefully develop every aspect of the support plan to ensure this balance is maintained throughout the operation. The distances are vast and the ability to leverage the local communities, without adversely affecting their ability to support themselves, is very limited.

The size of the forces we deploy is a critical factor in our planning. In 2010, we contracted the building of a temporary camp in Resolute Bay to house approximately 450 personnel. This year's NANOOK will see nearly double that number. There are many second- and third-order effects as the numbers increase. Namely, the complexity of the sustainment concept (camp size, dispersion of forces, transportation needs, camp services, etc.), land claims/Environment Canada regulations, ability to obtain site permits, potential impact on local communities, etc.

Another issue that we have struggled with is the development of "Northern-specific" equipment and material. This includes Arctic-suitable tents, land mobility platforms (ATV/snowmobiles), force protection measures (bear fences, etc.) and more robust communications systems. The CF continues to explore alternative options for all of these specific challenges and uses OP NANOOK as a venue for research and development.

Conclusion

Regardless of the challenges we face in the North, a common theme for the CF is the connection to the Northern peoples. We work very hard to incorporate the northern communities into all of our activities and endeavour to foster a close working relationship with the Canadian

Rangers (1 Canadian Ranger Patrol Group), the hamlets, private industry, and the territorial governments and agencies.

CANADIAN RANGERS

The Canadian Rangers (CR) were mentioned by name twice in the 2005 Defence Policy Statement (DPS). In the section on Domestic Operations, the DPS spoke of the involvement of the CR in assisting civilian authorities to respond to natural disasters and other incidents, including floods, forest fires, hurricanes, and plane crashes. The sovereignty task is the main effort of the Canadian Rangers and is the task to which the majority of their efforts are focused.

The Canadian Army has been active for decades in the Arctic, primarily through the Rangers — the "eyes and ears" of the Canadian Forces — providing a military presence in remote regions throughout Canada, including Canada's North. Recruited from 56 communities across Canada's North (in addition to 109 communities south of the 60th parallel), the Canadian Rangers play a key role in protecting Canada's sovereignty by conducting surveillance and sovereignty patrols, reporting unusual activity or sightings, and collecting local data of significance to the CF.

They assist CF activities by: providing local expertise, guidance, and advice during operations and exercises; conducting North Warning System patrols; and providing local assistance to search and rescue activities. In August 2007, the government announced an expansion of the Canadian Rangers throughout Canada from 4,100 to 5,000 members, enabling the addition of new patrols and the strengthening of existing ones.

When interviewed, CWO D.W. Mahon said that the popular misconception is that the Rangers are just located north of the 60th parallel:

A much more accurate descriptor is — from coast to coast to coast — the Rangers are located in 170 Patrols from the east coast (NL) to the west (BC) to the north

(NWT and the Yukon). Nor is it a program — You will hear people commonly refer to the CR as a program. They are reserve force members employed in the Army in units identified by their CF Organization Order as units of LFC. To refer to them as a program is misleading.

The JCR program is a youth organization similar to other cadet organisations throughout Canada. CR mentor, instruct and supervise this program. The primary role of this part-time force was to conduct surveillance or sovereignty patrols and act as guides and scouts when southern forces were in their area of operations with some units also inspecting the North Warning System (NWS) sites.

OPERATION NUNALIVUT 10 saw 1 Canadian Ranger Patrol Group establish an ice camp 90 kilometres north of CFS Alert. Establishing the ice camp on the sea ice allowed the Canadian Rangers the opportunity to extend their patrol range, to gain experience in setting up a patrol base on the ice, and to conduct trials of new equipment. "The Canadian

Photo by Corporal Shilo Adamson, Canadian Forces Combat Camera.

A Canadian Forces CC-177 Globemaster rests on the tarmac at Canadian Forces Station Alert during OPERATION NUNALIVUT 10.

Rangers are ambassadors of the North," said the Honourable Eva Aariak, premier of Nunavut. "I am very proud of the reconnaissance and surveillance patrols the Rangers have undertaken throughout the high Arctic region and their ability to use their intimate knowledge of the land to work with other members of the Canadian Forces to ensure protection and safety of Nunavummiut."

Sergeant Peter Moon held the distinction of being the oldest sergeant in the Canadian Forces, having joined the forces after retiring in 1999 from a long and successful career in journalism. Originally from Scotland, Sergeant Moon completed his national service with the Royal Air Force before migrating to Canada in 1957. He wrote the following article when doing Public Affairs for 3rd Canadian Ranger Patrol Group:

SOVEREIGNTY PATROL BATTLES ELEMENTS
TO MAKE ARCTIC HISTORY

In the spring of 2007, a 24-member CF sovereignty patrol made Arctic history by travelling a record 5589 kilometres in 17 days in brutal weather conditions.

One of its three eight-person teams became the first in history to cover the 785 km, between the weather station at Eureka and CFS Alert by travelling across the northern coast of Ellesmere Island. The team made the epic journey over nine days, eight of them in blinding blizzards that frequently reduced visibility to inches. It erected a metal Canadian flag at Ward Hunt Island and placed a record of their visit in a cairn left by explorer Robert Peary in 1906 at Cape Aldrich, Canada's most northerly point.

"The three teams did fantastically well," said Major Chris Bergeron, patrol leader. "I can say we have done something that has never been done. Its mission accomplished. I am so proud of everyone. It taught us how to operate in the North." Major Bergeron's team made the

trip from Eureka to Alert in temperatures that dropped
to -50 ℃ and in winds gusting from 80 to 115 kilometres per hour. "We had no visibility whatsoever," he
said. "We fought our way inches by inches. It was hell.
In seven years in the Arctic I have never experienced
anything like it." Setting up a tent often took up to two
hours in white-out conditions, and simple tasks like
refueling snowmobiles became an ordeal.

All three teams encountered difficulties negotiating
ridge ice, rocks and challenging terrain. Snowmobiles
were damaged and komatiqs (sleds) had to be repaired.
One Canadian Ranger had to be evacuated after he was
thrown from his snowmobile and injured.

The patrol's three teams, made up of seven Regular
Force members and 17 Canadian Rangers began the
patrol at Resolute Bay on March 17 and reached Alert
on April 9. One team travelled north through central
Ellesmere Island to Alert. Major Bergeron's team travelled along the northern coastal route. And a third
team, accompanied by an RCMP officer, travelled to
Alexandra Fiord on the east coast of Ellesmere Island.

The eastern team became the first ever joint
CF-RCMP sovereignty patrol. It conducted patrols along
the coast checking for evidence of Inuit from Greenland
travelling to Canada to hunt polar bears.

The three teams were supported by two CC-138
Twin Otters from 440 Transport Squadron, based in
Yellowknife. The planes provided food and fuel caches
and spare parts for the patrol. Further support was
provided by a 20-person command post, based first in
Resolute and then Eureka, and another 20 personnel at
Joint Task Force North headquarters in Yellowknife. "It
was the trip of a lifetime," said Ranger Sgt Allen Pogotok
of Holman, N.W.T. "I'm very proud and honoured to
have done this for Canada."

In February 1994, the DND announced that CFS Alert would be converted to remote operations. As a remotely operated facility, staffing was reduced from 215 to 74 personnel, of whom only seven were directly employed in operations. The remaining 67 personnel are employed in airfield, construction engineering, food services, and logistical/administrative support functions. Canadian Forces personnel, both men and women, from the navy, army, and air force are employed in these support functions.

But a new war, defined by the attacks of September 11, 2001, meant the Canadian northern front took on a high level of importance and Alert is seen today as one of Canada's most important assets. Ottawa spent $32 million in 2003 to update the station's communications equipment and where once reels of recording tape were gathered and flown out, today's raw data is sent directly to intelligence experts at CFS Leitrim outside Ottawa via a satellite link.

The Canadian Air Force officially took over the responsibility of Alert on April 1, 2008. The CC-177 Globemaster made its inaugural landing at CFS Alert on April 14, 2010 and operates regularly to the Arctic ever since. With its much greater carrying capacity, the CC-177 can move approximately three times more cargo to CFS Alert on each trip than was done with the CC-130 Hercules. During OPERATION BOXTOP — the annual resupplying of Alert — the Canadian Air Force runs supplies to the station each spring and fall. Over the last 20 years, the mission has averaged an annual delivery of approximately 294,000 kilograms of dry goods and 2.5 million litres of fuel into CFS Alert.

Major Bill Chambré was posted to CFS Alert in 2006 as part of a planning trip for OP HURRICANE — the annual maintenance of the High Arctic Data Communications System (HADCS) — the vital microwave link between Alert and Eureka that enables communication with a geostationary satellite, which cannot be reached from Alert due to its northerly latitude (82° 30' N). To humanize what a posting is like for the "Frozen Chosen" in the most northerly inhabited part of the world, this is his journal for a week.

2 March

I went out at about 11:15 to see if I could see the sun. The sun is supposed to be at its peak here at 11:21 or 11:22 am. Not quite able to peek over the mountains just yet. A few minutes later, I watched the Herc take off to return to Trenton. As its engines revved up, I heard the sound of an Arctic Wolf down by the runway. By the time the Herc was taxiing down the runway, there was a chorus of wolves howling. It was like they were saying "good-bye."

3 March

I was able to participate in one of the annual traditions up here — the Annual Sunrise Carnival. A day of games and events that included a tournament of "blind volleyball" — like regular volleyball but with sheets over the net so you can't see the ball coming, plus all players had to play with their heavy arctic mitts on their hands. It made for an interesting game. Other contests included a tug of war, snowshoe race (that resembled short-track speed skating) and egg tossing contest. The snowshoe race seemed to capture the interest of the local wolves who came to the parking lot to check things out after we had gone back inside. During the subsequent egg toss, I heard the wolves howling above the din of the egg tossing participants. I went over to the edge of the parking lot and saw one of the wolves about 50 metres away from me. I didn't get any closer as I heard enough warnings about this pack of wolves that I did not want to antagonize them. The one I saw didn't seem to upset by my presence. He stood up and stretched, and then curled up in the snow to go back to sleep.

4 March

For the past couple of days I have been advertising for new participants in the "North of 80 Running Club." Astonishingly (?), only one person has come out to join me so far. It was about -25 deg when we ran out to the end of the runway and back. While down by the airstrip I took a GPS measurement so I can measure the exact distance from Alert to my home in Williamstown, Ont. A sign-making friend has offered to make a sign indicating the distance to Williamstown to go with the many other similar signs up here by the airstrip. Our run was uneventful. I was probably a bit too warm. It would appear that I was dressed for -35. I saw no wolves on this trip, and no wolf footprints. I saw where several foxes crossed the runway recently, and may have heard wolves but not sure. With the number of layers of clothing covering my ears, about all I could really hear for certain was the sound of our footsteps and my own breathing. My running partner told me that this was his first time outdoors this year. We ran with a camera, a "puppy pounder" (a baton that would be used to tap a wolf on the nose if he got too close), and a can of pepper spray that would be used to temporarily blind any wolves that got too aggressive. The effects of the pepper spray wear off after about 20 minutes. Interestingly enough, pepper spray is considered banned by the Geneva Convention. Fortunately we are not bound by the Geneva Convention since we are not at war with the wolves, and do not even consider them to be "enemy combatants."

5 March

Temperature is down to -33 deg today. Started the "North of 80 Walking Club." Just one other person joined that club — an American civilian technician who is up here for a couple of weeks. She is from Colorado, so at least has experience with some winter, plus she has been up here several times over the years. We walked to the end of the runway and back. It was too overcast to see the sun when we started out at 11:30, but on the way back the fog cleared and we saw the last of the sunset. Still haven't really seen the sun yet, but maybe tomorrow. It worked out to be a 7 km walk and was the first time I made use of all the military Arctic clothing I have been issued with. I must say, it stood up to the -33 deg temperature quite nicely. Made it back to the Station by 1310 hrs, giving me enough time to change into my running clothes for the "North of 80 Running Club." No sightings of wolves or any other wildlife today. It was just a pleasant day to enjoy the afterglow of the sunset, the absolute stillness of the environment and the fresh crisp Arctic air. So far, the North of 80 Running Club has only 2 members, but I have had 2 others express an interest and ask when I am going out next.

6 March

I saw the sun today! It was like this bright yellow ball in the sky. Well, I guess you don't need me to tell you what the sun looks like, but for a lot of people here it was the first time they saw it since October. I saw it at about 10:30, then it ducked behind the mountains for a while and I saw it again at about noon. Amazing just how white everything looks when the sun is actually up. After the sun goes down, the afterglow stays around for a while, gradually shifting from the east to the southern sky. It takes a few hours for the sun to go well below the horizon and become dark. I went out running between 5 and 6 pm. It was a pleasant -38 deg. Had a new running partner today — a young Reservist from BC who is up here for a few months to save some money before heading out on a world backpacking tour. He was getting a little cold on the way back so we stopped in at the weather forecasting building on the airstrip to warm up. Nobody was there, but one of the unwritten rules of the North is that doors are never locked, since access to a warm building can be a matter of life or death.

As the Arctic ice melts away, Canada's internal waters are becoming more navigable throughout the year. Along with the movement of goods, tourism is expected to grow, especially from cruise ship travel in the near term. In 2003, seven cruise ships operated in Canadian Arctic waters; by 2008, this number had increased to 15. In August, 2010, the *Clipper Adventurer*, operated by Adventure Canada and carrying 200 passengers and crew, ran aground about 55 nautical miles from Coppermine, Nunavut, in "three meters of water." The cruise operator claimed that the cruise ship had run aground on an "uncharted rock." This ship had come to the rescue when another cruise ship the *Ocean Nova*, ran aground on Antarctica the year before.

As a consequence of the increase in maritime traffic, and the escalating exploration of natural resources, there is a potentially greater risk of criminal activity, illegal entry of people and goods, human- and drug-smuggling, and foreign military activities. Environmental concerns and search-and-rescue needs will also increase. While other government departments and agencies, such as the CCG and the RCMP, remain responsible for dealing with most security issues in the North, the Canadian Forces continue to play a significant role exercising sovereignty.

Commander Alistair Harrigan, director of Maritime Strategy, helps coordinate all entities in the Arctic for the navy. Six to eight Arctic Offshore Patrol Vessels are to be built, he explained, dependant on National Shipbuilding Procurement Strategy and they were looking at 2015–16 "to cut steel." When asked why the navy went to the Arctic so infrequently in the past, Commander Harrigan says:

Warships are not designed for ice — as there was no threat in the Arctic so Canada didn't build ships to go there. These are internal waters so this is a Coast Guard and RCMP matter and the navy supports them. We need a ship that will operate in "first year ice" — a metre thick — which will give us seasonal capability, meaning we will able to work there during the shipping season. The problem is that you also get multi-year ice with the first year ice. So taking a ship that is not designed to operate in ice and putting it in ice is a risk — it could puncture your hull and you need specialized engineering — this is why the navy did not go there because our ships were not designed for ice. Plus where's the threat? What the military threat up there?

Asked about the Russians, the commander said, "There is no naval threat. No one's building icebreaking war ships — the Russians are not sailing around in our waters. They have icebreakers but not icebreaking warships. You have to look at where is the threat. There is no naval threat."

But with global warming, the ice is melting away and that is opening up the Arctic to new threats. Harrigan says:

We have to look at what's the threat? We're looking at crime, increased trade, immigration problems, but not really a military threat per se. The other problem is that the ice is not going away — it will still freeze and it will still be dark in the winter. The ice will form so you are going to need something that will operate in some level of ice. There will still be big chunks floating around so the sea routes in the Arctic — it is unlikely that the traditional Northwest Passage will open up first. What we will see is the northern sea route over Russia or the transpolar route — shorter for transit. Even in North America there's very few places where going through the Northwest Passage makes sense. If you are going from Ketchikan, Alaska to Halifax, it is the shorter route — other than that for everywhere else, it is shorter to go through the Panama Canal. It is one of the myths that it is shorter to go through the Northwest Passage — not a lot of people realize that. Plus you are going through waters that are dangerous — even if the ice melts, there are always big bits floating around. And it is not just first year ice — there are sections of multi-year ice in the Passage. The shipping season is June to September — that's it — and they still need icebreakers to escort them through. So the Arctic Offshore Patrol Vessel does not need to be built as a warship. It's going to be built as a constabulary/support vessel. It will be designed to handle the ice in the shipping season and be big enough to handle a helicopter and carry extra personnel like the RCMP, Rangers, you name it.

When asked about the Nanisivik Naval Facility, Commander Harrigan says, "Once we get up there is not a lot of places to get fuel so that is why we are building it. We will bring the fuel in by barge."

But why Nanisivik? Harrigan continues, "It is one of the few deepwater harbours in the Arctic. Again, most people don't realize that there is not a lot of deep water in the Arctic — there is some where the passages are but most of it is shoaled. When you look at the Arctic as a maritime environment it is unique."

What disputed areas there are in the Arctic are dealt with these days by diplomats rather than the navy. Besides the perennial Northwest Passage disagreement with the United States (in which they contend it is an international strait), there is the Beaufort Sea dispute over the seaward border between Yukon and Alaska, concerning a zone of 6,250 square nautical miles.

The first of two sovereignty disputes with Denmark is in the Lincoln Sea on the seaward border north of Ellesmere Island, consisting of two tiny maritime zones of 31 and 35 square nautical miles. The second has received a lot more publicity and concerns the ownership of Hans Island — a small 1.3-square-kilometre unpopulated island just south of the 81st parallel in the Kennedy Channel between Greenland and Ellesmere Island. In 1973, Canada and Denmark drew up borders in the Nares Strait between Canada and Greenland, but delayed any decision regarding the sovereignty of Hans Island. Assisted by the Royal Danish Navy, on July 28, 1984, the Danes raised their national flag on the island. Canada responded with EXERCISE FROZEN BEAVER on March 30, 2004, with visits by Canadian Forces helicopters and Canadian Rangers (sometimes called Canada's "sovereignty soldiers"), who replaced the Danish flag with a Canadian one and left a plaque and an Inukshuk on the island.

In Ottawa, the Danish Ambassador to Canada, Poul E.D. Kristensen published a letter in the *Ottawa Citizen*, asserting Denmark's sovereignty over Hans Island and threatened to send HDMS *Tulugaq*, the Greenland-based, ice-strengthened cutter to the island. A series of negotiations followed within the United Nations General Assembly in New York to attempt to resolve the sovereignty question regarding Hans Island, but no resolution was reached.

Of all the sovereignty operations that Canada has routinely conducted in the Arctic, none gave more hope for a peaceful solution than OPERATION NUNALIVUT 10, which was completed at Alert on April 26, 2010. The Royal Danish Navy sent the HDMS *Vaedderen* and the HDMS *Knud Rasmussen* to participate in the CF exercises. They were joined by the United States Second Fleet destroyer USS *Porter* and the USCG cutter *Alder*.[9] On the sea ice off northern Ellesmere Island and Greenland, the Canadian Rangers completed a joint mission with the Danish (Greenland) Sirius Dog Patrol. In Ottawa, the two chiefs of defence staff, Canadian General Walt Natynczyk and Danish General Knud Bartels, signed a Memorandum of Understanding on Arctic Defence, Security and Operational Cooperation. The exercise and signing demonstrated that the sovereignty of the Arctic is the responsibility of no single nation. For a country whose prime minister was once awarded a Nobel Peace prize, such "quiet diplomacy" instead of confrontation to settle disputes is fitting. After all, we are Canadian.

On July 25, 2010, Parks Canada archaeologists began a sonar scan of Mercy Bay, Bank's Island, in the Northwest Territories. Within 15 minutes they found HMS *Investigator* sitting upright on the ocean floor under about eight metres of pristine, icy Arctic water. Captained by Robert McClure, it had been sent in 1850 to search for Franklin's crew and their two ships, the *Erebus* and *Terror*. After more than two years trapped in the ice at Mercy Bay, the *Investigator*'s crew was rescued by a Royal Navy sledge team. Also found at Mercy Bay were three graves of sailors who died of scurvy on the expedition. The Royal Naval ship remains the property of the British government, which was notified regarding the finds. Jim Prentice, the minister for the environment, said that the discovery supported Canada's sovereignty to the region.

Working with the Coast Guard and Canadian Hydrographic Service, Parks Canada's Underwater Archaeology Service began searching for Franklin's ships HMS *Erebus* and HMS *Terror* on August 18, 2010. The search area of interest included zones southeast and northeast of O'Reilly Island, located just west of the Adelaide Peninsula in the Queen Maud Gulf. Although no "targets of interest" were located that summer, the search brought Canadians closer to determining the final resting place of the two ships and the fate of Sir John Franklin, the man who began the search for Arctic sovereignty for Britain — and eventually Canada.

A short walk from Canada House in London is Waterloo Place. Within the square are a variety of memorials, and two with polar connections. On the east side is Kathleen Scott's statue of her husband, Robert Falcon Scott, the doomed Antarctic explorer. Scott's Arctic counterpart, Sir John Franklin, stands opposite on the west side of Waterloo Place, the two tragic figures eternally staring at one another across the London traffic. Schooled on the heroic deaths of national heroes like Wolfe and Nelson, both of whom had died with victory in their grasp, the Victorian public expected their government to erect such statues and Franklin's was sanctioned by unanimous vote in Parliament. The standing bronze figure of Franklin is in uniform, clutching in his right hand a roll of charts. Carved in bronze is the inscription:

TO THE GREAT ARCTIC NAVIGATOR AND HIS BRAVE
COMPANIONS WHO SACRIFICED THEIR LIVES IN
COMPLETING THE DISCOVERY OF THE NORTHWEST
PASSAGE, A.D. 1847–8.

Although sculpted by Matthew Noble in 1866, by which time events had proven otherwise, the statue honours Franklin as the naval officer who had discovered the Northwest Passage. Given the chain of events that followed his disappearance, in a way he had done just that.

Notes

INTRODUCTION

1. The reference is to Robert Service's poem "The Cremation of Sam McGee."

   > There are strange things done in the midnight sun
   > By the men who moil for gold;
   > The Arctic trails have their secret tales
   > That would make your blood run cold;

2. "Rethinking the Top of the World: Arctic Security Public Opinion Survey," January 2011 (Toronto: EKOS Research Associates).

CHAPTER ONE: BRITISH OBSESSION

1. Who is forgotten in place names is Captain Samuel Gurney Cresswell, the first British naval officer to cross the entire Northwest passage. One hopes that with the discovery of the wreck of his ship, HMS *Investigator*, in July 2010, he might be accorded this honour.
2. Although Beaufort was not to know it in his lifetime as the book came out in 1859, his greatest accomplishment was perhaps in finding an obscure naturalist named Charles Darwin to take a voyage on the *Beagle* departing for South America on a five-year survey in 1831.
3. Hugh N. Wallace, *The Navy, the Company, and Richard King* (Montreal: McGill-Queen's University Press, 1980), 125.
4. The fool's gold that Frobisher brought back was believed to be so valuable that Queen Elizabeth I ordered quadruple locks for the worthless cache in the Tower of London. The Inuit whom he had kidnapped and presented at court died within a month.
5. They did not get very far, and nearly half a century later, Samuel Hearne would discover the fate of the crews when he came across the wrecks and a cabin in a cove on Marble Island, near Rankin Inlet, Northwest Territories. After interviewing

the Inuit, Hearne confirmed that this was where the Knight expedition had been wrecked. The Inuit said that in the late fall of 1719, about 50 men built a house after their ships had been wrecked. By the end of a second winter, only 20 men were left. Five lived until the summer of 1721.

6. "A Bill for More Effectually Discovering the Longitude at Sea, and Encouraging Attempts to Find a *Northern* Passage Between the *Atlantic* and *Pacific* Oceans, and to Approach the *Northern* Pole." Ordered, by The House of Commons, to be Printed, 9 March 1818.

7. Hugh N. Wallace, *The Navy, the Company, and Richard King* (Montreal: McGill-Queen's University Press, 1980), 2.

8. Beechey has a Canadian connection other than this. He came from a family of artists (his father and brothers), but his daughter Francis Anne Hopkins married a Hudson's Bay Company officer and travelled with him across Canada by canoe and her paintings hang in the National Gallery of Canada.

9. Completely out of his depth on this expedition, Franklin may have been unaware that his men were murdering each other to save themselves from cannibalism on this expedition.

10. Wallace, Hugh et al., 13.

11. In 2009, Michael Palin, the former Monty Python troupe member and television presenter, was made the society's president.

12. Bomb vessels were floating artillery batteries, designed to remain stationary off shore and fire heavy mortars. Strengthened because of the mortar recoil, their shallow drafts and large holds for ammunition and stores suited them for polar expeditions.

13. When the vessel was new, *Terror* had taken part in the War of 1812, bombarding Fort McHenry with mortar and rocket, a display that inspired onlooker Francis Scott Key to compose a poem that would become "The Star Spangled Banner."

14. As the Franklin expedition was preparing to sail, the author Charles Dickens had just published *Oliver Twist*, in which he sets Fagin's den in Whitechapel. Dickens, like most Victorians, was morbidly fascinated by the reports of cannibalism in the expedition and in 1854 would comment on it in his *The Lost Arctic Voyagers*.

15. The Canadian Food Inspection Agency website warns that *Clostridium perfringens* bacterium grows in foods that are high in starch or high in protein, such as meat products, and that ordinary cooking will not kill its spores because strains can survive at the boiling point (100 °C or 212 °F) for up to an hour. Food-processing companies now claim that it takes 10 hours at 250 °F to kill the bacteria.

16. One of the crew was Canadian, having been born in Nova Scotia.

17. In 1846, of the 1,151 officers in the Royal Navy, only 172 were fully employed.

18. Although the men had died of tuberculosis and pneumonia — common enough in Victorian times — autopsies done in 1986 revealed that the scurvy-causing *Clostridium* spores were already at work in their bodies.

19. In the James Ross Strait lurk the Matty Island shoals, which almost finished the lighter *Gjøa* and *St. Roch*, both of which had a draft of 12 feet. The heavier *Erebus* and *Terror* would have foundered on them.

20. Scott Cookman, *Iceblink* (Toronto: John Wiley & Sons, 2000), 139.

21. In 1930, a Canadian government-sponsored party, led by Major L.T. Burwash and flown by bush pilot Walter Gilbert, found some artifacts on the northwestern side of King William Island. In 1931, William Gibson of the HBC searched the south coast of King William Island, discovering a number of skeletons and artifacts.

22. The evidence of cannibalism is overwhelming. In 1981, Dr. Owen Beattie discovered knife marks on a femur bone on the site and in 1993, the archaeologist Margaret Bertulli and anthropologist Anne Keenleyside found cut marks on the bones made by knives that indicated "defleshing" or removal of muscle tissue.

23. Copper Inuit groups travelling to Banks Island to hunt and fish first discovered the abandoned *Investigator*. They soon made annual visits to Mercy Bay to salvage metal and wood from the ship before it sank. Her wreckage was found in July 2010 by a team of Parks Canada archaeologists.

24. To protest what she saw as the government's abandonment of her husband, Lady Franklin replaced her mourning clothes for bright colourful ones to demonstrate her faith in her husband's "continued existence."

25. An oil portrait of Rae by Stephen Pearce is in the National Portrait Gallery, London. The relics from the Franklin expedition which Rae bought from the Inuit in 1854 are in the John Rae collection at the Royal Scottish Museum, Edinburgh.

26. Tennyson was Franklin's nephew by marriage and there were many who believed that Lady Franklin had composed the epitaph.

27. Peter Pigott, *Sailing Seven Seas: The History of the Canadian Pacific Shipping Line* (Toronto: Dundurn, 2010).

28. Erika Behrisch, ed., *As affecting the fate of my absent husband: Selected Letters of Lady Franklin Concerning the Search for the Lost Franklin Expedition. 1848–1860.* (Montreal: McGill-Queen's University Press, 2009), 19.

29. Wallace, 161.

CHAPTER TWO: ALL THAT GLITTERS

1. To its discredit, the HBC did not — and paid for that ever after. This was Simpson's own investment.

2. The Nootka Sound Conventions in which the British disavowed any colonial ambitions in South America (including adjacent islands) and then seized the Malvinas Islands in 1833 (renaming them the Falklands) forms the basis of Argentinean sovereignty claims.

3. G. Bennett, "Yukon Transportation: A History," *Canadian Historic Sites, Occasional*

Papers in Archeology and History, No. 19 (Ottawa: Parks Canada, Indian and Northern Affairs, 1978): 14.

4. Congressional opposition delayed the appropriation until 1868, when extensive lobbying and huge bribes to congressmen by the Russian ambassador secured the required votes.

5. The use of the term "City" by the stampeders in no way implies that there was a discernible organized structure either at Circle or Dawson, merely a congregation of people at a given time.

6. Pierre Berton, *The Klondike: The Last Great Gold Rush 1896–1899* (Toronto: McClelland & Stewart, 1972), 21.

7. Ken Coates and William R. Morrison, *Land of the Midnight Sun: A History of the Yukon* (Edmonton: Hurtig Publishers, 1988), 112.

8. A single bowhead whale, providing up to 100 barrels of oil and 2,000 pounds of baleen, would be worth up to $2,000. A good season could net $400,000 for a whaling ship, this at a time when the average American worker made $400 a year.

9. Coates, 70.

10. "On January 11, 1888, while stationed at Kootenay Ferry B.C., Steele jotted this wonderful note: 'Annual flogging administered to whores, adulterers, drunkards and gamblers.'" Charlotte Gray, "Faded Hero," *The Walrus* (October 2010).

11. Canada, Debates, House of Commons, 1898, 234.

12. *Ibid.*, 625.

13. Roy Minter, *The White Pass: Gateway to the Klondike* (Toronto: McClelland & Stewart, 1987), 151.

14. *Ibid.*, 152.

15. Peter Pigott, *Canada in Sudan: War Without Borders* (Toronto: Dundurn, 2008), 74.

16. Kenneth Charles Eyre, "Custos Borealis: The Military in the Canadian North" (Ph.D. diss., University of London King's College, 1981), 28.

17. *Ibid.*, 4795.

18. The purchases of the Lee-Enfield rifles were a result of Herbert's warning. The militia was still equipped with the Enfield-Snyder rifles from the Fenian raids.

19. It was different for the four nurses. On the day of departure, a church service was held in the chapel at Government House, after which each of them was taken into Lady Aberdeen's private boudoir for a heart-to-heart talk.

20. Berton, 230.

21. Brereton Greenhous, *Guarding the Goldfields: The Story of the Yukon Field Force* (Toronto: Dundurn, 1987), 163.

22. London had been loaned a dog called Buck who was St. Bernard/Scotch Shepherd mix, which he would later immortalize in his classic of the Yukon gold rush, *Call of the Wild*.

23. *Regimental History*, Vol. 1, 76.

24. *Militia Report*, 1898, 36–37.

25. *Dawson Daily News*, May 2, 1900.

26. Virtual Museum Canada website, "Fort Selkirk Virtual Museum, Power and Sovereignty: The Police and the Yukon Field Force," *www.virtualmuseum.ca/ Exhibitions/FortSelkirk/english/ps/psgov.html*.

27. Debates, 1900, 1209.

28. Debates, 1900, 6321–6322.

29. Eyre, 36.

30. Greenhous, 212–13.

31. Gray, 4.

32. All figures taken from M. Zaslow, *The Opening of the Canadian North 1870–1914* (Toronto: McClelland & Stewart, 1971).

CHAPTER THREE: EXPLORATION AND AIRCRAFT

1. Alan Rudolph Marcus, *Relocating Eden: The Images and Politics of Inuit Exile in the Canadian Arctic* (Lebanon, NH: University Press of New England, 1995).

2. M. Zaslow, *The Northward Expansion of Canada, 1914–1967"* (Toronto: McClelland & Stewart, 1988).

3. In 2010, the five main surface combatant ships of the Royal Norwegian Navy were of the Fridtjof Nansen class and one of which is called the *Otto Sverdrup*.

4. Zaslow, 260.

5. *Ibid.*, 262.

6. When Amundsen finally got to Herschel Island, he cross-country skied 500 miles to the nearest telegraph office in Alaska to tell the world of his exploits.

7. As soon as he got to Labrador, Peary sent a cable that made headlines around the world: "Stars and stripes nailed to the North Pole."

8. Kenneth Charles Eyre, "Custos Borealis: The Military in the Canadian North" (Ph.D. diss., University of London King's College, 1981), 41.

9. Zaslow, 18.

10. In 1921, the Department of the Interior chartered the *Nascopie* to sail to Loppen, Norway, and pick up a cargo of 550 reindeer to be delivered to Baffin Island. Caribou were dying out on the island and the Inuit were facing starvation. It was hoped that reindeer would supply meat and skins to them. Sadly, the venture was not a success.

11. R.A. Logan, "Report of Investigations on Aviation in the Arctic Archipelago carried out during the summer of 1922," Department of National Defence, Directorate of History, (74/414).

12. R. A. Logan, "Staking Canada's Claim," *Sentinel Magazine* (November/December b1970), 53.

13. R.A. Logan, "Pinpoints in the Past," *Roundel* magazine (June 1949), 12.

14. *Ibid.*, 2–3.
15. Logan, 55.
16. *Ibid.*, 56.
17. DND Report, 1925, 39.
18. S. Bernard Shaw, *Photographing Canada from Flying Canoes* (Burnstown, ON: General Store Publishing House, 2001), 97.
19. In 1973, the National Film Board made a 28-minute video, *The Aviators of Hudson Strait*, from George Valiquette's footage and a commentary was added by the then-retired Air Vice-Marshal T.E. Lawrence.
20. The next film to portray the Canadian Arctic and the Inuit was 1960's *The Savage Innocents*, in which Anthony Quinn and a Japanese actress played the Inuit couple. Peter O'Toole played the RCMP constable and had to have his accent dubbed into "Canadian."

CHAPTER FOUR: SOVEREIGNTY AND MACKENZIE KING

1. Ironically, the one resource industry in the North that did not prosper during the war was gold mining. Considered nonessential, men and machinery were withdrawn from the gold mines and allocated either to the war effort or to Port Radium to make the fissionable material for atomic bombs.
2. *The Ottawa Citizen*, January 6, 1938.
3. *Globe and Mail*, January 6, 1938.
4. The life and times of Grant McConachie are celebrated in the author's books: *Wingwalkers: A History of Canadian Airlines International* (Madeira Park, B.C.: Harbour Publishing, 1998) and *Flying Canucks Two* (Toronto: Dundurn, 1996).
5. The time-honoured story goes that an RCMP constable, after tracking a killer for a month through the winter, found him frozen to death in the snow. Wishing to prove that he had the right man, the constable cut off the man's head and put it in a sack. He then caught the YSAT plane to Edmonton. During the flight, a superstitious passenger remarked that there were only 13 persons onboard. To reassure him, the constable said: "Don't worry," and opened the sack whereupon — as the story goes — the contents rolled down the aisle.
6. Because of defence contracts, the Lockheed 14s came in one colour only — military green — a drawback for aircraft flying (and crashing) in the bush. But this worked in McConachie's favour. Whenever a YSAT airliner landed at a U.S. military base, because of the colour, it was filled up with precious gasoline without charge.
7. Aluminum was so strategic to Second World War aircraft production that in 1942, eight German saboteurs were landed by U-boats, four on Long Island and four south of Jacksonville, Florida, to destroy Alcoa's plants at Massena, New York, East St. Louis, and Alcoa, Tennessee.

8. Kingston Airport is named after him.
9. The 1940 film, *49th Parallel*, about survivors from a U-boat sunk in Hudson Bay making their way to the still neutral United States, played on such fears. It starred Laurence Oliver, Raymond and Vincent Massey, and Leslie Howard.
10. The situation was repeated with the French colony of St. Pierre and Miquelon, which Power also wanted Canadian troops (this time called "Force Q") to occupy.
11. The native names were too cumbersome, so the Greenland Stations were called "Bluies" in army code.
12. If any ship deserves to be honoured by a commemorative stamp it is the gallant *Nascopie*. In 1947, she struck an uncharted reef off of Beacon Island at the entrance to Cape Dorset Harbour and sank. On the 50th anniversary of the sinking in 1997, to honour the vessel, a team of scuba divers placed a plaque on the reef to commemorate the ship.
13. The historic railway car was also used by President Dwight Eisenhower on a state visit to Ottawa in 1953 and is now in a Florida museum.
14. The British also foresaw the need to fight in the Alps and the Apennines and in 1943 the British Lovett Scouts — a specialized mountain regiment — had been sent to Jasper to train for winter warfare. Although it had no such regiments, the Canadian military provided instructors for this.
15. Another imperial entanglement that Canada refused that year was providing a garrison for the Falkland Islands. Concerned that Japan might seize the Falkland Islands and hand them over to Argentina to gain South American support, Britain asked Canada to send troops to the islands. After having lost over 2,000 soldiers in the defense of the British colony of Hong Kong and suffered the American reaction to the proposed "Force X" to Greenland — the Falklands at least were in the western hemisphere — Ottawa once more refused.
16. At a critical time, King was forced to move Ian Alistair Mackenzie from the Defence portfolio to the position of minister of pensions because he was implicated in a scandal involving the awarding of a contract to manufacture the Bren Gun. But the Vancouver riding was important to the prime minister and he accommodated much of Mackenzie's anti-Japanese sentiments, particularly with the internment of Japanese Canadians.
17. Canada Treaty Series 1942/13.
18. The use of black (or as they were called then "coloured") troops in the North was a sensitive issue with the Canadian government. In 1948, Ottawa refused to accept black engineers because "the native population in the north is very susceptible to white men's diseases and the incidence of venereal disease in the Mackenzie District, N.W.T., following the assignment of coloured troops to the Canol project, was very discouraging." Foreign Affairs & International Trade website, Documents on Canadian External Relations, Vol. 14–990, *www.international.gc.ca/department/*

history-histoire/dcer/details-en.asp?intRefid=10678.

19. Vancouver *Province*, November 22, 1942.

20. McDonald related an incident that occurred when he was touring the project. One day, a Native chief appeared at the RCMP post and asked to meet him. He handed the British High Commissioner $393 that his village had collected, he said, for the children in London who had been orphaned in the air raids.

21. The story was used by Ernest K. Gann in his book *Fate is the Hunter* and made into the movie *Island in The Sky*, starring John Wayne.

22. D. Hist 181.009 (D3391) North West Air Command (RCAF) December 31, 1942–44; April 1944, "USAAF Control Towers on Hangars-NWSR," January 17, 1944.

23. S.G. French, "The North West Staging Route," *Roundel* magazine (in seven parts), 1955.

24. The Canadian military later reciprocated by installing Canadian-made radar at United States bases in the Panama Canal zone.

25. Hysteria was not confined to the coast. In the heartland, both Americans and Canadians were sure that enemy bombers or paratroopers would make for the locks at Sault Ste. Marie to destroy them and vast numbers of aircraft, guns, and troops were tied up throughout the war for their protection.

26. An excellent book on one of Canada's best-kept wartime secrets is *The Armoured Train in Canadian Service* by former foreign affairs colleague Roger V. Lucy.

27. When he later served in Europe, Boomer became the first Canadian to shoot down a German aircraft, an Italian aircraft, and a Japanese aircraft.

28. Labrador takes its name from the Portuguese explorer João Fernandes Lavrador, who as a landowner was allowed to use the title *lavrador* or "landholder" of the New World.

29. J.R.K. Main, *Voyageurs of the Air* (Ottawa: Queen's Printer, 1967), 179.

CHAPTER FIVE: DEW LINE AND DIEFENBAKER

1. Clothes were so rationed that when the Gouzenkos fled with only what they were wearing, in order to buy more from an Ottawa department store (Mrs. Gouzenko was heavily pregnant), the RCMP had to concoct a story that he was a war veteran whose house had burned down.

2. In 1958, Greenaway was senior navigator aboard the first airship to penetrate the Arctic in more than a quarter of a century, making the 4,700-nautical-mile round trip to evaluate the use of lighter-than-air craft in supporting arctic research in the United States. Navy ZPG-2, at an altitude of 2,100 feet above sea level.

3. Always modest and quietly spoken, Greenaway was the recipient of many polar exploration awards, including the President's Prize of the Royal Meteorological

Society, the Thurlow Award of the U.S. Institute of Navigation, and was made a Fellow of the Arctic Institute of North America. He died on May 21, 2010.

4.   All excerpts taken from Wilson's speech to the Empire Club of Toronto April, 18, 1946.

5.   Permission to quote this incident was given by the NWT Archives. It was written by Randy Freeman while employed by the archives.

6.   It was the perfect way to commemorate a great ship. After the Nares expedition, HMS *Alert* would be loaned to the U.S. Navy for polar exploration and then from 1885–93 would be transferred to the Canadian government for the exploration of Hudson Bay. She ended her days as a lighthouse supply ship on the St. Lawrence before being returned to the Royal Navy to be broken up.

7.   Elizabeth B. Elliot-Meisel, "Arctic Focus: The Royal Canadian Navy in Arctic Waters, 1946–1949," *The Northern Mariner/Le Marin du nord*, IX, No. 2 (April 1999): 23–398. Kenneth Charles Eyre, "Custos Borealis: The Military in the Canadian North" (Ph.D. diss., University of London King's College, 1981), 193.

9.   As told to Holly Bridges for *Air Force* magazine and reproduced here with Mr. Catton's permission.

10. This was kept secret by both governments until 2000.

11. Canada, House of Commons Debates, March 25, 1954, Vol. 4, 3344.

12. Canada, House of Commons Debates, April 12, 1954, Vol. 4, 3980.

13. Much of the information on the DEW Line is from "The Dew Line," by Flight Lieutenant R.B. Wybou, Directorate of Control Environment Operations, *Roundel* magazine (May 1960).

14. Canada, House of Commons Debates, June 20, 1956.

15. In April 1993, 40 years after the relocation, Canada's first Royal Commission on Aboriginal Peoples conducted public hearings in Ottawa. Televised across Canada, the public was shocked as the elders talked of the suffering caused by the relocations.

16. Hall might have been the first man to get to the North Pole had he not died at Hall Bay, Greenland. His body was exhumed in 1968 and neutron activation tests on his hair and fingernails, run by the Centre of Forensic Sciences Toronto, proved that during the last two weeks of his life he had ingested large amounts of arsenic. It was always suspected he had been murdered by members of his crew (on a previous voyage to maintain discipline, he had shot one of them), but Hall could also have overdosed himself. Incredibly, when the *Polaris* was crushed by ice, the remnants of Hall's crew drifted on an ice floe 1,300 miles to the coast of Labrador and survived.

17. The former government had assured the United States in January 1957 that the Canadian government believed that the USAF should continue to man and operate that portion of the DEW Line in Canada until 1963, subject to the understanding that Canada would be free to review this decision if conditions were to change.

18. Robertson had also accompanied W/C Keith Greenaway in the U.S. Navy airship over the Arctic in 1958.

19. Desmond Morton, A Military History of Canada (Edmonton: Hurtig Publishers, 1990), 240.

CHAPTER SIX: ON GUARD FOR THEE

1. The title of his book was *Damn the Torpedoes: My Fight to Unify Canada's Armed Forces* (Toronto: McClelland & Stewart, 1990).

2. But the media and public were more interested in how the associate defence minister was then handling a pair of Cold War spy scandals — that of George Victor Spencer, a Vancouver postal clerk who was not prosecuted for espionage because he was dying of cancer; and the sex-and-security case involving East German spy Gerda Munsinger.

3. Whether apocryphal or not, the story went that at one point during *Manhattan's* voyage, Inuit hunters stopped the tanker and demanded that its captain ask their permission to cross through their territory, which he did, and which they granted.

4. U.S. National Archives, RG 59, Central Files 1970-73, POL 33-8. Secret. Drafted by Neuman and cleared by Johnson, Stevenson, and McKernan, and with EUR/CAN, Defense, Interior, and Transportation.

5. F. Griffiths, ed., "Politics of The Northwest Passage," *Statements on Sovereignty* (1987), 270–71.

6. Whether the Canadian submarines were actually to be deployed under the Arctic ice was not the point. As the Royal Navy had demonstrated in the Falklands War, just having a nuclear submarine in the vicinity provided Canada with a deterrent.

7. What really had a $1 billion price tag for the Mulroney government was the Low Level Air Defence (LLAD) system sought in 1985 to provide an air defence system for the Canadian Mechanized Brigade Group in southern Germany.

8. Statutes of the Government of Canada, *Nunavut Land Claims Agreement Act, 1993*, c.29. Preamble.

9. USS *Porter* is named for Commodore David Porter (1780–1843), who by coincidence captured the British warship HMS *Alert* on August 13, 1812.

Bibliography

Anderson, Lieutenant-Commander Ian. "Northern Deployments: Naval Operations in the Canadian North." *Canadian Naval Review* Vol. 1, No. 4 (Winter 2006): 6–12.

Beardsley, Martin. *Deadly Winter: The Life of Sir John Franklin*. London: Chatham Publishing, 2002.

Beattie, Owen, and John Geiger. *Frozen in Time: Unlocking the Secrets of the Franklin Expedition*. Saskatoon: Western Producer Prairie Books, 1989.

Bennett, G. "Yukon Transportation: A History." *Canadian Historic Sites, Occasional Papers in Archeology and History*, No. 19. Ottawa: Parks Canada, Indian and Northern Affairs, 1978.

Berton, Pierre. *The Klondike: The Last Great Gold Rush 1896–1899*. Toronto: McClelland & Stewart, 1972.

Byers, Michael, and Suzanne Lalonde. "Our Arctic Sovereignty is on Thin Ice." The *Globe and Mail*, August 1, 2005, A11.

Carnaghan, Matthew, and Allison Goody. "Canadian Arctic Sovereignty." Library of Parliament, *www2.parl.gc.ca/Content/LOP/ResearchPublications/prb0561-e.htm* (accessed January 2010).

Chair: The Honourable William Rompkey, P.C., June 2008, *www.parl.gc.ca/Content/SEN/Committee/392/fish/rep/rep04jun08-e.pdf*.

"The Coast Guard in Canada's Arctic: Interim Report, Standing Senate Committee on Fisheries and Oceans." Fourth Report.

Coates, Ken, P. Whitney Lackenbauer, Bill Morrison, and Greg Poelzer. *Arctic Front: Defending Canada in the Far North*. Toronto: Thomas Allen, 2009.

Coates, Ken, and William R. Morrison. *Land of the Midnight Sun: A History of the Yukon*. Edmonton: Hurtig Publishers, 1988.

Cookman, Scott. *Iceblink*. Toronto: John Wiley & Sons, 2000.

Douglas, W.A.B. "The Creation of a National Air Force." *The Official History of the Royal Canadian Air Force, Vol. II*. Toronto: University of Toronto Press, 1986.

Elce, Erika Behrisch, ed. *As affecting the fate of my absent husband. Selected Letters of Lady Franklin Concerning the Search for the Lost Franklin Expedition. 1848–1860*. Montreal: McGill-Queen's University Press, 2009.

Elliot-Meisel, Elizabeth B. "Arctic Focus: The Royal Canadian Navy in Arctic Waters,

1946–1949." *The Northern Mariner/Le Marin du nord, IX*, No. 2 (April 1999).

French, S.G. "The North West Staging Route." *Roundel* magazine (in seven parts), 1955.

Hist, D. 181.009 (D3391) North West Air Command (RCAF), December 31, 1942–April 4, 1944; "USAAF Control Towers on Hangars-NWSR," January 17, 1944.

Eyre, Kenneth Charles."Custos Borealis: The Military in the Canadian North." Ph.D. diss. London: University of London King's College, 1981.

Granatstein, J.L. *Whose War is It? How Canada Can Survive in the Post 9/11 World.* Toronto: HarperCollins, 2007.

Greenhous, Brereton. *The Crucible of War, 1939–1945: The Official History of the Royal Canadian Air Force Volume III.* Toronto: University of Toronto Press, 1994.

Greenhous, Brereton. *Guarding the Goldfields: The Story of the Yukon Field Force.* Toronto: Dundurn, 1987.

Honderich, John. *Arctic Imperative: Is Canada Losing the North?* Toronto: University of Toronto Press, 1987.

Lackenbauer, Ph.D., P. Whitney, Matthew J. Farish, Ph.D., and Jennifer Arthur-Lackenbauer, M.Sc. *The Distant Early Warning (DEW) Line": A Bibliography and Documentary Resource List, Prepared for the Arctic Institute of North America.* Calgary: The Arctic Institute of North America, 2005.

Logan, R.A. "Pinpoints in the Past." *Roundel* magazine, June 1949.

_____. "Staking Canada's Claim." *Sentinel Magazine*, November–December, 1970.

_____. "Report of Investigations on Aviation in the Arctic Archipelago Carried Out During the Summer of 1922." Department of National Defence, Directorate of History, (74/414).

Main, J.R.K. "Voyageurs of the Air." Ottawa: Queen's Printer, 1967.

Marcus, Alan Rudolph. *Relocating Eden: The Image and Politics of Inuit Exile in the Canadian Arctic.* Lebanon, NH: University Press of New England, 1995.

Minter, Roy. *The White Pass: Gateway to the Klondike.* Toronto: McClelland & Stewart, 1987.

Morton, Desmond. *A Military History of Canada.* Edmonton: Hurtig Publishers, 1990.

"Rethinking the Top of the World: Arctic Security Public Opinion Survey." Final Report submitted to The Walter and Duncan Gordon Foundation and The Canada Centre for Global Security Studies at the Munk School of Global Affairs. Ekos Research Associates Inc., January 2011.

Shaw, S. Bernard. *Photographing Canada from Flying Canoes.* Burnstown, ON: General Store Publishing House, 2001.

Statutes of the Government of Canada, *Nunavut Land Claims Agreement Act, 1993*, c.29.

Wallace, Hugh N. *The Navy, The Company, and Richard King.* Montreal: McGill-Queen's University Press, 1980.

Zaslow, M. *The Opening of the Canadian North 1870–1914.* Toronto: McClelland & Stewart, 1971.

_____. *The Northward Expansion of Canada, 1914–1967.* Toronto: McClelland & Stewart, 1988.

Index